Cavendish
Publishing
Limited

CONVEYANCING
LAW & PRACTICE

London Guildhall-Cavendish
Legal Practice Course Companion Series

LONDON GUILDHALL
UNIVERSITY

TITLES IN THE SERIES

Assessment of Skills

Business Law & Practice

Civil Litigation

Commercial Law & practice

Conveyancing Law & Practice

Corporate Insolvency Law & Practice

Criminal Litigation

Employment Law & Practice

Evidence

Family Law & Practice

Immigration & Nationality Law & Practice

Intellectual Property with Competition Law & Practice

Introduction to the Legal Practice Course

Pervasive Subjects

Wills, Probate & Administration

Cavendish
Publishing
Limited

CONVEYANCING
LAW & PRACTICE

J Mills & J Willis

London Guildhall-Cavendish
Legal Practice Course Companion Series

LONDON GUILDHALL
UNIVERSITY

First published in Great Britain 1993 by Cavendish Publishing Limited, 23A Countess Road, London NW5 2XH.

Telephone: 071-485 0303 Facsimile: 071-485 0304

British Library Cataloguing in Publication Data

Mills, J and Willis, J
Conveyancing Law and Practice - (LPC Series)
I Title II Series
344.206438

ISBN 1-874241-98-8
Printed and bound in Great Britain

Outline contents

1   Introduction to conveyancing

1.1   What is conveyancing?   1

1.2   Course content   3

1.3   Stages in the conveyancing process   5

1.4   The National Conveyancing Protocol   6

2   The Land Register

2.1   The form of the Land Register   9

2.2   Protection of minor interests   10

2.3   Land and charge certificates   13

2.4   Inspecting the Register   13

2.5   Registration of title   14

3   Taking instructions

3.1   Obtaining instructions and information   17

3.2   Giving explanation and advice   17

3.3   Quoting on costs   18

3.4   Taking instructions from a seller   19

3.5   Taking instructions from a buyer   20

4   Professional conduct

4.1   Introduction   23

4.2   Rule 15: Solicitors' Practice Rules   23

4.3   Costs   24

4.4   Acting for more than one party   25

4.5   Contract races   28

4.6   Undertakings   30

4.7   Client account rules   33

4.8   Miscellaneous   35

5   Financial aspects

5.1   Costs of the transaction   37

5.2   Stamp duty   39

5.3   VAT   41

5.4   Mortgage interest relief   42

5.5   Mortgage finance   42

5.6   Financial services   45

5.7   Capital Gains Tax relief   46

6   Physical aspects

6.1   Surveys   49

6.2   NHBC   50

6.3   Planning   51

7   Drafting the contract

7.1   Who does what?   59

7.2   The form and content of the contract   59

7.3   Preparation for drafting the contract   60

7.4   The seller's common law duty of
      disclosure   60

7.5   The Standard Conditions of Sale
      contract form   61

7.6   Analysis of certain standard conditions
      of sale   64

7.7   Special conditions   67

8   Pre-contract searches and enquiries

8.1   Introduction   69

8.2   Their purpose   69

8.3   Pre-contract enquiries   70

8.4   Liability for misrepresentation   72

8.5   Local land charges search   73

8.6   Enquiries of the local authority   74

8.7   Special searches and enquiries   74

8.8   Inspection of the property   75

9   Deducing and investigating title

9.1	Deducing title	77
9.2	Investigating title	79
9.3	Dispositions by a sole proprietor	79
9.4	Dispositions by a surviving co-owner	80
9.5	Dispositions by mortgagees	82
9.6	Third party rights	84

10 Exchange of contracts

10.1	Preparation for exchange: buyer	89
10.2	Methods of exchange	92
10.3	Conditional contracts	94

11 Exchange to completion

11.1	The effect of a binding contract	97
11.2	Requisitions on title	100
11.3	Preparing documentation	100
11.4	Pre-completion searches	105

12 Completion and post-completion

12.1	Completion defined	107
12.2	Payment of the price	107
12.3	Performance by the seller	108
12.4	The completion process	108
12.5	Post completion	110

13 Remedies

13.1	Delayed completion	113
13.2	Non-completion	116
13.3	Misrepresentation	118
13.4	Post completion	119

14 Unregistered freeholds: deducing and investigating title

14.1	Deducing title	123
14.2	Investigation of title	127
14.3	Sale by a sole seller	128
14.4	Sale by a surviving co-owner	129
14.5	Sale by a mortgagee	130
14.6	Third party rights	131

15 Unregistered freehold title: 1

15.1	Taking instructions	133
15.2	Drafting the contract	133
15.3	Pre-contract searches and enquiries	135
15.4	Deducing and investigating title	137
15.5	Exchange of contracts	138

16 Unregistered freehold title: 2

16.1	The effect of a binding contract	139
16.2	Requisitions on title	139
16.3	Preparing the documentation	139
16.4	Pre-completion searches	143

17 Unregistered freehold title : 3

17.1	Completion	151
17.2	Post-completion	153
17.3	Remedies	156

18 Special dispositions

18.1	Dispositions by personal	
18.2	Dispositions by attorneys	163
18.3	Dispositions by companies	167
18.4	Voidable dispositions	168
18.5	Transaction at an undervalue	169
18.6	Miscellaneous dispositions	171
18.7	Dispositions other than sales	171
18.8	Auction sales	172

19 Sales of part

19.1	Creation of new covenants and easements	173
19.2	Procedures: registered title	175
19.3	Procedures: unregistered title	176

20 Estate conveyancing

20.1	Introduction	181
20.2	Seller	181
20.3	Buyer	186

21 Leasehold conveyancing

21.1	Introduction	191
21.2	Advantages of selling leasehold	191
21.3	The grant of a long lease of a house	193
21.4	Drafting the lease	194

22 Grant of a long lease

22.1	The draft contract	201
22.2	Exchanging contracts and investigating title	204
22.3	Preparing for completion	205
22.4	Completion	206
22.5	Post completion stages	207

23 Special problems relating to flats

23.1	Introduction	211
23.2	Parcels	211
23.3	Easements	212
23.4	Tenant's covenants	212
23.5	Landlord's covenants	213
23.6	Management company	213
23.7	Insurance	214
23.8	Statutory provisions for service charges	214

24 The assignment of a registered lease

24.1	Introduction	217
24.2	Taking instructions	217
24.3	Drafting the contract and deducing title	218
24.4	Making pre-contract searches and enquiries	219
24.5	Approving the contract	219
24.6	Investigating title	220
24.7	Preparing the purchase deed	221
24.8	Preparing for completion	221
24.9	Making pre-completion searches	
24.10	Completion	222
24.11	Post completion	223

25 The assignment of an unregistered lease

25.1	Introduction	225
25.2	Taking instructions	225
25.3	Drafting the contract and deducing title	225
25.4	Making pre-contract searches and enquiries	226
25.5	Approving the draft contract	226
25.6	Investigating title	227
25.7	Preparing the purchase deed	227
25.8	Preparing for completion	228
25.9	Making pre-completion searches	228
25.10	Completion	229
25.11	Post completion	229

Contents

1 Introduction to conveyancing

1.1 What is conveyancing? 1

  1.1.1 Creation and transfer of estates 1

  1.1.2 Creation of new estates 1
    Freehold titles
    Leasehold titles

  1.1.3 Transfer of existing estates 2

  1.1.4 The sale and purchase of land 2
    The seller's right to sell
    Knowledge about all third party
    interests in the land

  1.1.5 Creation of new third party interests 3

  1.1.6 Transfer of existing third party
    interests 3
    Benefit
    Burden

1.2 Course content 3

  1.2.1 Structure of the manual 4

  1.2.2 Main differences between registered
    and unregistered conveyancing 4

1.3 Stages in the conveyancing process 5

  1.3.1 Up to exchange of contracts 5

  1.3.2 Exchange to completion 5

  1.3.3 Post-completion 6

  1.3.4 Stages in a freehold conveyancing
    transaction 6

1.4 The National Conveyancing Protocol 6

  1.4.1 Main differences: traditional
    conveyancing and the protocol 7
    Pre-contract enquiries and searches
    Deducing title

  1.4.2 Some problems with the protocol 7
    In a depressed market
    Who pays for the searches?

  1.4.3 Terminology 8

2 The Land Register

2.1 The form of the Land Register 9

2.1.1 The Property Register 9

2.1.2 The Proprietorship Register 9

2.1.3 The Charges Register 10

2.1.4 The filed plan 10

2.2 Protection of minor interests 10

  2.2.1 Inhibitions 10

  2.2.2 Restrictions 10

  2.2.3 Cautions 11

  2.2.4 Notices 12

2.3 Land and charge certificates 13

2.4 Inspecting the Register 13

2.5 Registration of title 14

  2.5.1 Compulsory registration 14

  2.5.2 Completing the register 15

3 Taking instructions

3.1 Obtaining instructions and information 17

  3.1.1 The solicitor as agent 17

  3.1.2 Be thorough 17

3.2 Giving explanation and advice 17

3.3 Quoting on costs 18

  3.3.1 Items to be included if acting for
    buyer 18

  3.3.2 Items to be included if acting for
    seller 18

  3.3.3 Charging for other disbursements 18

3.4 Taking instructions from a seller 19

  3.4.1 Checklist 19

  3.4.2 Action following instructions 20

3.5 Taking instructions from a buyer 20

  3.5.1 Checklist 20

  3.5.2 Action following instructions 21

4 Professional conduct

4.1 Introduction 23

4.2   Rule 15: Solicitors' Practice Rules   23

4.3   Costs   24

4.3.1   Information on costs   24

4.3.2   Exceeding the estimate   24

4.3.3   Rendering the bill   24

4.4   Acting for more than one party   25

4.4.1   General rule   25

4.4.2   Rule 6: Solicitors' Practice Rules   25

4.4.3   Acting for seller and buyer   26
    Conflict of interest
    Undue influence

4.4.4   Acting for the seller's mortgagee   27

4.4.5   Acting for the buyer's mortgagee   27

4.4.6   Acting for more than one buyer   28

4.5   Contract races   28

4.5.1   The Law Society direction   28

4.5.2   The perils of contract races   29

4.5.3   Gazumping   30

4.6   Undertakings   30

4.6.1   Obtaining title documents from the
    seller's mortgagee   30

4.6.2   Bridging finance   31
    The deposit
    The completion money
    Discharge of seller's mortgage
    The solicitor's undertaking

4.6.3   Undertaking for discharge of
    seller's mortgage   32

4.6.4   Miscellaneous undertakings   33

4.7   Client account rules   33

4.7.1   Interest on client account   34

4.8   Miscellaneous   35

5   Financial aspects

5.1   Costs of the transaction   37

5.1.1   Solicitors' fees   37

5.1.2   Disbursements   37

5.1.3   Other items of expenditure   37

5.1.4   Typical costs   37

    Sales costs
    Purchase costs
    Overall budget

5.2   Stamp duty   39

5.2.1   Stamping of leases   40

5.2.2   Voluntary conveyances   41

5.3   VAT   41

5.4   Mortgage interest relief   42

5.5   Mortgage finance   42

5.5.1   Repayment mortgage   42
    Mortgage protection insurance

5.5.2   Endowment mortgage   43
    The capital sum
    Charging the policy
    Payment of the policy monies

5.5.3   Selling mortgaged property   45

5.6   Financial services   45

5.6.1   Disclosing commission   46

5.7   Capital Gains Tax relief   46

6   Physical aspects

6.1   Surveys   49

6.1.1   Surveyor's liability   49

6.2   NHBC   50

6.3   Planning   51

6.3.1   Development   52

6.3.2   The Use Classes Order   53
    Class A1
    Class A2
    Class A3
    Class B1
    Class B2
    Part C
    Part D

6.3.3   The General Development Order   54
    Class 1
    Class 2

6.3.4   Article 4 directions   54

6.3.5   Specific applications   55

6.3.6   Duration of planning permission   55

6.3.7   Enforcement of planning legislation   56

6.3.8   Building regulations   56

7   Drafting the contract

7.1   Who does what?   59

7.2   The form and content of the contract   59

7.2.1   The Standard Conditions of Sale   59

7.2.2   The open contract   60

7.3   Preparation for drafting the contract   60

7.3.1   Land/charge certificate   60

7.3.2   Office copy entries   60

7.3.3   Overriding interests   60

7.4   The seller's common law duty of disclosure   60

7.4.1   Extent of the common law duty   61

7.4.2   Breach of the duty   61

7.4.3   Modifying the common law duty   61

7.5   The Standard Conditions of Sale contract form   61

7.5.1   The agreement date   62

7.5.2   The parties   62

7.5.3   Property   62

7.5.4   Incumbrances on the property   62

7.5.5   Capacity in which the seller sells   63

7.5.6   Completion date   63

7.5.7   The contract rate   63

7.5.8   The purchase price   64

7.6   Analysis of certain standard conditions of sale   64

7.6.1   Standard condition 2.2: Deposit   64
Amount and purpose
Agent or stakeholder
Possible problems

7.6.2   Standard condition 9: Chattels   65

7.6.3   Standard condition 3.1: Freedom from incumbrances   66

7.6.4   Condition 4.2 : Proof of title   67

7.7   Special conditions   67

7.7.1   Void conditions   68

8   Pre-contract searches and enquiries

8.1   Introduction   69

8.2   Their purpose   69

8.3   Pre-contract enquiries   70

8.3.1   Boundaries   70

8.3.2   Disputes   70

8.3.3   Notices   71

8.3.4   Guarantees   71

8.3.5   Services   71

8.3.6   Facilities   71

8.3.7   Adverse rights   71

8.3.8   Occupiers   71

8.3.9   Restrictions   71

8.3.10   Planning   72

8.3.11   Mechanics of sale   72

8.3.12   Outgoings   72

8.4   Liability for misrepresentation   72

8.5   Local land charges search   73

8.5.1   Examples of local land charges   73

8.5.2   The official search   73

8.5.3   Search validation insurance   74

8.6   Enquiries of the local authority   74

8.7   Special searches and enquiries   74

8.7.1   Common registration search   75

8.7.2   Coal mining enquiries   75

8.7.3   Other mining enquiries   75

8.7.4   Other special enquiries   75

8.8   Inspection of the property   75

9   Deducing and investigating title

9.1   Deducing title   77

9.1.1   Method   77

9.1.2   Time   78

9.1.3   The seller who is not the registered proprietor   78
Mortgagee
Personal representatives
Re-sale

9.2   Investigating title   79
  9.2.1   Method   79
9.3   Dispositions by a sole proprietor   79
9.4   Dispositions by a surviving co-owner   80
  9.4.1   Legal co-ownership   80
  9.4.2   Death of a legal co-owner   80
  9.4.3   Beneficial joint tenants   80
  9.4.4   Beneficial tenants in common   80
  9.4.5   Type of beneficial holding   81
  9.4.6   Summary   81
  9.4.7   Beneficial interests which are not
            overreached   82
9.5   Dispositions by mortgagees   82
  9.5.1   When does the power arise?   83
  9.5.2   Order for possession   83
  9.5.3   Effect of a sale by mortgagee   83
  9.5.4   Second mortgages   84
  9.5.5   Equitable mortgages   84
9.6   Third party rights   84
  9.6.1   Mortgages   84
  9.6.2   Beneficial interests   85
  9.6.3   MHA rights   85
  9.6.4   Covenants and easements   86
  9.6.5   Estate contracts   86
  9.6.6   Local land charges   87

10 Exchange of contracts

10.1   Preparation for exchange: buyer   89
  10.1.1   Approval of the draft contract   89
  10.1.2   Satisfactory investigations   90
  10.1.3   Finance   91
  10.1.4   Signing the contract: buyer or seller 91
10.2   Methods of exchange   92
  10.2.1   Statutory requirements   92
  10.2.2   Methods of exchange   93
  10.2.3   The Law Society formulae   93
  10.2.4   Dating the contract   94
10.3   Conditional contracts   94

11 Exchange to completion

11.1   The effect of a binding contract   97
  11.1.1   Protecting the buyer's equitable title 97
  11.1.2   The risk in the property   97
  11.1.3   Standard condition 5.1   98
  11.1.4   Occupation by the buyer   99
11.2   Requisitions on title   100
11.3   Preparing documentation   100
  11.3.1   The Land Registry transfer   100
  11.3.2   The buyer's mortgage   102
  11.3.3   The seller's mortgage: undertaking
            for Form 53   103
  11.3.4   Statements of account   104
11.4   Pre-completion searches   105
  11.4.1   Search of the Land Register   105
  11.4.2   Inspection of the property   105
  11.4.3   Search of the Local Land
            Charges Register?   105
  11.4.4   Search of Company's Register?   105
  11.4.5   Mortgagee's Searches   106

12 Completion and post-completion

12.1   Completion defined   107
12.2   Payment of the price   107
  12.2.1   By telegraphic transfer   107
  12.2.2   By banker's draft or in cash   107
  12.2.3   Payment for chattels   108
12.3   Performance by the seller   108
12.4   The completion process   108
  12.4.1   The Law Society's Code for
            Completion by Post   109
  12.4.2   The effect of completion   109
12.5   Post completion   110
  12.5.1   Seller's solicitor   110
  12.5.2   Buyer's solicitor: stamping the
            transfer   110
  12.5.3   Buyer's solicitor: registering the
            transfer   110
  12.5.4   Custody of documents   111

13 Remedies

13.1	Delayed completion	113
13.1.1	The open contract approach	113
13.1.2	Damages	114
13.1.3	The standard conditions	114
13.1.4	Notice to complete	115
13.1.5	Specific performance	116
13.2	Non-completion	116
13.2.1	Damages recoverable by a buyer	117
13.2.2	Damages recoverable by a seller	117
13.2.3	The date for assessing damages	118
13.3	Misrepresentation	118
13.4	Post completion	119
13.4.1	The doctrine of merger	119
13.4.2	The covenants for title	12

14 Unregistered freeholds: deducing and investigating title

14.1	Deducing title	123
14.1.1	A good root of title	123
	Deals with the whole estate	
	The description of the property	
	Does not cast doubt on the title	
	Acceptable roots	
14.1.2	The age of the root	124
	The 15-year rule	
	Shorter roots	
	Registered land charges	
14.1.3	The abstract of title	125
14.1.4	Documents to be abstracted	126
14.2	Investigation of title	127
14.2.1	Examining the abstract	127
14.2.2	Stamping	127
14.2.3	Requisitions on title	128
	Barring requisitions	
14.3	Sale by a sole seller	128
14.4	Sale by a surviving co-owner	129
14.5	Sale by a mortgagee	130
14.5.1	Second mortgages	130

14.5.2	Equitable mortgages	130
14.6	Third party rights	131
14.6.1	Mortgages	131
	Discharge	
	Second mortgages	
14.6.2	Beneficial interests	132
14.6.3	MHA rights	132
14.6.4	Covenants and easements	132
14.6.5	Estate contracts	132
14.6.6	Local land charges	132

15 Unregistered freehold title: 1

15.1	Taking instructions	133
15.2	Drafting the contract	133
15.2.1	The particulars of sale	133
15.2.2	The root of title	134
15.2.3	Incumbrances	135
15.3	Pre-contract searches and enquiries	135
15.3.1	Inspection of the property	135
	Rights of persons in occupation	
15.3.2	Index map search	136
15.3.3	Land charges search: unregistered titles	137
15.4	Deducing and investigating title	137
15.5	Exchange of contracts	138

16 Unregistered freehold title: 2

16.1	The effect of a binding contract	139
16.2	Requisitions on title	139
16.3	Preparing the documentation	139
16.3.1	Deed of conveyance	139
	Commencement and date	
	The parties	
	Recitals	
	The testatum	
	The consideration and receipt clause	
	The parcels clause	
	Exceptions and reservations	
	The habendum	
	Co-ownership declaration of trust for sale	

Declarations
Express covenants
Acknowledgement and undertaking
Certificate of value
Schedules
Execution and attestation

16.3.2   Transfer under rule 72   142

16.3.3   The mortgage deed   143

16.3.4   Undertaking for discharge of the
         seller's mortgage   143

16.3.5   Statements of account   143

16.4   Pre-completion searches   143

16.4.1   Central Land Charges search   143
         Making the search
         Relying on previous land charges
            searches

16.4.2   Inspection of the property   146

16.4.3   Search of the Local Land
         Charges Register?   146

16.4.4   Company search   147

16.4.5   Mortgagee's searches   148

17 Unregistered freehold title : 3

17.1   Completion   151

17.1.1   Verifying the title   151

17.1.2   Documents to be handed over   152

17.1.3   The passing of the legal title   152

17.2   Post-completion   153

17.2.1   Seller's solicitor   153

17.2.2   Buyer's solicitor: stamping   153

17.2.3   Buyer's solicitor: first registration
         of title   154
         Documents to be produced   154
         Requisitions on title   154

17.2.4   The pre-registration deeds   155

17.3   Remedies   156

17.3.1   Post-completion   156

18 Special dispositions

18.1   Dispositions by personal
       representatives   159

18.1.1   Proof of the PR's title   159

18.1.2   Assents by PRs   159
         Registered titles
         Unregistered titles
         Memorandum
         PR as beneficiary

18.1.3   Sales by personal representatives   160
         The operation of s.36

18.1.4   PRs and beneficial joint tenancies   162
         Unregistered titles
         Registered titles

18.1.5   PRs and tenancies in common   163

18.2   Dispositions by attorneys   163

18.2.1   General and specific powers   163

18.2.2   Trustee's powers   164

18.2.3   Revocation of authority   164

18.2.4   Protection of buyers and other
         purchasers   164
         Protection available
         Buyer's actions

18.2.5   Execution of deeds by attorneys   16c

18.2.6   Proof of a power of attorney   166

18.2.7   Irrevocable security powers   166

18.2.8   Enduring powers of attorney   166

18.3   Dispositions by companies   167

18.3.1   Powers of directors to bind the
         company   167

18.3.2   Execution of deeds   168

18.4   Voidable dispositions   168

18.4.1   Dispositions by trustees to
         themselves   168

18.4.2   Dispositions affected by undue
         influence   169

18.5   Transaction at an undervalue   169

18.5.1   Definition   170

18.5.2   Setting aside the transaction   170
         Within two years
         Between two and five years
         More than five years

18.5.3   Protection of third parties   170

18.6   Miscellaneous dispositions   171

18.7   Dispositions other than sales   171

18.8   Auction sales   172

19 Sales of part

19.1   Creation of new covenants and
        easements   173

19.1.1   New covenants   173

19.1.2   Grant of new easements   173

19.1.3   Preventing new easements being
          granted by implication   174

19.1.4   Reservation of new easements   174

19.2   Procedures: registered title   175

19.2.1   Description of the property   175

19.2.2   Discharge of seller's mortgage   175

19.2.3   Pre-completion search   175

19.2.4   Form of the transfer   175

19.2.5   Placing the seller's land certificate
          on deposit   176

19.2.6   Registration of the transfer   176

19.3   Procedures: unregistered title   176

19.3.1   Description of the property   176

19.3.2   Discharge of the seller's mortgage   176

19.3.3   The deed of conveyance   177

19.3.4   Acknowledgements and
          undertakings   177

19.3.5   Marking the abstract and
          recording sales off   178

19.3.6   Registration of title   179

20 Estate conveyancing

20.1   Introduction   181

20.2   Seller   181

20.2.1   Title   181

20.2.2   Contract   182
          Seller's register of title
          Sale before completion of the
              property
          Services
          NHBC cover
          Form of transfer

20.2.3   Transfer   184

20.2.4   Documents provided with the
          contract   185
          Roads and drainage

20.3   Buyer   186

20.3.1   Contract   186

20.3.2   Transfer   186

20.3.3   Searches and enquiries   187

20.3.4   Exchange and after   187

20.3.5   Completion and post-completion   188

21 Leasehold conveyancing

21.1   Introduction   191

21.2   Advantages of selling leasehold   191

21.2.1   Rent   191

21.2.2   Continuing interest   191

21.2.3   Enforcing covenants   193

21.3   The grant of a long lease of a house   193

21.3.1   Taking instructions   193

21.3.2   Investigating title   194

21.3.3   Mortgagee's consent   194

21.4   Drafting the lease   194

21.4.1   Commencement, date and
          parties   194

21.4.2   Payment of premium and receipt   194

21.4.3   Operative words   194

21.4.4   Parcels   194

21.4.5   Term   195

21.4.6   Rent   195

21.4.7   Express covenants   195
          To pay rent
          To repair
          Prohibitive covenants
          Insurance
          Notice of dealings to landlord
          Quiet enjoyment

21.4.8   Covenant not to assign or underlet   197
          Requesting payment for consent
          Withholding or delaying consent

21.4.9   Forfeiture (or re-entry)   198

21.4.10 Certificate of value   198

21.4.11 Production to the Inland Revenue 199

22 Grant of a long lease

22.1   The draft contract   201

22.1.1   Deducing title   201
Types of registered leasehold title
Where the superior title is unregistered
Where the superior title is registered

22.1.2   Consideration of the draft contract   203

22.1.3   Insurance arrangements   204

22.1.4   Mortgagee's consent   204

22.2   Exchanging contracts and investigating title   204

22.2.1   Preparing for exchange: the buyer   204

22.2.2   Buyer and seller   204

22.2.3   Investigating title   205

22.3   Preparing for completion   205

22.3.1   Engrossing the lease   205

22.3.2   Execution   205

22.3.3   Pre-completion searches   206
Unregistered titles
Registered titles

22.4   Completion   206

22.4.1   Documents   206

23.4.2   Purchase monies   207

22.5   Post completion stages   207

22.5.1   Stamping   207

22.5.2   Registration   207
First registration
Dispositionary lease

22.5.3   Notice to landlord   208

22.5.4   Custody of the deeds and documents   209

23 Special problems relating to flats

23.1   Introduction   211

23.2   Parcels   211

23.3   Easements   212

23.4   Tenant's covenants   212

23.4.1   Enforceability of covenants   212
Enforcement by the landlord
Letting scheme

23.5   Landlord's covenants   213

23.6   Management company   213

23.6.1   Three-party leases   214

23.6.2   Freehold vested in the management company   214

23.7   Insurance   214

23.8   Statutory provisions for service charges   214

23.8.1   Payment required in advance   215

23.8.2   Payment for work already carried out   215

23.8.3   Payment of large sums   215

23.8.4   Further information   215

24 The assignment of a registered lease

24.1   Introduction   217

24.2   Taking instructions   217

24.2.1   Consent to assignment   217

24.2.2   Other documents   218

24.3   Drafting the contract and deducing title   218

24.3.1   Deducing title   219

24.4   Making pre-contract searches and enquiries   219

24.5   Approving the contract   219

24.6   Investigating title   220

24.7   Preparing the purchase deed   221

24.8   Preparing for completion   221

24.8.1   Seller's solicitor   221

24.8.2 Buyer's solicitor   221

24.9   Making pre-completion searches

24.10 Completion   222

24.10.I What the buyer must receive   222

24.10.2 Other documents   222

24.11 Post completion   223

24.11.1 Transfer document   223

24.11.2 Land Registry   223

24.11.3 Notice to the landlord   223

24.11.4 Custody of documents   223

**25 The assignment of an unregistered
     lease**

25.1   Introduction   225

25.2   Taking instructions   225

25.3   Drafting the contract and
       deducing title   225

25.3.1 Particulars of the lease   225

25.3.2 Deducing title   225
        The open contact rule
        Special conditions

25.4   Making pre-contract searches
       and enquiries   226

25.5   Approving the draft contract   226

25.6   Investigating title   227

25.7   Preparing the purchase deed   227

25.7.1 Recitals clause   227

25.7.2 Habendum clause   227

25.7.3 SC 8.1.4   228

25.7.4 Indemnity covenants   228

25.8   Preparing for completion   228

25.9   Making pre-completion searches   228

25.10 Completion   229

25.10.1 What the buyer must receive   229

25.10.2 Other documents   229

25.11 Post completion   229

25.11.I The assignment   229

25.11.2 Land Registry   229

25.11.3 Notice to landlord and custody of
         documents   229

Table of cases

Abbey National Building Society v Cann [1991] AC 56   82

Beard v Porter [1948] 1KB 321   117

Carne v Debono [1988] 1 WLR 1107   104

Domb v Isoz [1980] Ch 548   92
Dunning (A J) & Sons (Shopfitters) Ltd v Sykes & Son (Poole) Ltd [1987] Ch 287   121

Hadley v Baxendale (1854) 9 Exch 341   114
Hastingwood Property Ltd v Saunders Bearman Anselm [1990] WLR 623   107
Heron II, The (Koufos v C Czarnikou Ltd) [1969] 1 AC 350   114
Hunt v Luck [1902] 1 Ch 428   129, 136

Johnson v Agnew [1980] AC 367   116, 118

King's Will Trust, Re [1964] Ch 542   160

Midland Bank Trust Co v Greene [1981] AC 513   136

Oak Co-operative Building Society v Blackburn [1968] Ch 730   145

Palmer v Johnson (1884) 13 QBD 351   120

Raineri v Miles [1981] AC 1050   114
Rignall Developments v Halil [1987] 3 WLR 394   66

Schwann v Cotton [1916] 2 Ch 120   174
Smith v Eric S Bush [1990] 1 AC 831   49–50

Walker v Boyle [1982] 1 WLR 495   70
Wheeldon v Burrows (1879) 12 Ch D 31   174, 175
Wroth v Tyler [1974] Ch 30   86, 118

Table of statutes

Administration of Estates Act 1925
s.36   161–2, 171
s.36(5)   160
s.36(6)   160, 161–2, 162
s.36(7)   160
s.36(8)   160

Administration of Justice Act 1970
s.36   83

Enduring Powers of Attorney Act 1985   167

Insolvency Act 1986
s.336   86
s.339   170
s.342   170
s.345   170
s.423   170

Land Charges Act 1925   125
s.198   66
Land Charges Act 1969   125
Land Charges Act 1972   3, 106, 145, 147
s.4 181
Land Registration Act 1925   4, 14, 207
s.110   63, 67, 77, 79, 202, 219
s.123   4, 14, 15, 153
s.24   228
s.70(1)(g)   82, 105–6, 136
s.83   14, 105
Landlord and Tenant Act 1927   196
19(1)   197
19(2)   196
19(3)   196
Landlord and Tenant Act 1985
ss.11–14   195
ss.18–30   215
Landlord and Tenant Act 1988   198
Law of Property (Joint Tenants)
  Act 1964   129, 162, 163

Law of Property (Miscellaneous
  Provisions) Act 1989
s.1   102, 142, 168
s.2   84, 92, 97, 130, 172
Law of Property Act 1925   8
s.101   82, 83
s.104   83
s.115   131
s.199   129, 136
s.205   8
s.44   124
s.44(2)   202
s.47   99
s.48   68
s.49   100
s.49(2)   117
s.74   168
s.76   120
s.77   228
s.84   86
s.88(1)   83
Law of Property Act 1969
s.144   197
s.23   124
s.25   125, 144, 156
s.27(2)   160
s.62   140, 173, 174
s.64   177
Local Land Charges Act 1975   73
s.10   73

Matrimonial Homes Act 1967   132
Matrimonial Homes Act 1983   12
s.4   85
Mental Health Act 1983   171
Misrepresentation Act 1967
s.1   119, 120
s.2(1)   72, 119, 120
s.2(2)   72, 119
s.3 73   119

Planning (Listed Buildings and Conservation Areas) 1990	54	s.53	46
		ss.222–226	46
Planning and Compensation Act 1991	51	Town and Country Planning Act 1990	51
s.4	56	s.171B	56
Policies of Assurance Act 1867	44	s.172	56
		s.55	52
Powers of Attorney Act 1971		s.57	54
s.10	164	s.70	55
s.3	166	s.92	55, 56
s.4	166		
s.5(2)	164, 165, 166	Trustee Act 1925	
s.5(4)	164–5, 165	s.25	164
s.7	166		
s.9	164	Unfair Contract Terms Act 1977	49
		s.11(1)	119
Stamp Act 1891	40, 100	s.2	50
s.117	68		
		Water Industry Act 1991	
Taxation of Chargeable Gains Act 1992	46	s.104	186
s.38	46		

Chapter 1

Introduction to conveyancing

What is conveyancing?   1.1

Conveyancing is real property law in action. It is about the creation and transfer of estates and interests in land.

> *Note* _____
>
> It is important that you have a firm understanding of the principles of land law and the pre-course primer has focused on revision of these basic principles.

Creation and transfer of estates   1.1.1

There are only two estates which can exist as legal estates:

- The *fee simple absolute in possession*; and
- The *term of years absolute*.

They tend to be referred to by the tenure on which they are held as (legal) freehold and leaseholds titles. The word 'legal' is not generally stated and 'title' is also frequently omitted. So the terms 'freehold' and 'leasehold' are widely used to mean respectively a legal fee simple estate held on freehold tenure and a legal term of years absolute held on leasehold tenure.

Creation of new estates   1.1.2

Freehold titles
It is *not* possible to create any new freehold titles except by subdividing an existing title. Where there is a sale of part of a title the buyer will be registered as the first proprietor of the title in that part and given a new title number.

The seller will remain as registered proprietor of the title in the retained land and will keep the old title number but the property register and filed plan will be amended to show that the area sold has been removed from that title.

Leasehold titles
A new leasehold title may be created out of a freehold title and a new sub-leasehold (underlease) out of a leasehold title. Sub-underleases may be created out of sub-leases and so on.

The estate out of which a leasehold is created is called the reversionary estate, or the superior title.

1.1.3   Transfer of existing estates

Existing freeholds, leases and sub-leases may be trans-ferred as a result of:

- A contract of sale;
- A gift (which may be either a gift *inter vivos* or a gift taking effect on death);
- By operation of law – as in the event of bankruptcy; or
- By court order.

Note

Most conveyancing transactions take place where there is a *sale* of land and this manual will be primarily concerned with that event.

1.1.4   The sale and purchase of land

On a sale, the buyer will want to be satisfied that:

- The seller has the right to sell; and
- They know about all third party interests in the land.

The seller's right to sell

The seller will have to prove title to the estate that is the subject of the sale.

If the title to the estate is *registered* this can easily be done by obtaining an official copy, known as an *office copy*, of the entries on the Land Register. This will show who is regis-tered as proprietor of the title.

If the title is *unregistered* it will be more complex. The title will have to be traced back through the title deeds to a good *root of title* which is at least 15 years old (*see* Chapter 16).

Knowledge about all third party interests in the land

Some third party rights are removable and the buyer, having discovered their existence will take the necessary steps to ensure that they take free from them, eg. the buyer will not want to take the land subject to existing mortgages or MHA rights. Similarly, the buyer will not want to take the land subject to the rights of beneficiaries under a trust and will ensure that such rights are overreached.

Other third party rights, such as easements, covenants and local land charges are nor normally removable, nor can they be overreached. The buyer takes subject to them and will therefore want full details of them before enter-ing into the contract.

Thus, conveyancing largely involves:

- Ensuring that the seller has title, ie. the right to sell; and

- Checking for third party incumbrances to ensure that they are appropriately dealt with.

Creation of new third party interests   1.1.5

It is when land is sold that new third party rights are most often created, eg. the buyer may create a new mortgage over the land or may enter into new covenants and easements. It is possible, however, for new third party rights to be created at other times, eg. the owner of an unincumbered estate may mortgage it, or grant a neighbour a right of way over the land, or enter into covenants with a neighbour affecting the use of the land.

Transfer of existing third party interests   1.1.6

When an estate is transferred, the benefit and burden of third party interests (incumbrances) affecting the estate will generally also be transferred.

Benefit

Some third party rights are personal, eg. MHA rights and beneficiaries' rights, but others are designed to benefit specific land, eg. easements and covenants, and the benefit of these rights may pass with the dominant land.

Burden

Third party rights that have been protected by registration will generally bind a buyer. However, the rights of beneficiaries under a trust for sale or strict settlement will not bind the buyer even if protected by registration if the overreaching machinery is utilised. Others may be removable by the seller, eg. by repaying a mortgage loan and so conveying the property unincumbered.

Third party rights in *registered land* which have *not* been registered will still be bind the buyer if they constitute *overriding interests*. If the title is *unregistered*, third party rights which are not registrable under the Land Charges Act 1972 will be binding if they constitute legal interests or interests whose enforceability depends on the doctrine of notice, and the buyer has notice.

Course content   1.2

This course deals with residential conveyancing, commercial conveyancing is not included. You will, however, be able to utilise the skills and knowledge gained in studying residential conveyancing in other contexts and you will acquire an understanding of the conveyancing process which will be equally applicable to commercial conveyancing.

1.2.1 Structure of the manual

The main focus of the course is on *registered conveyancing*.

Chapters 2, 3 and 7–13 of this manual assume that the title being dealt with is a registered freehold. However, many of the matters considered and processes described will also apply to unregistered titles.

Chapter 14–17 deal specifically with unregistered freeholds, 18–20 consider both registered and unregistered titles.

Chapters 21–25 deal with leaseholds, both registered and unregistered.

Chapters 4–6 apply regardless of whether the title is registered or unregistered, freehold or leasehold.

1.2.2 Main differences between registered and unregistered conveyancing

Registered	*Unregistered*
Checking that the seller has title to the property	
Inspect the register to see who is registered as proprietor and the type of title which they have.	Investigate title back through the deeds to a good root of title at least 15 years old.
Checking for third party incumbrances	
Inspect the register to check for minor interests protected by notice or caution and check for overriding interests, and for local land charges.	Undertake a central land charges search to check for registered third party charges and a local land charges search to check for local land charges. Check for other non-registrable interests which, if legal, will be binding and, if equitable, will be binding if the buyer is fixed with notice of them.
Registration of title	
A disposition of a registered title must be registered otherwise the legal estate does not pass.	On completion legal title passes but if the transaction is one which leads to compulsory registration of the title then, following completion, an application must be made to the Land Registry for first registration within two months otherwise legal title reverts to the seller: s.123, LRA 1925.

Stages in the conveyancing process   1.3

A sale and purchase of land falls into three phases:

- Up to exchange of contracts;
- Exchange to completion;
- Post-completion.

Up to exchange of contracts   1.3.1

This stage includes:

- Taking *instructions* to act for seller or buyer;
- Organising the *financial aspects* of the transaction;
- Drafting/negotiating *amendments* to the contract of sale;
- Carrying out various *searches and enquiries* to enable the buyer to discover:
    - the physical state of the property;
    - third party rights affecting the land; and
    - other matters which may influence a buyer's decision whether or not to buy, eg. whether there are disputes with the neighbours and whether there are plans for new roads in the area;
- The *exchange of contracts*. Until this occurs either party may at any time withdraw from the transaction without any liability to the other side. Once contracts have been exchanged both sides are legally bound to complete, ie. to perform the contract – the buyer by paying the agreed price and the seller by transferring the agreed property.

Exchange to completion   1.3.2

This stage includes:

- Checking that the seller has *title to the property*. In modern conveyancing this is often done pre-exchange (*see* 1.4);
- Preparing the document necessary to *transfer the property*. This will be a land registry transfer (registered title), or deed of conveyance (unregistered title). (If the buyer is buying with the aid of a mortgage, the mortgage documentation will also have to be prepared.)
- Conducting certain *pre-completion searches* to check that there are no new third party rights/incumbrances;
- Ensuring that the *finance* is in place;
- *Completion* by payment of the price and the execution and handing over of the transfer/conveyance plus various other documents. (This is the performance of the contract, ie. the equivalent of the delivery of the goods under a sale of goods contract.)

1.3.3   Post-completion

To validate the transaction and ensure that the buyer gets legal title to the estate purchased, you must take the following steps:

- *Stamp* the transfer/conveyance;
- *Registration* – either registration of the dealing if the title was already registered or first registration if it was previously an unregistered title.

1.3.4   Stages in a freehold conveyancing transaction

Seller	Buyer
Take instructions.	Take instructions.
Investigate title and prepare draft contract.	Organise survey and finance, and await draft contract.
Answer buyer's pre-contract enquiries.	Make pre-contract searches and enquiries.
If Protocol is followed, supply buyer with searches and property information form and deduce title.	Check what is supplied and make any further searches and enquiries as necessary. Investigate title.
Negotiation of changes to the draft contract.	
Receipt of approved draft.	Approve draft contract.
Exchange of contracts.	
Deduce title if not done pre-exchange.	Investigate title.
Approve purchase deed.	Prepare purchase deed.
Preparation for completion.	Preparation for completion.
Completion	
Post-completion matters.	Post completion matters.

1.4   The National Conveyancing Protocol

There are certain aspects of the traditional conveyancing process which often give rise to delay or difficulty. The Protocol introduced amendments to the traditional process in the hope of speeding up the process and reducing the possibility of problems arising after contracts have been exchanged which might delay completion or even entitle the buyer to withdraw from the contract.

Note

The Protocol *only* applies if the parties agree to adopt it. If adopted, it should be adopted in its entirety but if there are to be any variations of it, they must be agreed in writing by both sides.

Main differences: traditional conveyancing and the protocol

Pre-contract enquiries and searches

Traditionally, it is for the buyer to initiate certain pre-contract searches and enquiries. This includes making enquiries of the seller and making a local land charges search and enquiries of the local authority. These all take time, especially the enquiries of the local authority which may take several weeks

Under the protocol, the seller assembles a 'property package', which includes a property information form, giving replies to the standard questions which buyers always ask and the replies to the local search and enquiries of the local authority and other relevant searches. If the package can be made available to the buyer as soon as they appear on the scene, an early exchange of contracts should be possible.

Note

It is always the buyer's responsibility to ensure that all necessary pre-contract searches and enquiries are made. The buyer may therefore decide to make further searches and enquiries.

Deducing title

Traditionally, title is not deduced by the seller until *after* the exchange of contracts. If it then transpires that the seller's title is defective and that the seller cannot transfer what they contracted to sell, the buyer will be entitled to withdraw from the contract. This will be very inconvenient, especially if the parties are in the middle of a chain transaction.

Where the title is *registered*, the process of deducing title is simple, ie. providing copies of the entries on the register. Hence, even before the introduction of the Protocol it was common practice for registered titles to be deduced pre-exchange. However, with *unregistered* titles the traditional process tended to be followed.

Under the protocol, title is *deduced by the seller* and *investigated by the buyer* before contracts are exchanged.

Some problems with the protocol

In a depressed market

There is no point in putting the property package together as soon as the property is marketed if a buyer may not appear for a very long time and by then the information in the package may be out of date. Sellers therefore tend not to put the package together until a buyer appears and so the saving in time may be insignificant.

Who pays for the searches?

Sellers have been reluctant to incur an expenditure which has traditionally been for the buyer's account. The Protocol does provide that if the buyer takes up and utilises the searches provided then, at exchange, the seller is entitled to be reimbursed by the buyer. This, however, presents several problems:

- Will the buyer honour this obligation?
- What if an exchange never materialises?
- What if the buyer decides not to rely on the searches provided but to make fresh searches?

1.4.3   **Terminology**

The Protocol sought to make the conveyancing process more user-friendly by adopting the terms 'seller' and 'buyer' in place of the traditional 'vendor' and 'purchaser'. This change in terminology is also found in the Standard Conditions of Sale (*see* Chapter 7) which were introduced at the same time as the Protocol and which can be, and are, used in transactions to which the Protocol is not applicable. The problem is that the terms 'buyer' and 'purchaser' are not synonymous. Many statutory provisions protect a 'purchaser' and s.205, LPA 1925 defines a purchaser to include a lessee, mortgagee or other person who for valuable consideration acquires an interest in the property. When dealing with such provisions the term 'purchaser' must be used and it cannot be replaced with 'buyer'.

Self-assessment questions

1   What is the significance of the exchange of contracts?
2   What are the two main legal issues which the buyer's solicitor is employed to investigate?
3   What is the National Conveyancing Protocol?
4   What are the two main differences between a transaction following the traditional pattern and one where the Protocol is adopted?

Chapter 2

The Land Register

The form of the Land Register

2.1

There is no central land register but a number of district land registries (17 as at the end of 1992), where titles to land served by each district registry are registered.

More than one title in any one piece of land can be registered as the freehold title, the leasehold title and any sub-leasehold title will all be separately registered, each title having a separate title number which is set out at the head of the register.

The register is then divided into three parts:

- The Property Register;
- The Proprietorship Register;
- The Charges Register.

The Property Register

2.1.1

This gives a brief description of the property and refers to the land registry plan, called the filed plan, which exists for each registered title. It states whether the title is freehold or leasehold.

If *leasehold*, it will give brief particulars of the lease but not its full terms.

Note

The lease itself, therefore, remains an essential title document in any dealing with the leasehold title.

If the property enjoys the benefit of rights of way over neighbouring land, these are sometimes expressly stated but, even if they are not, the proprietor will be entitled to all appurtenant rights.

The Proprietorship Register

2.1.2

This states the class of title, which may be:

- Absolute;
- Possessory;
- Qualified; or
- Good leasehold.

The register gives the names and addresses of the registered proprietors. Up to four persons can be registered as proprietors and up to three addresses may be given for each.

Note

It is important that proprietors keep the land registry informed of any change of address as, should the land registry need to communicate with the registered proprietors, it will do so at the addresses listed.

It is in this part of the register that inhibitions, restrictions and cautions appear. (These are all devices for protecting minor interests.)

2.1.3   The Charges Register

This part of the register records registered charges, ie. legal mortgages and notices protecting minor interests.

2.1.4   The filed plan

After the Charges Register there is a copy of the filed plan. This is based on the Ordnance Survey map for the area and marks in red the property in question.

2.2   Protection of minor interests

All minor interests need to be protected by entry on the register. There are four different devices for protecting them:

- Inhibitions;
- Restrictions;
- Cautions;
- Notices.

2.2.1   Inhibitions

An inhibition is entered in the Proprietorship Register by the court or by the Chief Land Registrar.

The principal type is a *bankruptcy inhibition*. This is entered where a bankruptcy order has been made against a registered proprietor. It prevents the proprietor dealing with the title.

Note

A bankruptcy inhibition is usually preceded by a creditor's notice which is entered where a bankruptcy petition has been lodged against a registered proprietor.

Most *notices* appear in the Charges Register but a creditor's notice is an exception and appears in the Proprietorship Register.

2.2.2   Restrictions

Restrictions are entered in the *Proprietorship Register* at the request of the proprietor.

Where the proprietor is a corporation a restriction may indicate the particular officers of the corporation who are authorised to act on its behalf.

Where the registered proprietor is a *tenant for life* under a settlement, a restriction will indicate this and give the names of the trustees of the settlement to whom any purchase money will have to be paid.

Where the registered proprietors are holding on *trust for sale*, a restriction in the following terms is sometimes entered:

'No disposition by one proprietor of the land (being the survivor of joint proprietors and not being a trust corporation) under which capital money arises is to be registered except under an order of the registrar or of the court'.

The restriction will appear where the proprietors are holding for themselves as tenants in common or if they hold for other beneficiaries. It will ensure that a purchaser does not deal with the sole survivor alone but insists on the appointment of second trustee so as to overreach any other beneficial interest.

This restriction will *not* appear where the proprietors are holding on trust for sale for themselves as beneficial joint tenants because the right of survivorship will apply in that situation to both the legal and equitable titles and the sole surviving trustee will be entitled to deal with the property alone.

Where the proprietors hold for themselves as *beneficial joint tenants* and, in consequence, no restriction is entered, it is essential that if they subsequently sever the beneficial tenancy application be made to the Registry for the entry of the restriction. Severance can be effected unilaterally by one tenant simply serving notice of severance on the other(s). If the restriction is not entered then any purchaser is entitled to assume that they have continued as beneficial joint tenants and that the survivor can deal with the property alone.

Cautions 2.2.3

A caution against dealing can be entered in the *Proprietorship Register* by a third party to protect their interest.

Note

The main device for protecting minor interests is the notice.

In contrast to registering a *notice*, registering a caution does not require production of the land certificate. Thus, the co-operation of the registered proprietor is unnecessary. A caution is therefore fundamentally a hostile entry.

A caution simply indicates the name of the cautioner and the date it is lodged. This contrasts with a notice which indicates the type of interest it is intended to protect.

The cautioner has the right to be notified by the Land Registry of any application made to register any dealing with the property or to make any entry on the Register. The cautioner can then appear before the Registrar to assert their interest and, if it is established, the application for registration will be made subject to the cautioner's right.

A caution can be 'warned off' at any time. This means that the registered proprietor requires the Land Registry to give the cautioner 14 days within which to substantiate their right. If the cautioner fails to do so the caution will be removed.

The 'warning-off' mechanism prevents the title being clogged by unsubstantiated third party entries. The existence of a caution against the title will impede any dealing with that title as prospective purchasers will not be prepared to proceed until they have details of and are satisfied as to the right protected by the caution.

Note

An improperly lodged caution will entitle the registered proprietor to claim compensation for any resulting loss.

2.2.4   Notices

Notices are entered in the *Charges Register* to protect minor interests such as leases, restrictive covenants, estate contracts, rights under the Matrimonial Homes Act 1983, equitable mortgages and equitable easements.

To enter a notice the land certificate held by the registered proprietor must generally be produced. The most important exception is a notice of a spouse's right of occupation under the MHA. As production of the land certificate is not required, this type of notice can be entered as a hostile entry.

A creditor's notice and a notice of a lease at a rent without a fine, ie. without a premium, can also be entered without production of the land certificate.

Note

If a registered charge exists, the Land Registry will already hold the land certificate. The charge certificate held by the chargee will only have to be produced to register a notice if the notice adversely affects the chargee's title.

Where a notice protects a right of which there are lengthy details, these are usually set out in a separate schedule to the Charges Register. This commonly arises in relation to restrictive covenants. Thus, following the Charges Register there may be a schedule of several pages setting out details of the covenants.

Land and charge certificates   2.3

When the title is registered, the proprietor is issued with a land certificate which contains a copy of the entries on the register. This has to be produced to the Land Registry to register any disposition of the property and for the entry of restrictions and most notices – but not for the entry of a caution or inhibition. The land certificate may therefore not show the up to date state of the register. It can be sent to the registry at any time for up-dating and the date on which the certificate was last compared with the register is stamped inside the front cover of the certificate.

This means that when you need to know the current state of the title you should not rely on the entries in the land certificate as these may be out of date. You should obtain from the Land Registry an official copy of the entries on the Register. These are known as *office copies*.

If there is a registered charge against the title, the land certificate is kept by the Land Registry and only returned to the registered proprietor when all registered charges have been discharged. The chargee is issued with a charge certificate in its place. This is very similar to a land certificate in that it contains copies of the entries on the register but it also contains the original mortgage deed. If a second mortgage is created that too will be registered in the Charges Register and the chargee issued with a certificate of second charge which includes a copy of the entries on the Register and the original second mortgage deed.

Inspecting the Register   2.4

Since 3 December 1990 the Land Register has been open to the public and anyone can get details of any title by applying for a set of office copies. If you do not know the title number of the land in which you are interested, you can first apply for a search in the public index map.

This will tell you whether or not a title in a particular piece of land is already registered and, if it is, the title number. You can then apply for a set of office copies of the title.

In a sale of a registered title, it is usual for the seller to send the buyer a set of up to date office copies with the draft contract. If, at a later date, you want to check whether there have been any new entries made on the register, it is unnecessary to pay for a fresh set of office copies. You simply apply for a free official search of the register, asking whether there has been any new entries made since the date of issue of the office copies.

If office copies or official search certificates are inaccurate, eg. if they fail to reveal something that was actually on the register, then the purchaser will still be bound by the entry but will be entitled to seek compensation from the State Indemnity Fund: s.83, Land Registration Act 1925.

2.5   Registration of title

The present system of registration of title has existed since 1925 and in many urban areas most titles are now registered. Compulsory registration of title was extended to the whole of England and Wales on 1 December 1990.

However, even in areas in which registration has been in force for many years, there are still some unregistered titles, as registration is only compulsory when certain events take place which require an application for first registration of title.

2.5.1   Compulsory registration

Following completion of any of the transactions listed below, the freehold title in (a) and the leasehold title in (b) and (c) must be registered within *two* months: s.123, Land Registration Act 1925.

(a) A conveyance on sale of the freehold;

(b) The grant of a lease for more than 21 years out of an unregistered freehold title

(c) The assignment on sale of an unregistered lease with more than 21 years still to run at the date of the assignment;

Note

In situations (b) and (c) it is only the lease which is being granted or assigned which has to be registered. The superior reversionary title may remain unregistered until it is itself dealt with in circumstances rendering registration compulsory.

Registration is also compulsory where a lease for more than 21 years is granted out of a registered freehold title. This constitutes a disposition of an existing registered title and such a lease is consequently called a dispositionary lease. The two-month time limit for registration under s.123 does not apply in this case but the lessee only acquires legal title when the title is registered, not on the granting of the lease.

Completing the register

Voluntary registration can be applied for at any time.

The more recently the area became an area of compulsory registration the higher will be the proportion of remaining unregistered titles. In rural areas there is still a high but, with compulsory registration, progressively diminishing percentage of unregistered titles.

At the end of 1992 there were nearly 14 million registered titles, approximately two-thirds of the estimated number of separate titles in England and Wales. The Land Registry is considering strategies for speeding up the process of registration of the remaining unregistered titles and completing the register. The amendment of s.123 to provide new 'trigger mechanisms' for compulsory registration is the most likely method.

Registration may become compulsory whenever there is a change of ownership even if it does not occur 'on sale'. If there is a sale of part of an unregistered title, at present only the part sold has to be registered and the part retained can remain unregistered. This might change. Ways of encouraging public bodies, whose land rarely change hands, to register title voluntarily are also under consideration. However, for some years to come, conveyancers will have to deal with unregistered titles from time to time and those who can do so with confidence will be in demand.

Self-assessment questions

1   What is the difference between the Property Register, the Proprietorship Register and the Charges Register?
2   What are minor interests and will they bind a buyer?
3   What is the difference between a land certificate and a charge certificate?
4   Registration of title is now compulsory throughout England and Wales, so why do unregistered titles still exist?

Chapter 3

Taking instructions

Obtaining instructions and information   3.1

If a seller or buyer wishes you to act on a sale or purchase, you will have to take instructions from the client. Often you will be acting for a person who is both selling and buying and will therefore need to take instructions on *both* transactions.

The solicitor as agent   3.1.1

A solicitor acts as *agent* for the client and must therefore act within the authority (mandate) given by the client (the principal). You must never accept instructions to do anything which is illegal or which would constitute a breach of the rules of professional practice for example, the:

- Solicitors' Practice Rules;
- Solicitors' Accounts Rules;
- Solicitors' Publicity Code.

Note

These matters are considered in detail in Chapter 4 and in the manual on Professional Practice. They *must* be followed at all stages of the conveyancing transaction.

There are certain things that the solicitor will have *implied authority* to do unless otherwise instructed, eg. to effect an exchange of contracts by any usual method.

Be thorough   3.1.2

You must obtain clear and precise instructions as to what the client wishes and authorises you to do and all the information you will need to carry through those instructions. You must keep your client informed as to the progress you are making throughout the transaction. Matters may arise on which you will need to obtain further instructions, but if you obtain full instructions and information at the outset this should reduce the need to refer frequently to your client.

Giving explanation and advice   3.2

When taking instructions you will be asked to explain the transaction, or specific aspects of it, to the client and to give advice; in particular:

- *General explanation* of the sale/purchase process. What you will be doing for the client, what they will need to do themselves, the various stages in the transaction – especially the significance of exchange of contracts and of completion.
- How *long* it is likely to take.
- The *costs* of the transaction.
- The *financing* of the purchase. This may include general financial services advice and advice on types of mortgage and on mortgage interest relief.
- Explanation of the differences between *joint tenancy* and *tenancy in common* and which is appropriate to the clients' circumstances;
- On a sale, advice on possible *capital gains tax* liability.

3.3   Quoting on costs

This may form part of the initial interview with the client when you take instructions but may well arise at an earlier stage when a potential client asks for a quotation on costs before deciding whether or not to instruct you. It is important to distinguish between a fixed quote and an estimate.

3.3.1   Items to be included if acting for buyer

These are:

- Your fees plus VAT;
- If also acting for the buyer's mortgagee, are you making a separate charge, if so what?
- Stamp duty;
- Land Registry fees for registering the transfer;
- Search fees:
    - Local search and enquiries of local authority;
    - Bankruptcy search if acting for mortgagee;
    - Any other special searches.

3.3.2   Items to be included if acting for seller

These are:

- Your fees plus VAT;
- Office copy entries;
- Search fees if the Protocol is being followed and the buyer does not reimburse them.

3.3.3   Charging for other disbursements

Should you charge for each separate phone call, photocopying of documents etc? Generally, these are included in your fee. If separately billed they will attract VAT.

Taking instructions from a seller   3.4

Checklist   3.4.1

(a) Names, addresses, phone numbers (home and work) of seller(s).

   Capacity in which they are selling?

(b) Details of buyer(s) as far as they are known.

(c) Was the sale arranged through an estate agent? If so, obtain the estate agent's name and address and a copy of their particulars.

   Ascertain what arrangements the client has made with the agent regarding commission and whether, if the sale goes through, the client will wish you to settle the agent's bill directly out of the proceeds of sale.

(d) Details of the property:

   - Address.
   - Freehold/leasehold.
   - Registered/unregistered – the whereabouts of the title deeds, or the land or charge certificate.

   Get the client to complete the property information questionnaire.

(e) The price – what does it include?

   - Are any chattels included in the price or to be purchased for a separate consideration?
   - Are any fixtures to be removed?
   - Get the client to complete the fixtures and fittings form.
   - Has any preliminary deposit been paid by the buyer? If so, to whom?

(f) Does the seller have a mortgage on the property? If so, obtain details of the mortgagee and the account number and an estimate from the client of the amount outstanding on the mortgage. Check whether there are subsequent mortgages on the property.

(g) Instructions regarding proceeds of sale.

(h) Is there a related purchase and, if so, is it dependent on the sale proceeds? If it is, you will need to synchronise the exchange of contracts and generally have the same completion date on both contracts.

(i) Completion date – what target date would the client like you to work towards?

(j) Ask for any correspondence that exists between the client and the prospective buyer and with any other party involved.

(k) Are there any other special instructions that you require, given the circumstances of the case, or other issues that the client wishes to raise?

3.4.2 Action following instructions

(a) Confirm instructions in writing to the client and to the other side. Advise other side whether or not you intend to follow the Protocol.

(b) Obtain the charge certificate from the mortgagee by giving an undertaking (*see* Chapter 4).

(c) Obtain a set of office copy entries from the district land registry.

(d) Examine the seller's title and then draft the contract.

(e) Conduct local and other searches if the Protocol is being followed.

(f) Send the buyer (preferably with the draft contract):
- Two copies of the draft contract;
- Office copy entries;
- The results of the searches;
- The property information form;
- The fixtures and fittings form.

3.5 Taking instructions from a buyer

3.5.1 Checklist

(a) Names, addresses, phone numbers (home and work) of buyer(s).

Capacity in which they are buying?

(b) Details of seller(s) as far as they are known.

(c) Was purchase arranged through an estate agent? If so, obtain the estate agent's name and address and a copy of their particulars.

(d) Details of the property:
- Address.
- Freehold/leasehold.

(e) The price – what does it include? Has any preliminary deposit been paid by the buyer? If so, to whom?

(f) How is the purchase to be financed? It may be necessary to give the client advice on sources and types of mortgage finance (*see* Chapter 5).

(g) Is there a related sale? If there is, is it essential to synchronise the exchange of contracts on the two transactions and must the completion dates coincide?

(h) If there are more than two purchasers, how are they going to hold the beneficial title? Advice will need to be given on the two forms of co-ownership and the advantages and disadvantages of each and which is more appropriate to the clients' circumstances.

> *Note*
>
> If a conflict of interest arises between the purchasers then you cannot act for both or all of them (*see* Chapter 4).

(i) Completion date – what target date would the client like you to work towards?

(j) Ask for any correspondence that exists between the client and the prospective seller and with any other party involved.

(k) Are there any other special instructions that you require, given the circumstances of the case, or other issues that the client wishes to raise?

Action following instructions 3.5.2

(a) Confirm instructions in writing to the client and to the other side. Confirm adoption of Protocol if appropriate.

(b) Ensure that the client progresses the mortgage application and any separate survey that the client has decided is to be done.

(c) If the Protocol is not being followed and searches will not be provided by the seller, institute a local land charges search and enquiries of the local authority, plus any other appropriate searches.

(d) Await receipt from the seller of the draft contract and, if Protocol is being followed, the property package.

Self-assessment questions

1 What is the legal relationship between a solicitor and client, and what governs the terms of that relationship?

2 On what particular issue will you need to advise co-purchasers?

3 When acting for a client who is both selling and buying, what particular problem will you face?

4 Clients frequently ask how long the transaction will take. How will you reply?

Chapter 4

Professional conduct

Introduction

4.1

Throughout the conveyancing transaction you must at all times observe the Solicitors' Practice Rules and the other rules, codes, written standards and guidelines issued by the Law Society. Many issues of professional practice arise at the very outset of the transaction when taking instructions to act.

Note

You should refer to texts on professional practice for a full treatment of this topic.

Rule 15: Solicitors' Practice Rules

4.2

This comparatively new rule introduces the concept of *client care*.

Rule 15 (Client Care)

1   Every principal in private practice shall operate a complaints handling procedure which shall, *inter alia*, ensure that clients are informed whom to approach in the event of any problem with the service provided.

2   Every solicitor in private practice shall, unless it is inappropriate in the circumstances:

(a) ensure that clients know the name and status of the person responsible for the day to day conduct of the matter and the principal responsible for its overall supervision;

(b) ensure that clients know whom to approach in the event of any problem with the service provided; and

(c) ensure that clients are at all relevant times given any appropriate information as to the issues raised and the progress of the matter.

After taking instructions you will write to the client to confirm your instructions and the costs quoted. In that letter you must ensure that you comply with Rule 15(2).

Note

The Law Society has issued a good practice guide on client care which gives practical advice to solicitors on compliance with Rule 15 and also with the written professional standards on costs.

4.3   Costs

4.3.1   Information on costs

The Law Society has issued a set of written professional standards concerning information on costs. It provides that:

- On taking instructions you should give the client the best information possible about the likely cost of the matter and discuss with them how the charges and disbursements are to be met;

- When confirming instructions in writing you should record whether any fee has been agreed and, if so, what it is, what it covers and whether it includes VAT and disbursements;

- The final amount payable should not vary substantially from the estimate unless clients have been informed of changed circumstances in writing.

In conveyancing solicitors do not normally charge an hourly rate but give the client a price for the job.

Note

Many conveyancing transactions do not proceed to completion. The solicitor should make it clear at the outset whether or not they will charge for uncompleted transactions and the basis on which the charge will be made.

4.3.2   Exceeding the estimate

The price quoted may be an estimate or a fixed quote.

You should be careful to ensure that you do not bind yourself to a fixed fee, unless that is your intention, as a fixed fee cannot be increased if the transaction turns out to be more complex than you anticipated.

In the case of an estimate you should inform your client immediately it appears that the estimate will be or is likely to be exceeded and you should not wait until you submit the bill of costs.

4.3.3   Rendering the bill

You are under a duty to render a bill of costs to your client within a *reasonable time of concluding the matter* to which the bill relates.

It is good practice to submit it as soon as possible, especially where you are holding sums of money on behalf of the client and await their approval of the costs before accounting to the client for the balance. This is a common situation in conveyancing as you will often be holding sale proceeds for your client.

You may *not* move the costs from client account to office account unless the client has previously agreed the amount and it has in writing been made clear to the client that money held for them is being or will be applied towards such costs.

You must not sue, or threaten to sue, without first informing your client in writing of their right to require a remuneration certificate and/or to seek taxation of your bill. In any event, you may not sue your client until the expiration of a month from the delivery of your bill.

Acting for more than one party 4.4

General rule 4.4.1

There is a general principle of professional conduct that a solicitor or firm of solicitors should not accept instructions to act for two or more clients where there is a conflict or a significant risk of a conflict, between the interests of those clients.

Rule 6: Solicitors' Practice Rules 4.4.2

In conveyancing the chance of there being a conflict of interest is high and therefore Rule 6 deals specifically with this issue.

Rule 6 (Prohibition against acting for seller and buyer, or for lender and borrower in a private mortgage)

1   Without prejudice to the general principle of professional conduct that a solicitor shall not accept instructions to act for two or more clients where there is a conflict between the interests of those clients, a solicitor or two or more solicitors practising in partnership or association shall not act for both seller and buyer on a transfer of land for value at arm's length, or for both lessor and lessee on the grant of a lease for value at arm's length, or for both lender and borrower in a private mortgage at arm's length.

2   Provided no conflict of interest appears, and provided the seller or lessor is not a builder or developer selling or leasing as such, and provided the solicitor or any solicitor practising in partnership or association with that solicitor is not instructed to negotiate the sale of the property concerned, the rule set out in paragraph 1 of this rule shall not apply if:

(a) the parties are associated companies; or

(b) the parties are related by blood, adoption or marriage; or

(c) both parties are established clients (which expression shall include persons related by blood, adoption or marriage to established clients); or

(d) on a transfer of land, the consideration is less than £5,000; or

(e) there is no other solicitor or other qualified conveyancer in the vicinity whom either party can reasonably be expected to consult; or

(f) two associated firms or two offices of the same firm are respectively acting for the parties, provided that:

> (i) the respective firms or offices are in different localities; and
>
> (ii) neither party was referred to the firm or office acting for him or her from an associated firm or from another office of the same firm; and
>
> (iii) the transaction is dealt with or supervised by a different solicitor in regular attendance at each firm or office.

3 In this rule:

(a) 'association' refers to a situation where two or more firms of solicitors have at least one common principal; and where either firm is a recognised body 'principal' means a director or member of that body, or the beneficial owner of any share in the body held by a member as nominee, or the body itself; and

(b) 'private mortgage' means any mortgage other than one provided by an institution which provides mortgages in the normal course of its activities.

Note

1 The ban on acting for both parties imposed by Rule 6(1) applies even if there is no conflict of interest. The exceptions provided for in Rule 6(2) only apply if there is *no* conflict of interest.

2 A transaction is a transaction 'at arm's length' when it is intended to be a proper commercial transaction at full market value.

3 The test of whether someone is an 'established client' is an objective one, ie. whether the ordinary, reasonable and fair minded solicitor would regard a person as an established client. An *existing* client is not the same as an *established* client.

4.4.3 Acting for seller and buyer

Conflict of interest

A conflict of interest between seller and buyer may arise over any issue, eg. over the amount of the deposit or over the date for completion. The potential for a conflict arising is so great that extreme caution must be exercised before you accept instructions to act for both. The consent of both clients to the arrangement must always be obtained.

If at any time during the course of a transaction where you may properly act for both parties a conflict arises between them, you must *not continue* to act for both. You may continue to act for one of them provided you are not in possession of confidential information obtained while acting for the other. The consent of the other client must be sought and, in the absence of consent, you should only continue to act for the other if the withholding of consent is unreasonable. Generally you will continue to act for the more established client.

Undue influence

One particular situation in which you should never act for both, even if one of the Rule 6(2) exceptions applies, is where there is a possibility that one party may exercise *undue influence* over the other (*see* Chapter 18, para. 18.4.2). If there is any possibility of undue influence later being alleged it is vital that the parties are separately represented. This applies not only between seller and buyer, lessor and lessee and mortgagor and mortgagee, but also between co-buyers (*see* 4.4.6) and co-mortgagors.

Acting for the seller's mortgagee   4.4.4

Where the seller has a mortgage on the property they are selling, it will have to be redeemed at completion; usually out of the proceeds of sale. It is acceptable and usual for the seller's solicitor also to act on behalf of the mortgagee and to receive the purchase money on their behalf as well as on the seller's behalf. The mortgagee does not generally issue specific instructions to the seller's solicitor to act on their behalf but it is implied when the seller's mortgagee releases the title documents to the seller's solicitor for the purpose of sale.

Sometimes the mortgagee will insist on being separately represented, eg. by a firm that always acts for them. In such a case completion is likely to be at the office of the mortgagee's solicitor rather than at the office of the seller's solicitor as normally occurs.

Note

Increasingly, building societies will not release the title documents to sole practitioners. Similarly, on a purchase many building societies will not instruct sole practitioners.

Acting for the buyer's mortgagee   4.4.5

In the majority of transactions the buyer buys with the aid of a mortgage. It is quite usual for the same solicitor to act for the buyer and for the buyer's mortgagee, provided that the mortgagee is an institutional lender, eg. a bank or building society and not a private individual.

Acting for both is acceptable as:

- There is identity of interest between the buyer and their mortgagee as they are both concerned to ensure that the buyer obtains a good title from the seller and that therefore the title is a good security for the mortgagee to lend against;

- An institutional lender will have their own mortgage deeds which cannot generally be modified. The solicitor will have to explain to the buyer the terms of the mortgage but will not have to negotiate or draft the terms of the mortgage.

4.4.6 Acting for more than one buyer

If there is more than one buyer then there could be a conflict of interest as to how the beneficial title is to be held; whether as *joint tenants* or *tenants in common*.

The two forms of co-ownership will have to be carefully explained to the buyers and their wishes ascertained. They will probably ask for your advice. The generally accepted view is that in the case of a married couple a beneficial joint tenancy may be appropriate but that in other situations, a tenancy in common is probably preferable.

If the parties are contributing unequally then you must address the question of whether they should hold in shares which reflect their respective interests. This is obviously a situation in which a conflict of interest may arise.

If there is any hint of disagreement between them, or of undue influence being exercised by one over the other, then you must ensure that they are separately advised on this issue. This does not mean that you cannot continue to act for both in connection with their purchase, just that they must be separately advised on the issue of their beneficial holding.

4.5   Contract races

A contract race occurs when a seller sends out a draft contract to more than one prospective buyer on the understanding that the seller will exchange contracts with whichever buyer is ready to exchange first.

4.5.1 The Law Society direction

The Law Society has issued the following direction on contract races.

'The Council recognise that a solicitor acting for a Seller may sometimes be instructed by his client to deal with more than one prospective buyer at the same time.

The Council have accordingly directed that where a Seller instructs his solicitor to submit (whether simultaneously or otherwise) forms of contract to more than one prospective Buyer, the following steps by the solicitor are obligatory:

(A)Where solicitor is acting for Seller

The solicitor (with the client's authority) must at once disclose the Seller's decision direct to the solicitor acting for each prospective Buyer or (where no solicitor is acting) to the prospective Buyer(s) in person and such disclosure, if made orally, must at once be confirmed in writing. If the Seller refuses to authorise disclosure, the solicitor must cease acting for the Seller forthwith.

(B) Where solicitor is entitled to act for both Seller and Buyer

Notwithstanding the exceptions contained in para (2) of Rule 2 of the Solicitors' Practice Rules 1988, a solicitor cannot act for both Seller and Buyer if a conflict of interest arises. Where there is more than one prospective Buyer, the Council consider that the danger of a conflict of interest is greatly increased. The Council are reluctant to issue a general prohibition against acting in such cases and they therefore warn all solicitors concerned to consider most carefully whether, and if so to what extent, they can properly act in these cases.'

If, in an exceptional case, a solicitor decides that he can properly act for both vendor and one of the prospective purchasers, then (in addition to the steps he must take under paragraph (A) above) the solicitor must at once disclose his decision direct to those two clients and also to the solicitor acting for every other prospective purchaser or (where no solicitor is acting) to the prospective purchaser(s) in person and such disclosure, if made orally, must at once be confirmed in writing.

(C)Where solicitor is asked to act for more than one purchaser

Where forms of contract are submitted to more than one prospective purchaser, a solicitor must not accept instructions to act for more than one prospective purchaser.'

Note

This direction applies to all sales and purchases of freehold and leasehold property and any solicitor who is found to be in breach of the Direction is liable to face proceedings before the Solicitors' Disciplinary Tribunal.

The perils of contract races   4.5.2

Although a contract race may at first appear attractive to a seller who has more than one interested buyer it does have its dangers. In particular:

- Buyers may not be prepared to participate in a race and thereby risk their time and money in surveys and legal costs. All the buyers may withdraw.

- The seller must make sure that they impose a deadline on the exchange of contracts otherwise their offer to exchange with whichever buyer is ready first may have to remain open indefinitely until a buyer is eventually ready to exchange.

4.5.3 Gazumping

Gazumping occurs when a seller has accepted an offer from one buyer – but contracts have not yet been exchanged and the parties are therefore not yet legally bound – and then accepts a higher offer from another buyer. Sometimes this will result in the draft contract that was submitted to the first buyer being withdrawn; sometimes it will result in a contract race. There are no special rules applicable to gazumping. Provided the direction on contract races is followed it is not unprofessional to act for a client who seeks to secure a higher price.

Note

The fact that gazumping is possible clearly demonstrates that there is no legally binding contract until contracts are exchanged.

4.6 Undertakings

For the effect of undertakings generally you are referred to manuals on professional conduct.

Remember:

- A solicitor who fails to honour an undertaking is *prima facie* guilty of professional misconduct;

- An undertaking is still binding even if it is to do something outside the solicitor's control (therefore never undertake to do anything you may not be able to do);

- Before undertaking to deal with the client's money in a particular way you must have the client's authority to do so.

In conveyancing, undertakings are frequently used at various stages of the transaction.

4.6.1 Obtaining title documents from the seller's mortgagee

When acting for a seller whose property is mortgaged you

must obtain the charge certificate (or title deeds in the case of an unregistered title) from the mortgagee. Immediately after receiving instructions to act you will therefore write to the mortgagee requesting the charge certificate/title deeds for the purpose of sale. In that letter you will undertake to hold the documents to the order of the mortgagee and to return them to the mortgagee or demand pending completion of the transaction. You will further undertake that if the transaction is completed you will pay to the mortgagee the amount of the mortgage money.

Note

Bank mortgagees often require more extensive undertakings in which they are promised the whole of the sale proceeds less estate agent's commission and the legal costs and disbursements, and they will generally not permit any variation of the terms of their standard undertakings.

In recent years some mortgagees have decided not to release title documents to sole practitioners.

Bridging finance 4.6.2

This is short term borrowing to bridge (cover) a period of time before certain other funds become available. It is readily provided by banks if they can see a source from which the borrowing will be repaid in the not too distant future. It is, however, expensive both in terms of the interest rate and the bank's arrangement fee. It is therefore to be avoided if at all possible.

It may, however, be necessary to raise bridging finance at various stages of the transaction.

The deposit
The buyer may be funding the purchase entirely from the proceeds of sale of an existing property and/or a mortgage on the new property. Neither of these sources of finance will be available until completion. However, at exchange of contracts a 10% deposit will normally have to be paid and funding this may be a problem. It may be possible to persuade the seller to agree to a smaller deposit and where an existing property is being sold it may be possible to use the deposit received on that sale towards the deposit on the related purchase, but sometimes it will be necessary to raise bridging finance for the deposit.

The completion money
If there is a delay on a buyer's related sale or on the arrival of the mortgage funds then the buyer will not have the money to

complete. They will either have to delay their purchase, which will involve them in liability to the seller, or they will have to raise bridging finance in order to complete.

Discharge of seller's mortgage

A seller with a mortgage on the property they are selling will generally need to obtain the proceeds of sale before they can pay off the mortgage. If they are required to pay it off before completion and therefore before their sale proceeds are available, they may have to raise bridging finance to do so (but *see* 4.6.3 below).

The solicitor's undertaking

When a client obtains bridging finance the bank will require an undertaking from the client's solicitor with respect to the repayment of the loan. The undertaking will, for example, promise that the loan will be repaid by paying over to the bank the proceeds of a related sale less certain specified deductions. There are certain forms of undertaking which have been agreed between the Law Society and the Clearing Banks.

Note

Before giving an undertaking to pay over the client's money you must ensure that you have the client's written authority to give the undertaking.

4.6.3   ### Undertaking for discharge of seller's mortgage

To pay off their mortgage before completion may necessitate the seller raising expensive bridging finance. Buyers are generally reasonable about this and do not insist on the seller discharging the mortgage pre-completion but permit them to do so post-completion out of the proceeds of sale.

It is safe for a buyer to agree to this because of the great value of solicitors' undertakings.

The seller's solicitor will undertake to forward the money necessary to redeem the mortgage to the mortgagee and then when they receive from the mortgagee the proof of discharge (which will be a Form 53 if the title is registered and a receipt endorsed on the mortgage deed where it is unregistered) to forward it to the buyer's solicitor.

The Law Society has approved the following form of words for use in relation to building society mortgages:

'In consideration of your today completing the purchaser of ... WE HEREBY UNDERTAKE forthwith to pay over to the ... Building Society the money required to redeem the mortgage/legal charge dated ... and to forward the receipted mortgage/legal charge to you as soon as it is received by us from the ... Building Society.'

A similar undertaking can be used where the mortgagee is a bank but in the case of a private mortgage the buyer's solicitor should not complete on the basis of an undertaking but should insist on the mortgage being discharged pre-completion and the evidence of discharge handed over at completion (*see* Chapter 11, para. 11.3.3).

Note

The vast majority of domestic conveyancing transactions involve the discharge of a seller's mortgage and completion on the basis of the seller's solicitor giving an undertaking with regard to the discharge of the mortgage. The undertaking is a vital mechanism for the smooth functioning of the conveyancing process.

Miscellaneous undertakings 4.6.4

There are many other situations in which undertakings are used, for example they are:

- Embodied in the Law Society formulae for exchange of contracts (*see* Chapter 10, para. 10.2.3).
- Embodied in the Law Society Code for Completion by Post (*see* Chapter 12, para. 12.4.1).
- Given by the seller's solicitor to assist with any requisitions (queries) which the Land Registry may raise on an application for first registration of title (*see* Chapter 17, para. 17.2.3).

Client account rules 4.7

Conveyancing involves the handling of very large sums of money. The Solicitors' Accounts Rules 1991 must be scrupulously applied at all times.

The following must all be paid into client account and separate ledger entries must be maintained for each client:

1 Proceeds of sale;

2 Mortgage advance cheques;

3 Funds supplied by the client;

4 Deposit received on a client's sale including a deposit received on a stakeholder basis (*see* Chapter 7, para. 7.6.1).

The client's money can only be used on the client's authority for:

1 Payment of the deposit on their purchase;

2 Payment of the balance of the price;

3 Fees of third parties, eg. estate agents, counsel;

4 Stamp duty and land registry registration fees;

5   Costs, including VAT and other disbursements such as search fees (*see* 4.3.3 above).

Note

Items 3 and 4 must be paid directly from client account and the amounts must not be moved to office account prior to the payment of these items.

Client money must *never* be used for:

- Other client's transactions;
- The firm's expenses.

4.7.1   Interest on client account

Money held in client account will earn interest and a solicitor must account to the client for that interest in accordance with the following table:

Number of weeks held	Minimum amount held
8	1,000
4	2,000
2	10,000
1	20,000

Where the solicitor holds a sum of money exceeding £20,000 for less than a week they shall account to the client for the interest if it is fair and reasonable to so account having regard to all the circumstances.

In conveyancing very large sums are frequently held but usually only for a couple of days. In such cases the cost of working out the interest earned and making the payment may well outweigh the amount involved and if the amount involved is less than £20 the solicitor will not be expected to account for it.

In the case of money held as a stakeholder the solicitor shall pay interest in accordance with the above rules to the person to whom the stake is eventually paid, ie. if completion takes place it will be payable to the seller.

Nothing in the Accounts Rules shall affect any arrangement in writing between a solicitor and client as to the application of the client's money or interest thereon, including interest on stakeholder money.

On the face of it, this seems to entitle a solicitor to contract out of the interest provisions. However the Law

Society has issued a guidance note which demonstrates that caution should be exercised and that it is considered improper for a solicitor to request a client to enter into an arrangement in writing with a view to paying no interest at all. A stipulation for a £20 *de minimis* exception would nevertheless be acceptable.

So far as money held as stakeholder is concerned it may be acceptable to include a special provision in the contract that the solicitor stakeholder retains the interest on the deposit to cover their charges for acting as stakeholder. The guidance note states that this is only acceptable if it will provide fair and reasonable remuneration for the work and risk involved in holding a stake.

Miscellaneous   4.8

The conveyancing transaction may give rise to many other issues of professional conduct which are subject to specific Law Society rules. Full consideration of all of these is beyond the scope of this companion but they are covered in the following Law Society publications.

- Council Statement on Dealing with Licensed Conveyancers (1987)
- Council Statement on Dealing with Unqualified Conveyancers (1988, revised 1990)
- Council Statement on Property Selling by Solicitors (1990)
- Council Statement on the Financial Services Act 1986: Life Policies and Tied Agents (1988, revised 1990)
- Solicitors' Investment Business Rules (1990)
- Receipt of Commissions from Third Parties (Rule 10 Solicitors' Practice Rules 1991)

Some of these issues are considered further in Chapter 5, *Financial aspects.*

Self-assessment questions

1 In what circumstances may the same solicitor or firm of solicitors act for both seller and buyer?

2 Where there is more than one buyer interested in the property the seller may institute a contract rate. What are the advantages and disadvantages of this for (a) the seller and (b) the buyer?

3 Explain why solicitors' undertakings are so valuable and give three examples of their use in conveyancing.

4   When can you take out of client account:

(a) Your costs

(b) The money to pay the stamp duty to the Inland Revenue

(c) The money required to repay a bridging loan taken out by the client?

Chapter 5

Financial aspects

Costs of the transaction   5.1

Solicitors' fees   5.1.1

There are no fixed (scale) fees for solicitors' conveyancing
charges. Solicitors are free to charge what they think the
market will bear.

Over the past decade conveyancing fees have not increased, so in real terms they have fallen considerably.
Indeed in many cases they have actually fallen and solicitors today are charging less than they were 10 years ago.
Cut-price conveyancing is widely available and is causing
considerable concern. It is feared that when charging very
low fees conveyancers may have to cut corners and that
negligence may result. Another problem is that conveyancing, which traditionally subsidised certain other areas of
practice, eg. legal aid work, no longer provides a reasonable
fee income. The recent long recession in the property market has greatly exacerbated such problems.

Solicitors' fees are subject to VAT.

Disbursements   5.1.2

During the course of the transaction the solicitor will have
to pay out certain items of expenditure on the client's
behalf. These disbursements, eg. Stamp Duty, Land Registry Fees, Search Fees, will be included in the solicitor's bill.

Disbursements do not attract VAT (*see* 5.3).

Other items of expenditure   5.1.3

There will be a number of other expenses which a client will
need to take into account. These will often be payable by the
client directly to the payee, eg. survey fee to the mortgagee.

Note

See Chapter 4, para. 4.2 for the professional practice issues
regarding information on costs.

Typical costs   5.1.4

The following table of costs is for *illustration only*. There is
considerable variation in solicitors', mortgagees', surveyors' and estate agents' fees, and Land Registry fees and
search fees are subject to frequent change.

Assume that your client is selling a property for £80,000 and buying another for £120,000. There is a £30,000 mortgage outstanding on the property being sold and a mortgage of £70,000 will be taken out on the new house.

Sales costs

1	Estate agent's fees, say 2% (could be more)	1,600.00
	+ VAT	280.00
2	Solicitor's fees	250.00
	+ VAT	43.75
3	Office copy entries	16.00
4	Mortgagee's administrative charges in connection with the redemption of the mortgage (this is an increasingly common and very variable item), say	50.00
		2,239.75

Purchase costs

1	Solicitor's fees	300.00
	+ VAT	52.50
2	Stamp Duty at 1%	1,200.00
3	Land Registry fees (These are on a scale depending on the amount of the consideration.)	260.00
4	Search fees – Local Search (variable)	50.00
	Bankruptcy Search	2.00
5	Telegraphic transfer (The charge made by the bank for transmitting purchase price to seller at completion.)	25.00
6	Mortgagee's administrative charge (This is an increasingly common and variable charge. Building Societies tend to be moderate but banks may charge up to 1% of the loan. If the mortgagee instructs a different solicitor there will be a further large item for their solicitor's fees + VAT.)	100.00
7	Survey Costs (variable and depends on type of survey, eg. basic valuation survey £60–70, home buyer's survey £200, full structural survey 1% of the value of the property).	200.00
	+ VAT	35.00
		2,224.50

Overall budget

Sale price	80,000.00
Less outstanding mortgage	30,000.00
	50,000.00
Less costs of sale	2,239.75
Balance of sale proceeds	47,760.25
Purchase price	120,000.00
Plus costs	2,224.50
	122,224.50
Less mortgage advance	70,000.00
	52,224.50
Less sale proceeds	47,760.25
Balance outstanding	4,464.25

Removal costs, possible retentions from the mortgage advance and the possible costs of reconnecting services, eg. the telephone line to the property, have been ignored.

Stamp duty   5.2

The levying of stamp duty on certain documents is a means by which the government raises revenue. At one time there were many conveyancing and non-conveyancing documents that attracted stamp duty but over the years it became increasingly non-cost-effective to collect small amounts of duty, eg. at one time all receipts had to have a 2d (that is two *old* pence) duty, and many stamp duties have been abolished.

In conveyancing large sums of money are involved and there is consequently the scope for the government to raise substantial amounts of money by way of stamp duty. All transfers on sale of either freeholds or leaseholds are subject to stamp duty at 1% of the consideration but if the consideration does not exceed £60,000 and the transfer contains a certificate of value to that effect then a nil duty will be charged.

The certificate of value will say 'It is hereby certified that the transaction hereby effected does not form part of a larger transaction or of a series of transactions in respect of which the amount or value or the aggregate amount or value of the consideration exceeds £60,000'.

Note the reference here to *series* of transactions. It is not possible to sell a property worth £100,000 by transferring it in two halves for £50,000 each and inserting a certificate of value in each transfer and thereby paying nil duty.

If the transfer does not contain a certificate of value, duty at 1% will be payable even though the consideration does not in fact exceed £60,000.

Note

Where duty is payable it is payable on the full amount of the consideration and not just on the amount over £60,000. For example, if the price is £70,000 then the stamp duty will be £700.

Where chattels are being sold it may be preferable to buy them for a separate consideration rather than including them in the price of the land. This may save stamp duty as stamp duty is only payable on the consideration paid for the land. Any figure put on the chattels must be reasonable. Over valuing the chattels would constitute a fraud on the Inland Revenue.

The principal Act governing the payment of stamp duty is the Stamp Act 1891 but the rate of stamp duty and the point at which the nil band operates is varied from time to time by annual Finance Acts. In the past the basic rate of stamp duty was 2% but then there were lower bands of 1½%, 1% and ½% as well as a nil band. You may therefore find when looking back at old conveyances that the amount of duty that has been paid is not 1% of the consideration and you may also find certificates of value referring to a variety of considerations and not necessarily to £60,000.

A document which attracts stamp duty should be stamped within 30 days of its execution. Late stamping is possible but a penalty may be payable.

A document that requires stamping is if unstamped inadmissible in evidence. It will not be a good root or link in a chain of title to unregistered land and it will not be accepted for registration by the Land Registry.

5.2.1   Stamping of leases

On the sale of an existing lease the stamp duty position is exactly the same as on the sale of a freehold. However, when a lease is first granted the stamping position is different because duty is assessed not only on the premium, ie. the lump sum that the lessee may initially pay to acquire a lease, but also on the annual rent.

The premium will attract duty at 1% but if it does not exceed £60,000 a certificate of value to claim the benefit of the nil band can be inserted but only if the amount of the rent does not exceed £600 per annum.

On the rent the amount of duty will depend not only on the amount of the rent but also on the length of the lease. The longer the lease the higher the rate of duty will be. Bear in mind, however, that long leases are generally granted for a substantial premium and a comparatively small annual ground rent.

When a lease is granted there will be two identical documents – the lease and the counterpart lease. The *lease* is executed by the lessor and handed to the lessee and it is the lessee's responsibility to stamp it in accordance with the above rules. The *counterpart lease* is executed by the lessee and handed to the lessor. The counterpart attracts a fixed rate stamp duty of 50p and it is the lessor's responsibility to stamp it.

Voluntary conveyances 5.2.2

A conveyance by way of gift at one time attracted stamp duty on the value of the property. Such conveyances had to be sent to the Inland Revenue for adjudication, ie. for the Inland Revenue to determine the value of the property and therefore the amount of duty payable. Since 1 May 1987 such transfers are exempt from duty provided they contain the following certificate 'It is certified that the transaction hereby effected falls within Category L in the schedule to the Stamp Duty (Exempt Instruments) Regulations 1987'.

VAT 5.3

Solicitor's bills attract VAT at 17½%. When quoting costs to a client you must always make it absolutely clear that VAT will be added to your fees.

If items such as phone calls and photocopying are charged separately rather than being included in the overall fee charged, these items are also subject to VAT as they constitute the provision of services by you.

Note

In conveyancing the general view is that these items should be included in the estimate or quote and not added on as disbursements.

During the course of the transaction the solicitor will pay out various items of expenditure on the client's behalf such as stamp duty, land registry fees, and search fees. These items will feature on the solicitor's bill as disbursements and do not attract VAT.

5.4   Mortgage interest relief

Tax relief is obtainable on certain mortgage interest payments in order to encourage home ownership . Interest on a loan for the purchase of land is eligible for relief if the property is the *only* or *main residence* of the borrower. The relief is granted at the standard rate of tax on the interest payable on a loan of up to £30,000.

Note

The relief is not £30,000 per annum, it is a relief on the interest payable on £30,000.

The relief is granted under the MIRAS (Mortgage Interest Relief At Source) scheme. This means that the borrower does not pay the full rate of interest on the first £30,000 of their borrowing and then reclaim the tax relief, but pays the mortgagee the *net* interest, ie. the gross interest less the tax relief.

Note

At one time when two or more people purchased a property jointly they could each claim the benefit of the mortgage interest relief but it is now a relief on loans of up to £30,000 per property.

If a buyer is not already utilising their full mortgage income relief on an existing property and they borrow in order to pay the deposit on a new property then the interest on that borrowing for the deposit will be eligible for relief provided the money is borrowed on a loan account rather than simply as an overdraft facility.

5.5   Mortgage finance

The two main sources of mortgage finance are banks and building societies. As institutional lenders their mortgage requirements and documentation will be well worked out and a solicitor acting for them will receive precise instructions on their requirements.

There are two principal types of mortgage:

● An ordinary repayment mortgage;

● A mortgage coupled with an endowment policy.

5.5.1   Repayment mortgage

In the ordinary repayment mortgage the mortgagor not only pays the mortgagee interest on the loan but also makes repayment of capital, so that throughout the life of the mortgage the capital outstanding will gradually be reduced. At the end of the term, eg. at the end of 25 years, the mortgage debt will be paid off.

In the early years of the mortgage the monthly payments that the mortgagor makes will primarily be interest payments and the capital element being repaid will be small but as the years pass the proportion of capital to interest being paid each month will increase.

Mortgage protection insurance

In the case of a *straight repayment mortgage*, on the death of the mortgagor the remaining capital sum will still be outstanding and the mortgagor's estate will remain liable for the debt. It will probably be necessary to sell the mortgaged property in order for the estate to discharge this debt.

If the mortgagor has no dependants who will be prejudiced by this diminution in the value of the estate this may not be a matter of concern but generally it is advisable in the case of a straight repayment mortgage for the mortgagor to take out a mortgage protection policy.

This will not be an endowment insurance which will, should the mortgagors survive for a fixed period of years, provide a capital sum, but a life policy taken out for the life assured's life (a whole life policy) or for the duration of the mortgage term (term insurance) and only payable in the event of the mortgagor's death. Both are relatively cheap forms of life insurance. With term insurance, if the mortgagor survives for the full term of the mortgage, the policy produces nothing and in order to keep premiums low, such policies frequently secure only the declining balance of the mortgage advance.

Endowment mortgage   5.5.2

In the endowment mortgage the mortgagor makes payments to the mortgagee of interest only throughout the life of the mortgage. At the end of the term of the mortgage the full capital sum is still owing. This, however, is repaid out of the proceeds of a life insurance policy that the mortgagor will have taken out at the time of the granting of the mortgage.

This obviously means that throughout the mortgage term the mortgagor will not only be paying interest on the mortgage debt but will also be paying life insurance premiums. At one time these too were eligible for tax relief.

Note _____

As a result of the abolition of tax relief on premiums, endowment mortgages are less common than they were, particularly for older purchasers when premiums will be higher and alternative investments more attractive.

The capital sum

There are many different forms of life insurance policy on the market and a borrower needs to ensure that the policy taken out will provide a guaranteed capital sum at the end of the mortgage term. In recent years many people have taken out so-called *low-cost endowment mortgages* that are based on an anticipated capital value at the end of the term. Where the insurance company's investments have not performed as well as anticipated this has resulted in these policies not producing at maturity the anticipated capital sum. Borrowers in such circumstances find themselves left with a shortfall where the amount of the insurance policy does not pay off the amount of the mortgage debt.

Charging the policy

In the case of an endowment linked mortgage, the mortgagee may take a charge over the life insurance policy, in which case there will be two charges involved in the mortgage transaction:

- A charge over the land; and
- A charge over the life policy.

A charge over the life policy is created by *assigning the benefit* of the life policy to the mortgagee in accordance with the Policies of Assurance Act 1867, which requires notice in writing of the assignment to be given to the insurance company. The insurance company will then record that the mortgagee has rights in the policy and in the event of the policy monies becoming payable will make payment to the mortgagee.

If ever the mortgage is redeemed then, of course, the rights under the life policy need to be assigned back to the borrower. There will need to be a reassignment of the policy and a further notification to the life assurance company to let them know that the mortgagee no longer has any interest in the policy. It is increasingly common for mortgagees not to bother to take an assignment of the life policy.

Note

The assignment of the policy and the reassignment both form part of the chain of title to the policy and *must* be retained with the policy.

Payment of the policy monies

Under endowment insurance the policy monies become payable:

- When the policy matures after the specified number of years for which it is taken out; or
- On the death of the life assured should that happen earlier.

If, therefore, the mortgagor dies during the mortgage term their family will not be left with the outstanding mortgage debt to repay as it will be paid off from the proceeds of the endowment policy.

Selling mortgaged property   5.5.3

The mortgage when taken out will be planned to run for a fixed number of years, eg. 25 years. However, most people do not stay in the same house for that length of time. (On average people move every seven years.) The seller redeems, ie. pays off the mortgage on the house that they are selling out of the proceeds of the sale and takes a new mortgage on the new property that they are buying. The new mortgage may or may not be with the same bank or building society. If they have an endowment mortgage on the first property then the same life insurance policy can be used as the basis for an endowment mortgage on the new property, although if the amount being raised by way of mortgage on the new property is greater than on the old property there will be a need to increase the amount of life insurance cover.

Financial services   5.6

Any person carrying on investment business must be authorised under the Financial Services Act 1986.

Investment business does *not* include generic advice on whether a repayment or an endowment mortgage is the more suitable form of mortgage for a client but does include making arrangements for, or giving advice on, any life insurance with an investment element.

Generally, investment business which is incidental to legal business does not constitute discrete investment business (DIB), ie. mainstream investment business, and is not subject to most of the rules applicable to investment business. However, this exception does not apply to *life policies* and *unit trusts* and advice on an endowment policy which is incidental to a conveyancing transaction therefore still amounts to discrete investment business.

The majority of solicitors who are authorised to give investment advice are authorised via the Law Society which is a Recognised Professional Body (RPB) under the Act. Solicitors who are granted an investment business certificate by the

Society are required to comply with the Solicitors' Investment Business Rules 1990. These rules are very detailed and extremely complex. Consequently, unless a firm is of substantial size and has its own specialist investment department, it is unusual for it to engage directly in investment business. Instead many firms act through an organisation called The Solicitors' Financial Services Company. This company was established under the auspices of the Law Society to provide independent financial advice. The requirements imposed on firms are then more limited as the solicitor is only acting as a referral agency for the client and the independent financial advice is actually being given by the company.

5.6.1 Disclosing commission

Rule 10 of the Solicitors' Practice Rules 1988 provides that solicitors shall account for any commission received of more than £20 unless, having disclosed to the client in writing the amount or basis of calculation of the commission or an approximation thereof, they have the client's agreement to retain it.

Note

Commissions on arranging life insurance policies are substantial.

5.7 Capital Gains Tax relief

You should refer to the Pervasives companion for the general principles of Capital Gains Tax.

In calculating any chargeable gain you deduct from the consideration received for the disposal of the asset the acquisition cost, or if the property was acquired prior to 31 March 1982 its value at that date. The taxpayer will be entitled to offset against the gain the acquisition and disposal costs and any expenditure incurred in enhancing the value of the property: s.38, TCGA 1992. The gain will also be indexed in accordance with s.53 to take account of rises in the retail price index.

There is one particular relief from Capital Gains Tax which is of great importance in domestic conveyancing – ss.222–226, Taxation of Chargeable Gains Act 1992 .

Sections 222–226 provide that a gain accruing to an individual on the disposal of a dwelling house or part of a dwelling house including grounds of up to 0.5 of a hectare shall not be a chargeable gain if it has been occupied as the individual's only or main residence throughout their period of ownership.

Where an individual has two or more residences they can elect as to which is to be regarded as their main residence by giving notice to the Inspector of Taxes. There are certain time limits for giving this notice. In the absence of election the question shall be concluded by the determination of the Inspector although the taxpayer has a right of appeal against the determination.

Note

Spouses living together can have only one main residence for both.

Where the taxpayer has not occupied the house throughout their period of ownership then a fraction of the gain will not be chargeable but a fraction will be. In calculating the fraction of time during which the house is to be regarded as the taxpayer's main residence and consequently the fraction of the gain that is not chargeable, there are certain periods of absence from the property which will be disregarded and which will be treated as if the taxpayer were in occupation. The following periods are disregarded:

- The last three years of ownership;
- Periods before 31 March 1982;
- Periods of absence not exceeding three years;
- Periods of absence in employment overseas;
- Periods of absence not exceeding four years in which the taxpayer was required to reside elsewhere by reason of the demands of their work.

These periods are *cumulative* so that there could in fact be a period of many years during which the taxpayer did not occupy the property and yet their absences would be disregarded and they would still be entitled to this relief.

In respect of any chargeable gain the taxpayer will be entitled to an annual exemption. In the case of married couples each spouse is entitled to the annual exemption.

A disposal of part of the grounds of the dwelling house up to the permitted area will be exempt provided that the grounds are disposed of before the dwelling house itself.

If any part of the property has been used exclusively for business purposes only a part of the gain will be exempt.

Self-assessment questions

1 You are acting for a client who is buying a house for £62,000 to include all carpets, curtains, cooker, fridge,

freezer, dishwasher and washing machine. What particular matter should you consider?

2   What is MIRAS? Who can claim it and how much is it worth?

3   What is the difference between a repayment mortgage and an endowment mortgage?

4   Your client owns a London house and a country cottage which she originally used as a holiday home. Five years ago she retired and moved permanently to the country but did not sell the house as her adult children were still occupying it. They have now left and she is selling. Will she be liable to Capital Gains Tax?

Chapter 6

Physical aspects

Surveys

6.1

The seller does not owe any duty to the buyer to disclose physical defects in the property. The maxim caveat emptor (let the buyer beware) applies, so the buyer must ensure that they check the physical state of the property.

When the buyer is buying with the aid of a mortgage the prospective mortgagee will do a survey in order to decide whether the value of the property constitutes sufficient security for the loan which is being granted. The mortgagee will require the survey fee from the prospective buyer before they institute the survey.

Mortgagees generally offer buyers a choice between a simple valuation survey and a somewhat more detailed (and more expensive) home buyer's survey.

You must advise your client, however, that neither of these is a full structural survey and that they may not reveal all defects in the property, eg. on a mortgage survey the surveyor will probably not go into the loft or remove carpets to examine the floorboards.

The age and nature of the property will largely determine whether or not a full structural survey is advisable. For example, buying an eighteenth-century country house is a very different proposition from buying a 1980s 'semi' and a full survey will probably be advisable in the former case but not necessarily in the latter. A full structural survey is, however, very expensive.

Surveyor's liability

6.1.1

Where the buyer commissions their own survey, the surveyor is under a contractual duty to them to carry out the survey with the requisite degree of care and skill. If the survey fails to reveal certain defects in the property then the surveyor may possibly be liable for breach of contract. If the contract with the surveyor contains exclusion clauses then the reasonableness of those clauses under the Unfair Contract Terms Act 1977 will have to be considered.

In the case of the mortgagee's survey there is no contractual relationship between the buyer and the surveyor. However, in *Smith v Eric S Bush* (1990) the House of Lords held that 'the valuer who values a house for the purpose of a mortgage, knowing that the mortgagee will rely and the mortgagor will probably rely on the valuation, knowing that the purchaser mortgagor has in effect paid for the valuation, is under a duty to exercise reasonable skill and care and that duty is owed to both parties to the mortgage for which the valuation is made'.

The House of Lords also considered whether a disclaimer of liability was reasonable under s.2, Unfair Contract Terms Act 1977. In concluding that the disclaimer was not reasonable their Lordships took account of the factual circumstances in which domestic valuations for mortgage purposes are conducted and the fact that the valuer knows that 90% of purchasers rely on the mortgage valuation and do not commission their own survey. The fact that the valuer knows full well that failure on their part to exercise reasonable skill and care may be disastrous to the purchaser, may also have influenced the Law Lords' decision. They made it clear that their decision was:

'in respect of a dwelling house of modest value in which it is widely recognised by surveyors that purchasers are in fact relying on their care and skills';

but reserved their position:

'in respect of valuations of quite different types of property for mortgage purposes such as industrial property, large blocks of flats or very expensive houses. In such cases it may well be that the general expectation of behaviour of the purchaser is quite different. With very large sums of money at stake prudence would seem to demand that the purchaser obtains his own structural survey to guide him in his purchase and in such circumstances with very much larger sums of money at stake it may be reasonable for the surveyors valuing on behalf of those who are providing the finance, either to exclude or limit their liability to the purchaser'.

6.2   NHBC

The National House-Building Council is an organisation of house builders and developers. It sets minimum standards of construction, inspects properties as they are built to ensure compliance with those standards and operates a scheme known as Buildmark which provides protection for buyers of new houses for up to ten years after construction. Over 90% of new homes are constructed by builders who are members of NHBC. Those who are not will find that they probably need to take out similar forms of insurance cover in order to make their properties marketable. There are a number of commercial insurers who provide cover similar to that provided under the Buildmark Scheme.

Under the Buildmark Scheme a buyer's protection falls into three phases.

1   The first phase runs up to the completion of the construction of the property. During this period the buyer is protected against the risk of the builder going into liquidation and failing to complete the construction. They will be covered for any loss of deposit or for the cost of completing the property to NHBC standards.

2   The second phase runs for two years following the completion of the construction and the issue of the 10 year notice of cover. This is known as the *initial guarantee period*. If during this period faults appear in the property then the buyer must contact the builder to rectify them but if the builder has gone into liquidation or otherwise fails to carry out the necessary repairs, then the buyer can claim on the insurance policy that backs the guarantee.

3   The third phase runs from 2 to 10 years after construction. This is known as the *structural guarantee period*. The buyer is only protected in respect of major damage caused by *structural faults* in the property or by *subsidence or heave*. During this period there is no obligation on the buyer to first seek out the builder and try and get him to rectify the fault but the buyer can immediately make a claim on the NHBC insurance cover.

Thus, under the NHBC Buildmark Scheme there are varying degrees of insurance cover in respect of the physical state of the property for up to 10 years after its construction. If the first buyer sells the property before ten years then the benefit of the Buildmark cover will be transferred to the next buyer and so on.

Note

Where mortgage finance is being raised in order to buy a newly-constructed property or one constructed within the last 10 years, it will be a normal condition of the mortgage offer that there is NHBC cover. If this does not exist the mortgagee will have to be notified and it may require some alternative commercial structural guarantee insurance to be effected.

Planning   6.3

Town and country planning is regulated by the Town and Country Planning Act 1990 and the Planning and Compensation Act 1991. Planning is the responsibility of the local planning authority, ie. the local council.

The local planning authority must produce plans setting

out their policy for the area for which they are responsible. In metropolitan areas including London these are known as unitary development plans, whereas in non-metropolitan areas there are structure and local plans. Structure plans are prepared by the county council and approved by the Secretary of State for the Environment and local plans are prepared by district planning authorities. All these plans are written statements of the authorities' policy and proposals for the area for which they are responsible.

In the non-metropolitan areas where there are the two tiers of planning authority, the purpose of the local plan is to develop the structure plan at a more detailed level but it must fall within the general policy framework of the structure plan.

These plans will give you an indication as to whether you are likely to obtain planning permission for a particular type of development in a particular area.

6.3.1   Development

Planning permission is needed for anything that constitutes development. Development means 'the carrying out of building, engineering, mining or other operations in, on, and over or under land, or the making of any material change in the use of any buildings or other land': s.55, Town and Country Planning Act 1990.

Development therefore has two aspects to it:

- The *operational* aspect, and
- The *change of user* aspect.

The following activities do *not* involve development.

1   The carrying out for the maintenance, improvement or other alteration of any building of works which affect only the *interior* of the building or do not materially effect the *external appearance* of the building.

2   The use of any building or other land within the curtilage of a dwelling house for any *purpose incidental to the enjoyment* of the dwelling house as such.

There is no hard and fast definition of *curtilage*. It is defined in the Oxford English Dictionary as 'a small court, yard, garth, or piece of ground attached to a dwelling house and forming one enclosure with it, or so regarded by the law; the area attached to and containing a dwelling-house and its outbuildings'.

Since 'use' does not include building operations this provision does not authorise the erection of sheds, greenhouses or other buildings within the curtilage, but development of this type may be permitted development under the General Development Order depending on the size and location of the building.

3   In the case of buildings or other land which are used for a purpose of any class specified in an order made by the Secretary of State, the use thereof for any purpose of the same class.

Note

The Act specifically provides that the use as two or more separate dwelling houses of any building previously used as a single dwelling house does involve a material change in use.

The Use Classes Order 6.3.2

The Town and Country Planning (Use Classes) Order 1987 provides for 16 different classes of user divided into four groups: A, B, C and D. Where someone wishes to change the user of their premises to another user within the same class under the 1987 Order that does not constitute development and therefore does not require planning permission, eg. changing within Class A1 from a toy shop to a clothes shop, changing within Class A2 from a solicitor's office to a building society.

Class A1
Class A1 includes most types of shop other than those selling hot food. It includes hairdressers, travel agencies and dry cleaners.

Class A2
Class A2 covers financial and professional services which it is appropriate to provide in a shopping area where the services are provided principally to visiting members of the public.

Class A3
Class A3 covers premises selling food and drink for consumption on the premises or of hot food for consumption off the premises.

Class B1
Class B1 covers use as an office other than a use within Class A2, and the use of premises for research and development of products or processes or for any industrial process which can be carried on in a residential area without detriment to the amenity of the area.

Class B2
Class B2 comprises general industrial user and there are

further classes under Part B dealing with other special industrial groups.

Part C
Part C includes classes covering hotels and hostels and residential institutions and dwelling houses.

Part D
Part D comprises non-residential institutions and assembly and leisure premises.

> *Note*
>
> Although a change of user does not involve development and therefore does not require planning permission, if building operations are also involved then planning permission may be required for the building work. Also, if the building is of special historic or architectural interest there are special controls under the Planning (Listed Buildings and Conservation Areas) Act 1990 and even minor interior alterations will require special permission.

6.3.3   ## The General Development Order

Planning permission is required for anything that constitutes development. s.57, Town and Country Planning Act 1990. However, you do not always have to apply for a specific permission because it may fall within the permitted development under the Town and Country Planning (General Development) Order 1988. This provides a ready-made permission for development in 23 specified classes.

Class 1
Class 1 permits development within the curtilage of a dwelling house so long as certain restrictions are observed, ie. as to the height and size of the extended building. Erecting a garage is sometimes treated as an enlargement of the house depending on the proximity of the garage to the house. Adding a porch to the front of the house may similarly come within this permitted development. Many ordinary domestic extensions fall within this class of permitted development.

Class 2
Under Class 2 many minor operations such as erecting fences, gates, walls etc or painting the exterior of the property are permitted, but again the restrictions imposed by the GDO must be observed, eg. as to the height of fences, particularly those that abut the highway.

Article 4 directions   6.3.

The Local Planning Authority may direct that all or any of

the permissions granted by the GDO shall not apply to the whole or part of the area for which it is responsible. The pre-contract enquiries of the local authority will reveal whether there is an Article 4 direction in force affecting the area in which the property is situated. For example, a local author-ity may decide that in relation to a particular area, eg. a new estate, it does not want everyone to have the benefit of the development permitted by the GDO but wishes even minor developments to be the subject of specific applications for planning permission.

Specific applications　　6.3.5

An express application for planning permission must be made for any development that does not come within the development authorised by the GDO. Where the permis-sion being sought is permission to erect a building the initial application does not need to be a detailed one but can be an application for outline permission only. This means a plan-ning permission which is granted subject to the reservation for subsequent approval by the Local Planning Authority or the Secretary of State of certain reserved matters. For example, permission may be granted for the construction of a new block of flats of a certain size and height but the detail of what the block will look like so far as the type of brick, roof tiles, windows etc to be used may be the subject of a reservation: s.92, Town and Country Planning Act 1990.

If you are not sure whether particular proposals constitute development and therefore require planning permission and, if so, whether or not they fall within the GDO, you can apply to the local authority for a determination on these issues.

If your proposals do necessitate an application for plan-ning permission then the Local Planning Authority must keep a register of all applications and of the authority's decisions on those applications. The register is open to public inspection. The pre-contract enquiries of the local authority will reveal where the register is kept and its opening hours. Where planning permission is granted it is not generally personal to the applicant but attaches to the land so that the land carries with it the benefit of the planning permission. When granting permission the Local Planning Authority may impose such conditions as it think fits: s.70, Town and Country Planning Act 1990. Such conditions constitute local land charges.

Duration of planning permission　　6.3.6

An ordinary planning permission lasts for five years so the development must be commenced within that time. An outline planning permission is subject to conditions that:

- The application for approval of reserved matters is made within three years; and
- Development must be begun within five years of the grant of the outlined permission or within two years of the approval of reserved matters whichever is the later: s.92, Town and Country Planning Act 1990.

6.3.7   Enforcement of planning legislation

Carrying out development without the required planning permission or failing to comply with any condition or limitation subject to which planning permission has been granted constitutes a breach of planning control.

Where it appears to the Local Planning Authority that there has been a breach of planning control, the Local Planning Authority may issue an enforcement notice: s.172, Town and Country Planning Act 1990.

An enforcement notice requires the breach to be remedied, eg. it requires the condition attached to the consent to be complied with or requires the discontinuance of an unauthorised user or the removal of an unauthorised building.

There are time limits within which the local authority must issue an enforcement notice if it is going to do so. The time limit is four years where the breach consists of the carrying out of operations or the change of use of any building to use as a single dwelling house. For all other breaches the time limit is 10 years: s.171B, Town and Country Planning Act 1990 as amended by s.4, Planning and Compensation Act 1991.

Where an enforcement notice is not complied with within the compliance period, the local authority may enter the property and take for itself the steps necessary to comply with the enforcement notice. Reasonable costs for doing so can be charged to the owner of the land.

Non-compliance with an operative enforcement notice also constitutes a criminal offence.

6.3.8   Building regulations

Even where planning permission is not required, compliance with the building regulations will be necessary. These are regulations which ensure that the property is built or altered according to certain health and safety standards.

Building regulations deal with matters such as the materials to be used in the construction, the depth of the foundations and drainage and ventilation of the building. During the course of the construction/ alteration, the work will be inspected either by a local authority inspector or by some other approved inspector such as NHBC to ensure compliance with the Building Regulations.

Self-assessment questions

1 What is the difference between the initial guarantee period and the structural guarantee period under the Buildmark scheme?

2 What is the difference between the Use Classes Order and the General Development Order?

3 On behalf of a prospective buyer you have made certain pre-contract enquiries of the local authority. These have revealed that the property in question is within an area affected by an Article 4 direction. What practical effect will this have on your client?

4 What time limits apply to:

(a) the commencement of development;

(b) the service by the local authority of an enforcement notice?

Chapter 7

Drafting the contract

Who does what?

7.1

The seller's solicitor drafts the contract of sale and sends two copies to the buyer's solicitor, keeping a further copy on file for reference purposes. Amendments may be negotiated over the telephone or by correspondence. If on the telephone, it is important for both sides to keep an accurate attendance note of the conversation and for what was agreed to be confirmed in writing. All agreed amendments to the draft contract are incorporated by the buyer's solicitor into the two copies of the contract which they hold.

Note

It is vital that the two copies are identical.

The buyer's solicitor returns one copy of the contract containing the agreed amendments to the seller's solicitor so that each side can sign one part of the contract. When both sides are ready to be legally bound the signed parts of the contract will be exchanged.

The parties become legally bound at the moment of exchange.

The form and content of the contract

7.2

The contract has to be in writing, incorporate all the agreed terms. The parties can draft their own form of contract as no particular form is required but generally a standard form of contract is used with amendments and additions being made to it as the circumstances require.

The Standard Conditions of Sale

7.2.1

These conditions of sale have been approved by the Law Society and can be used for all types of sale, ie for registered or unregistered titles, freehold or leasehold titles, domestic or commercial properties.

Note

Throughout this course you can assume that the contract incorporates the Standard Conditions of Sale. Special conditions are added to amend or supplement the Standard Conditions as appropriate.

7.2.2   The open contract

Where a contract is concluded without anything being agreed on a particular issue then the open contract rules will apply. These constitute a sub-stratum of statutory and common law implied terms which will operate in the absence of any contrary agreement. For example, if a contract says nothing about whether a deposit is payable on exchange, under the open contract rules no deposit is payable.

A knowledge of the open contract rules is essential in order to appreciate what provisions need to be expressed in the contract. (The open contract rules will be referred to in context where appropriate in this manual.)

7.3   Preparation for drafting the contract

In order to draft the contract, the seller's solicitor must first take certain preparatory steps.

7.3.1   Land/charge certificate

Obtain from the seller the land certificate or, if the property is mortgaged, the charge certificate from the mortgagee. If there is more than one mortgage on the property then all the charge certificates should be obtained as they will all have to be handed over to the buyer at completion.

To obtain a charge certificate, the seller's solicitor will need to give the mortgagee an undertaking to hold the certificate to the mortgagee's order and to return it at any time should the mortgagee require it.

7.3.2   Office copy entries

Obtain from the relevant district land registry a full set of office copy entries, including a copy of the filed plan. The office copy entries will show the current state of the Register.

7.3.3   Overriding interests

Check for any overriding interests that incumber the property. This will be done primarily by questioning the seller, eg. asking who else is in occupation of the property.

7.4   The seller's common law duty of disclosure

The open contract rule is that it is an *implied term* of the contract that the seller is selling an absolute freehold title free from incumbrances. If the title is not absolute and/or if there are any incumbrances/burdens on the property, these should be disclosed by the seller.

Extent of the common law duty   7.4.1

The duty of disclosure it limited to disclosing *latent* defects
in/or burdens on the title, so there is in theory no duty to
reveal patently obvious matters. However, there may well
be room for argument as to whether or not a particular
burden is patent or latent. Thus, to be on the safe side, the
seller should disclose all defects or burdens.

Similarly, there is no duty to disclose matters that the
buyer already knows about but again there could be argument as to what the buyer did or did not know about at the
time of exchange of contracts. The fact that a particular
encumbrance is registered, eg. as a local land charge, is not
enough at the pre-contract stage to fix the buyer with
knowledge of it, so the seller should disclose it.

At common law the seller's duty is absolute. It is a duty
to disclose *all* latent defects and incumbrances that are not
already known to the buyer, it is not limited to matters that
the seller knows or ought to know about.

> *Note*
>
> The duty of disclosure does *not* extend to anything relating to
> the physical state of the property. Here the rule is *caveat emptor*
> (let the buyer beware). However, if the buyer actually asks
> questions about the physical stage of the property they must be
> answered truthfully otherwise the seller will be liable for
> misrepresentation.

Breach of the duty   7.4.2

Non-disclosure constitutes a breach of the implied term. It
will depend on the seriousness of the breach whether the
buyer's remedy is only damages, ie. for breach of warranty,
or whether the buyer may also terminate the contract, ie. for
breach of condition.

Modifying the common law duty   7.4.3

The standard conditions modify the common law duty of
disclosure both as regards the extent of the duty and the
consequences of non-disclosure (*see* standard conditions
3.1 and 7.1).

The Standard Conditions of Sale contract form   7.5

The front page of the contract form will have to be completed and special conditions added to the back of the form
as appropriate.

7.5.1   The agreement date

This will be left blank when the contract is initially drafted and only inserted when contacts are finally exchanged.

7.5.2   The parties

The full names and present addresses of sellers and buyers are inserted.

7.5.3   Property

The description of the property to be sold is sometimes referred to as the 'particulars of sale'. In the case of registered titles this part of the contract form can be completed by simply taking the description of the property from the property section of the Register and also stating the title number.

If the title is not an absolute one this should be clearly stated.

Delete the printed words leasehold and root of title.

7.5.4   Incumbrances on the property

This is where third party burdens that are going to bind the buyer should be disclosed. Look at the charges section of the Register to see what notices there are of third party rights and then state that the property is sold subject to those entries on the Charges Register. Where there are registered charges listed in the Charges Register, the seller will be discharging these, at or before completion, and they will not therefore bind the buyer. Consequently, they should not be stated as incumbrances subject to which the property is sold.

If there are overriding interests affecting the property these too constitute incumbrances and must be disclosed.

If there is insufficient room on the front of the agreement to set out all the incumbrances, the front page can simply state that the property is sold subject to the incumbrances set out in a special condition. Then on the reverse of the form, and on a separate sheet if necessary, the incumbrances can be set out in full.

Note

Apart from the incumbrances specifically mentioned on the face of the contract, the property is also sold subject to the incumbrances specified in standard condition 3.1.2 (*see* para. 7.6.3).

The pre-printed special condition 2 on the reverse of the form states that the property is sold subject to the incumbrances on the property and the buyer will raise no requisitions on them. This means that once contracts have been exchanged the buyer cannot raise questions about the incumbrances. The buyer must therefore ensure that all details of the incumbrances are supplied prior to the exchange of contracts and that any questions that the buyer wishes to raise are raised at the *pre-contract stage*. The seller will, of course, supply with the draft contract a set of office copy entries and where there are overriding interests affecting the property then the seller must provide such documentation as exists or oral information regarding them: s.110, Land Registration Act 1925.

Capacity in which the seller sells   7.5.5

There are various capacities in which a seller may sell, as:

- Beneficial owner;
- Trustee – this is the capacity in which trustees for sale and a tenant for life under a strict settlement sell;
- Personal representative – this is the capacity in which executors or administrators sell;
- Mortgagee.

Depending on the capacity in which the seller sells, and subsequently transfers the property, there will be certain implied promises given in the transfer. These are known as implied covenants for title. If, after completion, a defect or incumbrance comes to light the buyer may possibly be able to sue the seller on these implied covenants. The most extensive covenants are given where somebody sells as beneficial owner, but even these are not as extensive as may at first appear (*see* Chapter 13).

Completion date   7.5.6

This will be left blank until just before exchange of contracts when the parties agree on the completion date.

The contract rate   7.5.7

If completion does not take place at the contractually agreed date, the party responsible for the delay will have to pay compensation to the other. This is calculated at the contract rate on the purchase price (see Standard Condition 7.3). The rate of interest can be stated by reference to a clearing bank's base rate, eg. 4% above the base rate from time to time of Lloyds Bank plc, or can be stated as being the Law Society contract rate. The Law Society rate is fixed at 4% above Barclays Bank's base rate and is published each week in the *Law Society Gazette*.

7.5.8   The purchase price

The full purchase price is inserted followed by any deposit that is to be payable on exchange of contracts. The customary deposit is 10%. If any chattels are being purchased for a separate consideration, ie. they are not included in the overall sale price, then the amount payable for chattels should be separately stated. The balance will be the balance of the purchase price less the deposit payable on exchange. It does not include the amount payable separately for chattels.

7.6   Analysis of certain standard conditions of sale

7.6.1   Standard condition 2.2: Deposit

Amount and purpose

The open contract rules do not provide for the payment of any deposit but standard condition 2.2 provides for a deposit of 10% to be paid no later than the date of the contract. If this figure is to be varied, a special condition needs to be added.

The deposit acts as a partial payment so that, at completion, the buyer will only have to pay the balance of the purchase price. It also serves as a guarantee that the buyer will complete if the buyer breaks the contract by failing to complete then the seller will be able to retain the deposit. This is so even though the seller may suffer no loss as a result of the breach because the property can be resold at the same or a higher price.

> *Note*
>
> You should not agree to the deposit being less than the normal 10% without the client's express authorisation as in the event of the buyer defaulting there will then be a smaller deposit to be forfeited by the seller. Where the seller suffers a loss as a result of the buyer's default, the reduced deposit may not cover that loss, whereas the normal 10% might have done so. An action in negligence could be brought for the shortfall.

Agent or stakeholder

The deposit is not normally paid to the seller personally but to a third party, eg. the seller's solicitor. There are two capacities in which a third party may receive a deposit, either as agent for the seller or as a stakeholder.

If it is received as *agent for the seller* then the seller can ask for it to be handed over and may use it for any purpose, not necessarily for use in connection with a related purchase. There could then be problems for the buyer if the seller defaults and fails to complete. In such circumstances the buyer is entitled to the return of the deposit, but if the seller has already spent it, there may be problems in recovering the amount.

A *stakeholder* holds the deposit as agent for both parties to await the outcome of the transaction. If completion takes place, or if the buyer defaults, the stakeholder will pay the deposit to the seller. If the seller defaults, the stakeholder will return the deposit to the buyer with interest.

From the buyer's point of view the stakeholder basis is preferable, but the practical reality is that the seller may need to use the deposit money as a deposit on a related purchase and therefore needs to receive it on an agency basis. Under the open contract rule a solicitor receives a deposit as agent for the seller, but standard condition 2.2 modifies this and reaches a compromise solution under which the deposit can be used as a deposit on the purchase of another residence but not for any other purpose, and if not so used it is to be held on a stakeholder basis.

Possible problems

A practical problem may arise where contracts are exchanged under Law Society Formula B (*see* Chapter 10). This incorporates an undertaking to forward the deposit by the following day but it is frequently not fulfilled as in a chain situation the buyer is relying on receiving the deposit on a related sale and then passing it on up the chain. There appears to be no satisfactory solution to this problem.

A further problem arises where the deposit is paid by a cheque which bounces. Standard condition 2.2.4 makes it clear that the requirement that a deposit be paid is a term of the contract and not a condition precedent to the existence of the contract. It provides that the seller may either treat the contract as discharged by the breach or treat it as subsisting and sue for the deposit.

Standard condition 9: Chattels 7.6.2

This makes it clear that, regardless of whether or not a separate price is paid for the chattels, there is in addition to the contract for the sale of land also a contract for the sale of goods. Under the sale of goods contract, ownership of the chattels will pass to the buyer on actual completion. The chattels being sold should be precisely listed and special condition 3 (on the reverse of the contract form) provides for this to be done in an attached list.

Conversely, if there are any fixtures which are not to be included in the sale, a special condition needs to provide for this and specify the fixtures, if necessary in an attached list. The Protocol requires the seller to provide the buyer with a fixtures and fittings form.

7.6.3   Standard condition 3.1: Freedom from incumbrances

This states that the seller is selling the property free from incumbrances other than those mentioned in condition 3.1.2. This specifies the incumbrances subject to which the property is sold, specifically:

- Those *mentioned in the agreement*, ie. those that have been disclosed by the seller on the face of the contract;

- Those discoverable by *inspection of the property* before the contract, ie. those which are patently obvious.

  At common law the duty of disclosure is limited to the disclosure of latent incumbrances and this provision is therefore in line with the common law duty of disclosure. Many overriding interests will fall within this category;

- Those the seller *does not and could not know about.* At common law the seller's duty is to disclose all latent defects whether known about or not.

  This provision therefore constitutes a reduction of the common law duty but it is nevertheless regarded as an acceptable reduction.

  Note _____

  A provision that absolved the seller from the need to disclose matters that were actually known about would not be permissible;

- *Entries* made before the date of the contract in *any public register* except those maintained by HM Land Registry or its Land Charges department or by Companies House.

  This seeks to fix the buyer with knowledge of matters registered in the local land charges register and public registers other than those specified. Before exchanging contracts the buyer will search these registers (*see* Chapter 8, paras. 8.4 and 8.6). The provision does not, however, accord with the decision in *Rignall Developments v Halil* (1987) in which Millett J refused to equate *notice* imposed under s.198, Land Charges Act 1925 with the *knowledge* of the buyer which would preclude the seller's duty of disclosure. He held that notice and knowledge were not synonymous and that a seller with knowledge of a local land charge was under a duty to disclose it.

- *Public requirements* (defined in Standard Condition 1.1)

The affect of this provision is uncertain. If the seller actually knows of the public requirement, it probably should be disclosed by specifying it in the agreement and the seller should not be able to shelter behind this contractual provision. Standard condition 3.1.4 provides that after the contract is made the seller is to give the buyer details without delay of any new public requirement. It would therefore be strange if condition 3.1.2(e) were interpreted to mean that the property was sold subject to public requirements that were known to the seller before contract but which were not disclosed.

Condition 4.2 : Proof of title   7.6.4

The Land Registration Act 1925, s.110 requires a seller to deduce title by providing the buyer with:

- A copy of the subsisting entries in the register and of any filed plan;
- Copies or abstract of any document noted on the Register;
- Copies, abstracts and evidence (if any) relating to any subsisting rights and interests appurtenant to the registered land as to which the register is not conclusive must be provided. (This latter requirement covers overriding interests.)

Note

Section 110 does not require the seller to supply the buyer with office copies of the entries on the Register – a copy of the entries in the land certificate would suffice – but standard condition 4.2.1 modifies s.110 and requires the use of office copies.

Special conditions   7.7

These may be required to modify or supplement the standard conditions, eg. to specify fixtures to be removed or to modify the provisions regarding the deposit.

On a sale of the entirety of the land comprised in a registered title there is often no need for any special conditions, whereas in a sale of part there will probably be easements to be granted and reserved and covenants to be imposed. These will all be set out in special conditions (*see* Chapter 19).

Where the national conveyancing protocol is being followed and the seller is deducing title before exchange of contracts there should be a special condition stating that title has been deduced and that the buyer will raise no further requisitions on the title.

7.7.1   **Void conditions**

The following conditions will be void if inserted in the contract:

- A condition restricting the buyer's choice of solicitor: s.48, LPA 1925.
- A condition restricting the buyer's right to object to any stamping deficiencies: s.117, Stamp Act 1891.

Self-assessment questions

1 What is the difference between the open contract rules and the Standard Conditions of Sale?

2 Why does the seller's solicitor need to investigate the seller's title before drafting the contract?

3 What is the purpose of a deposit and should it be paid to an agent of the seller or to a stakeholder?

4 If there are incumbrances on the property which are not specified in the contract:

   (a) If the property is transferred to the buyer, will the buyer be bound by them?

   (b) Is the buyer bound by the contract and obliged to complete?

Chapter 8

Pre-contract searches and enquiries

Introduction   8.1

It is the seller's duty at common law to disclose all latent defects in and incumbrances on the title. The seller is not obliged to disclose patent defects or incumbrances nor to disclose anything regarding the physical state of the property.

Standard condition 3.1 seeks to modify the common law duty of disclosure and to absolve the seller from the duty to disclose matters that the seller does not and could not know about, and also entries on the register of local land charges and some other public registers (*see* Chapter 7, para. 7.6.3).

Their purpose   8.2

The buyer's pre-contract searches and enquiries are designed to find out about the physical state of the property and those title matters that the seller is not obliged to disclose, and also about a whole range of other matters that may influence the buyer's decision whether or not to buy, eg. whether the property enjoys mains drainage; whether there have been any disputes with the neighbours; whether a new motorway is planned near the property.

As a result of the pre-contract searches and enquiries the buyer may decide not to proceed at all, or may seek to negotiate a reduction in the price, or may insist on the draft contract being amended to incorporate some special condition.

Note _____

Where the National Conveyancing Protocol is being followed it is for the seller to provide the buyer with a conveyancing package which includes the property information form, the result of the local land charges search, the replies to the enquiries of the local authority, and the result of any other special searches that may be appropriate in the circumstances. It is, however, ultimately the buyer's responsibility to see that all the necessary searches and enquiries are made and that the results are satisfactory before proceeding to exchange contracts. If the buyer takes up and uses the searches supplied by the seller, the buyer must reimburse the seller the costs incurred (*see* Protocol steps 5.5 and 6.3).

8.3   Pre-contract enquiries

Where the Protocol is *not* being followed, the buyer will send to the seller a list of pre-contract enquiries. There is no obligation on the seller to reply to these questions but if the seller refuses to do so the buyer will probably not proceed. If the questions are answered then the answers must be truthful. An incorrect reply may constitute an actionable misrepresentation.

Where the protocol is being followed, the seller anticipates the usual questions that a buyer will raise and supplies the answers to those stock questions without waiting to be asked them. The questions are set out and the answers provided on the *property information form*. The seller's solicitor will need to go through this form with the client in order to obtain the information required to answer the questions.

Under the Protocol, the buyer may raise further enquiries but they should be kept to a minimum.

The standard pre-contract enquiries deal with the following matters.

8.3.1   Boundaries

The Land Registry operates a general boundary rule, ie. the Register and the filed plan give only a general indication of the extent of the property and do not give precise boundaries or state responsibilities for maintaining boundaries.

Standard condition 4.3 provides that the seller need not prove the exact boundaries of the property or who owns fences, ditches, hedges and walls. Nevertheless the buyer will want to have as much information as possible with respect to boundaries and who maintains them.

Note

The pre-registration deeds can sometimes be useful in providing more detailed information about boundaries.

8.3.2   Disputes

The buyer does not want to buy a dispute. This question therefore asks whether there have been any disputes with the neighbours, either about the property which is the subject of the sale or about neighbouring properties. In *Walker v Boyle* (1982), for example, it was incorrectly stated that there had been no disputes with the neighbours when in fact there was an ongoing dispute. The buyer discovered the true position before completion and was able to rescind the contract for misrepresentation.

Notices 8.3.3

This asks what notices, if any, relating to the property have been served. Local authority notices regarding planning issues are the most frequently encountered notices.

Guarantees 8.3.4

The buyer wants to know what guarantees go with the property, eg. guarantees for central heating, double glazing, against dry rot or wood worm and, most importantly, any NHBC guarantee.

Services 8.3.5

Mains services that run across private property do so by virtue of statutory rights. If, therefore, the property is served by mains services that run over someone else's land, the buyer does not have to worry about whether easements exist in respect of those services. Where the services are not mains services, easements in respect of them must exist and the buyer will need to be satisfied about this.

Facilities 8.3.6

This asks for details of shared facilities and the cost of, and arrangements for, maintaining them.

Adverse rights 8.3.7

This question asks the seller to give details of all overriding interests and other rights affecting the property. In answering it, the seller will be going beyond the common law duty of disclosure and giving details not just of latent but also of patent rights.

Occupiers 8.3.8

This question to some extent overlaps with the previous question as, if there is someone in occupation, their rights in the land will constitute an overriding interest. When dealing with a sole seller, the buyer will be especially concerned to discover if there is anyone in occupation who has a beneficial interest in the property and, if so, will ensure that a second trustee is appointed so that on sale the beneficial interest is overreached. Anyone in occupation, even where their interest will be overreached, should be joined in the contract of sale in order to agree to vacate the property at completion. If they have so contracted, then they will probably vacate and this will avoid possible unpleasantness in having to evict them.

Restrictions 8.3.9

This seeks to discover whether there are any outstanding

breaches of restrictions affecting the property and also to discover who has the benefit of restrictive covenants affecting the property.

8.3.10   Planning

This question refers to developments within the last four years as, if more than four years has elapsed since an unauthorised development other than change of user has occurred, a local authority can no longer serve an enforcement notice (*see* Chapter 6).

8.3.11   Mechanics of sale

These questions about the seller's related transaction should only be answered by the seller's solicitor after receiving the *client's authorisation* to reveal the position.

8.3.12   Outgoings

This question is asked so that the buyer has a good idea of likely future liabilities in relation to the property.

8.4   Liability for misrepresentation

All answers given by the seller on the property information form must be correct. An incorrect answer will constitute a false statement of fact and, if it induces the buyer to make the contract (it need not be the sole inducement), it will constitute an operative misrepresentation. At common law, a misrepresentation – whether it be fraudulent, negligent or innocent – renders the contract voidable. If the buyer discovers the misrepresentation pre-completion, the buyer may seek rescission, ie. restoration to the pre-contract position. At common law, the buyer may also be able to claim damages in tort for deceit or for negligence.

The Misrepresentation Act 1967, s.2(2) provides that where rescission is sought, but the misrepresentation was not fraudulent, the court may award damages in lieu of rescission. Section 2(1) of the Act provides that where the misrepresentation is not innocent, the party misled may claim damages as if the misrepresentation were fraudulent.

Note

In an action under s.2(1) the burden of proof is on the *defendant* to show that the misrepresentation was innocent. This contrasts with an action in tort where the burden of establishing fraud or negligence is on the plaintiff.

Standard condition 7.1 seeks to modify the remedies that would otherwise be available for misrepresentation. It provides that the contract can only be rescinded where the error or omission results from fraud or recklessness, or where the injured party 'would be obliged to his prejudice to transfer or accept property differing substantially (in quantity, quality or tenure) from what the error or omission had led him to expect'. Whether this is reasonable under s.3, Misrepresentation Act 1967 has not yet been tested, but it probably is.

Local land charges search 8.5

Under the Local Land Charges Act 1975, each local authority (LA) keeps a register of local land charges. It is divided into twelve classes. The vast majority of registrable charges consist of rights which the LA has in the property. There are also some statutory bodies which may have rights, eg. the Civil Aviation Authority. The only class of charge which can be entered by an ordinary person is a *light obstruction notice*. This is lodged in order to prevent a neighbour acquiring an easement of light by prescription.

Examples of local land charges 8.5.1

Examples include:

- *Financial charges.* These may be for a specific amount or general. For example, where a council tenant buys their home with the benefit of a discount, the LA will have a charge on the property for the amount of the discount which reduces over the next three years. Properties fronting a private unmade road may be subject to a charge for the making up and adoption of the road as a public highway.
- *Planning charges,* ie. where planning permission is granted subject to conditions.
- *Preservation orders* on buildings or trees.

The official search 8.5.2

The Register is open to public inspection and a personal search can be made but an official search is usually instituted. The result of the search is not conclusive and registered charges which it fails to reveal, and local land charges which have not yet been registered, will still be binding. However, the advantage of the official search is that a buyer relying on an inaccurate search result will be entitled to compensation: s.10, Local Land Charges Act 1975. An official search also protects you from a possible negligence claim.

Note _____

The buyer need not have instituted the search. It is sufficient that the buyer or their agent has knowledge of the contents of the official search certificate. Under the Protocol, the search will be instituted by the seller and the certificate supplied to the buyer.

8.5.3 Search validation insurance

The official search does not carry with it any priority period. If a new charge comes into existence the day after the search, it will bind the property and the buyer.

To overcome this problem, a local search validation insurance scheme has been established by the Law Society for residential properties where the purchase price does not exceed £500,000. For a small premium the buyer will be compensated if there is any diminution in the market value of the property between the date of the search and the date of exchange of contracts as a result of new adverse charges. It is a condition of the insurance that contracts are exchanged within six months of the date of the search. The insurance also applies to the replies to the enquiries of the LA which are made on form CON.29.

8.6 Enquiries of the local authority

At the same time as the application for the local land charges search is submitted, enquiries about the property are made of the local authority on form CON.29. They deal mainly with the status of the roads and drains which serve the property and with various planning matters (see Chapter 6).

The enquiries will reveal very little about matters beyond the property. To discover what plans there are for the surrounding area, eg. whether a petrol filling station is about to be built next door, other investigations will have to be made, such as asking questions of neighbours, residents' associations and staff at the LA offices. It is *not* part of the solicitor's normal function to undertake such investigations.

Note

The client must be advised of the limitations of the searches and enquiries which a solicitor normally makes. If the client has reason to suspect that there may be some particular problem in the surrounding area, the solicitor will normally assist in trying to obtain further information.

8.7 Special searches and enquiries

The location of the property may necessitate special searches and enquiries.

Common registration search   8.7.1

Registers of common land and town and village greens are kept by county councils. If the property adjoins an open space which might possibly fall into these categories then a search should be made to ensure that no part of the property is registered as publicly owned land.

Coal mining enquiries   8.7.2

If the property is in a mining area, enquiries should be made of British Coal to discover:

● If there are any old, existing or proposed shafts, or other mine workings, in the vicinity of the property;

● Whether there is a risk of subsidence; and

● Whether any claim for subsidence damage has already been paid.

British Coal produces a directory showing the areas of the country in which enquiries should be made and a standard form for making them.

Other mining enquiries   8.7.3

Similar enquiries should be made if the property is in an area where other minerals are abstracted from the land, eg. tin in Cornwall, salt in Cheshire.

Other special enquiries   8.7.4

There are many other special enquiries which may be appropriate in particular cases, eg. enquiring about flood levels if the property is near a river or enquiring about proposed railway lines.

Inspection of the property   8.8

This is important not only to discover the physical state of the property, including what fixtures there are on the property, but also to discover overriding interests. At common law, the seller is not obliged to disclose patent incumbrances and, similarly, under standard condition 3.1.2 the property is sold subject to incumbrances discoverable by inspection of the property before contract even if they are not mentioned, ie. disclosed in the contract.

Note

It is generally not practicable for the buyer's solicitor to inspect the property personally. The buyer's own inspection is relied on. However, the solicitor should advise the buyer as to what to look for, eg. evidence of anyone other than the seller being in occupation, and evidence of rights of way over the property.

Self-assessment questions

1   What enquiries of the seller is the buyer entitled to raise pre-contract?

2   A buyer will be bound by overriding interests. How does a buyer discover what overriding interests, if any, exist?

3   What is the difference between the local land charges search and the enquiries of the local authority?

4   To what extent is the buyer's solicitor absolved from the responsibility for making pre-contract searches and enquiries where the National Conveyancing Protocol is adopted?

Chapter 9

Deducing and investigating title

Deducing title   9.1

The seller must deduce title to the estate being sold, ie. the seller must prove that they are capable of transferring title to the buyer.

Generally this is proved by showing that the seller is the registered proprietor. Sometimes the property is registered in someone else's name but the seller can nevertheless prove the right to sell it (*see* 9.1.3).

They must also provide details of incumbrances which affect the title and subject to which the property is being sold. There must be no other incumbrances on the title other than those provided for in the contract.

Method   9.1.1

Title must be deduced in accordance with s.110, LRA 1925. This requires the seller to provide the buyer with:

- A copy of the subsisting entries in the register;
- A copy of any filed plan;
- Copies or abstracts, ie. summaries, of any documents or any part thereof noted on the register so far as they affect the land to be dealt with;
- Subject to any contrary stipulation, copies, abstracts and evidence (if any) in respect of any subsisting rights and interests appurtenant to the registered land as to which the register is not conclusive, and of any matters excepted from the effect of registration, eg. overriding interests.

Section 110 does not require the copies of the entries in the register, which the seller provides, to be Office Copies, ie. official copies issued by the Land Registry. Photocopies of the entries in the land/charge certificate would satisfy s.110. However, the certificate may not reflect the current state of the register as certain entries can be made without the production of the certificate (*see* Chapter 2, para. 2.2). Although a seller will normally provide office copies, a buyer should nevertheless always ensure that the contract requires the seller to provide them so that the buyer is given proof of the up to date state of the register.

Note _____

Standard condition 4.2.1 requires the seller to provide Office Copies.

_____

9.1.2 Time

Traditionally title is deduced after the exchange of contracts and standard condition 4.1.1 still provides for this.

Where the title is registered the process of deducing title is straightforward and therefore it has long been the practice to deduce title pre-contract by providing office copies with the draft contract (or shortly thereafter).

Note _____

Where the National Conveyancing Protocol is being followed, step 4.2 requires the evidence of title to be sent with the draft contract.

_____

9.1.3 The seller who is not the registered proprietor

There are various situations where the title is not registered in the seller's name but where the seller may nevertheless be able to prove the right to dispose of the title.

Mortgagee

A mortgagee (registered chargee) whose power of sale has arisen is able to transfer the registered proprietor's (mortgagor's) title to a buyer. The buyer will need to see the mortgage deed to check that the power of sale has arisen (*see* 9.5).

Personal representatives

Where a sole or last surviving registered proprietor dies, title vests in their personal representatives (PRs) and by producing the grant of representation the PRs can be registered as the new proprietors. They can, however, dispose of the property without being so registered.

Title will then be proved by the PRs producing office copies showing the deceased as registered proprietor and the grant of representation proving their right to deal with the deceased's estate (*see* Chapter 18).

Re-sale

A buyer may contract to re-sell to a sub-buyer and may never themselves become the registered proprietor. The seller in the re-sale contract will prove title by showing that the head seller is registered as proprietor and that the sub-seller (the first buyer) has a binding contract with the proprietor (the head seller) for the transfer of the title. There will generally then be a transfer from the head seller directly to the sub-buyer.

Note

All these situations, ie. sales by mortgagees, personal representatives and re-sales, require the seller to produce further documents beyond those specified in s.110 in order to prove the right to deal with the title. Where the seller could have become the registered proprietor the buyer may insist that they do so, but this is rarely done. Thus, buyers do not usually insist on PRs or sub-sellers becoming registered as proprietors but are content to deal with them on proof that they could have been so registered.

Investigating title 9.2

The buyer's solicitor must:

- Check the *evidence of title* supplied by the seller to ensure that the seller can transfer title;
- Check for *third party rights* which will be binding on a buyer.

  Those which are removable or overreachable should be appropriately dealt with to ensure that the buyer will not be subject to them. Others which cannot be removed or overreached will bind the buyer and the buyer must therefore decide whether or not to proceed with the purchase.

Method 9.2.1

- Examine the Office Copies and other documents supplied by the seller (*see* 9.1.1). These will prove the seller's title and show the entries in the Register protecting minor interests. They should also provide such documentary evidence as exists of overriding interests.
- Make pre-contract enquiries of the seller and ensure inspection of the property to discover overriding interests, eg. legal easements and the rights of those in occupation.
- Do a local land charges search.
- Shortly before completion check, by means of a Land Registry Search and a further inspection, that the position has not changed (*see* Chapter 11, para. 11.4).

Dispositions by a sole proprietor 9.3

Where the title is registered in a sole name there may be other people who have a beneficial interest in the property. You must therefore check to see if there is any restriction or caution protecting such an interest and also check whether there is anyone in occupation with such an interest. If a beneficial interest is discovered you *must* ensure that it is overreached.

Whenever title is registered in a sole name there is also the danger of the existence of a MHA right. If there is a notice protecting such a right, you must ensure that it is removed by the spouse who entered it (*see* 9.6.3).

9.4　Dispositions by a surviving co-owner

9.4.1　Legal co-ownership

Up to four people can hold the legal estate and therefore be registered as proprietors of the legal title. Most cases of co-ownership involve only two co-owners, eg. husband and wife, but if there are three or four co-owners then they must *all* be party to any disposition and a disposition by two only will not be effective to transfer the legal title.

9.4.2　Death of a legal co-owner

Legal co-owners must hold as joint tenants on trust for sale. When one dies the right of survivorship automatically operates and the survivor(s) alone has legal title. The PRs of the deceased co-owner *never* acquire the legal title and therefore will not be involved in any subsequent disposition of it. Only on the death of the last surviving co-owner does the legal title pass to the deceased's PRs.

A sole surviving co-owner has sole legal title and can effectively dispose of the legal title on their own. Whether or not the buyer should insist on the appointment of a second trustee will depend on how the beneficial title was held.

9.4.3　Beneficial joint tenants

Where co-owners are holding on trust for sale for themselves as beneficial joint tenants, the right of survivorship will operate as regards both the legal and the beneficial title.

A sole surviving co-owner will therefore have both sole legal and sole beneficial title and a buyer can safely deal with the survivor alone. The appointment of a second trustee is unnecessary.

9.4.4　Beneficial tenants in common

Where co-owners are holding on trust for sale for themselves as beneficial tenants in common, the right of survivorship will operate as regards the legal title but *not* as regards the beneficial title. The deceased's beneficial share forms part of their estate and passes to their PRs.

A disposition by the sole surviving co-owner acting alone will be effective to transfer the legal title and their own share of the beneficial title but the buyer will still be subject to the beneficial interest of the deceased's estate.

To avoid this, you should insist on the appointment by the survivor of a *second trustee*. The buyer who pays the purchase money to two trustees will then take free from the interest of the deceased's estate. The beneficial interest is overreached and the PRs must claim the deceased's share of the proceeds of sale from the two trustees.

Type of beneficial holding   9.4.5

How does a buyer know whether joint proprietors are holding for themselves as beneficial joint tenants or as tenants in common, or whether they are holding on trust for other beneficiaries?

The right of a beneficiary under a trust for sale is a minor interest. The principal device for protecting a minor interest is a restriction, although a caution can also be used (*see* Chapter 2, para. 2.2.2). Where a co-ownership restriction appears in the proprietorship register a buyer should not deal with a sole survivor but should insist on the appointment of a second trustee.

Where there is no such restriction a buyer is entitled to assume that the co-owners hold for themselves as beneficial joint tenants and that a sole survivor therefore has sole legal and beneficial title and consequently that the appointment of a second trustee is unnecessary. However, if there is a caution protecting a beneficial interest or if there is anyone with such an interest in occupation, a second trustee is necessary.

When co-owners apply for registration of title, the Land Registry asks how the beneficial title is held and unless they hold for themselves as beneficial joint tenants a restriction will be entered. If a beneficial joint tenancy is later severed a restriction must be entered.

Summary   9.4.6

(a) If a joint proprietor dies a buyer never needs to deal with the deceased's PRs.

(b) If the proprietors held for themselves as beneficial joint tenants a buyer can deal with the sole surviving proprietor alone.

(c) If the proprietors held for themselves as beneficial tenants in common a buyer should insist on a sole survivor appointing a second trustee.

(d) If the proprietors held for beneficiaries other than them-selves a buyer should insist on a sole survivor appointing a second trustee.

Note

If there is more than one surviving proprietor in situations (c) and (d), nothing further needs to be done as there are still two trustees. Also, if the surviving trustee is a trust corporation, the appointment of a second trustee is not necessary, but this is not a situation which is often encountered in normal residential conveyancing.

(e) If the sole surviving proprietor dies then a buyer will have to deal with that proprietor's PRs. (*See* Chapter 18.)

9.4.7   Beneficial interests which are not overreached

Where a buyer does not pay the purchase money to a minimum of two trustees or a trust corporation and thereby overreach any beneficial interests, it does not automatically follow that the buyer will be bound by a beneficial interest. For such an interest to bind the buyer it must either:

- Be *protected as a minor interest* by some entry on the register; or
- Constitute an *overriding interest*.

As a *minor interest* it could be protected by the entry of a restriction or failing that a caution. In either case the pur-pose of the entry is to alert the buyer to the existence of the interest and the need to overreach it. If, however, the overreaching machinery is not utilised the buyer will take subject to the protected interest.

If the interest is not protected as a minor interest it may nevertheless be protected as an *overriding interest* under s.70(1)(g), LRA 1925.

Note

This will only apply if the beneficiary is in occupation at the time of the transfer: *Abbey National Building Society v Cann* (1991).

If the buyer is bound by a beneficial interest it will mean that the beneficiary is not only entitled to a share in the value of the property but is also entitled to occupy it.

9.5   Dispositions by mortgagees

The proprietor of a registered charge has a power of sale: s.101, LPA 1925.

When does the power arise? 9.5.1

The power arises when the debt is due. You must therefore examine the mortgage deed to see when this occurs.

Building society mortgages generally provide for the debt to be regarded as due, and therefore for the power of sale to arise, on a specific date shortly after the mortgage is created. *Bank* mortgages will provide for the debt to be payable on demand.

Provided that the power of sale has arisen, a buyer need not be concerned as to whether or not it has become exercisable under s.103 or any modification thereof contained in the mortgage deed: s.104, LPA 1925.

Note

If you are acting for a mortgagee who is selling, you must be sure that the power has become exercisable. If you do not, your client will be liable to the mortgagor for the premature exercise of the power.

Order for possession 9.5.2

In order to sell the property with vacant possession a mortgagee will (unless the mortgagor voluntarily vacates) first have to obtain a court order for possession. Under s.36, Administration of Justice Act 1970, the court has discretion to adjourn the proceedings for such period as it thinks reasonable where it considers that the mortgagor is likely to be able to pay the accrued sum, or remedy the breach of any other obligation under the mortgage, within a reasonable period.

Effect of a sale by mortgagee 9.5.3

A legal mortgagee is able to transfer the mortgagor's legal title: s.88(1), LPA 1925. As the buyer obtains title through the mortgagee the buyer will only be subject to third party interests that bound the mortgagee. If subsequent to the creation of the mortgage other incumbrances have been created, they will not bind the mortgagee, or the buyer from the mortgagee, even if they have been entered in the register. In particular, the buyer will take free from any *later mortgages*.

Sale by a mortgagee realises the security but the mortgagor remains liable for any part of the debt which is still outstanding. As the security has been realised the charge over the property has been extinguished and it is unnecessary for the buyer to lodge a Land Registry Form 53 to obtain its removal from the register.

9.5.4   Second mortgages

A sale by a first mortgagee extinguishes the second mortgagee's security, although the second mortgagee is of course still entitled to repayment of the outstanding debt. If the proceeds of sale are more than sufficient to repay the first mortgagee, the second mortgagee is entitled to the balance. Anything left after the second mortgagee has been repaid must be paid to the mortgagor (or subsequent mortgagees if there are any).

A sale by a second mortgagee will be subject to the first mortgage. To avoid this the second mortgagee will either pay off the first mortgagee or, where sufficient monies will be realised, persuade the first mortgagee to sell. The property can then be sold unincumbered.

9.5.5   Equitable mortgages

An equitable mortgage of a registered title can be created by the registered proprietor lodging their land certificate with a creditor with an accompanying memorandum which satisfies s.2, Law of Property (Miscellaneous Provisions) Act 1989 (*see* Chapter 10, para. 10.2). It will be protected by the entry of a notice of deposit in the Charges Register.

Such an arrangement is generally entered into to cover an informal short-term borrowing and it will avoid incurring land registry fees for registering a registered charge. (It is not commonly encountered in day-to-day residential conveyancing.) Such a mortgagee can only sell by first obtaining a court order for sale or converting the equitable mortgage into a registered charge. For example, a borrower may execute a registered charge at the outset but the lender may initially not register it but merely retain the land certificate and lodge a notice of deposit. Should it subsequently become necessary to realise the security, the charge can then be registered.

9.6   Third party rights

This section will consider the action you, as buyer's solicitor, must take when certain third party rights are encountered.

9.6.1   Mortgages

These can be removed by the seller paying them off. When this is done the mortgagee issues a Land Registry Form 53 which acknowledges the payment and the discharge of the security. It is lodged at the Land Registry to obtain the removal of the charge from the register.

Note

You must obtain from the seller's solicitor a Form 53 for *each* outstanding mortgage.

Beneficial interests   9.6.2

If someone who is not on the legal title has a beneficial entitlement, you must ensure that the purchase money is paid to at least two trustees (or to a trust corporation). The beneficial interest will then be overreached and the buyer will take free from it.

An alternative is to get the beneficiary to join in the contract to agree to the sale and to waive their beneficial interest.

MHA rights   9.6.3

A spouse's right of occupation under the MHA must be protected by a notice on the register; it can *never* obtain protection as an overriding interest. If protected by notice, it cannot be overreached.

Note

1   A spouse who is on the legal title does not have a MHA right. They don't need it.

2   The MHA gives a right to occupy but does not give a right to a share in the value of the property.

3   A spouse who has contributed to the value of the property will, in addition to the MHA right, have a beneficial interest which must be separately dealt with by overreaching it.

For the buyer to take free from the MHA right you must ensure that it is removed from the Register. This will require an application to the Land Registry for its removal signed by the spouse who entered it. If the notice exists pre-contract, you should not exchange contracts unless you are certain that the seller can secure its removal, ie. that the seller already holds the removal form signed by the spouse. The notice might, however, be entered after contracts have been exchanged. In this case, the seller will still be bound to secure its removal but might not be able to do so.

Section 4, MHA 1983, provides that where there is a sale with vacant possession it is an implied term of the contract that the seller will secure the cancellation of any MHA charge. A seller will often have to give a spouse some financial inducement to remove it.

If the seller cannot secure the removal of the entry, the seller will be in breach of contract and the buyer will be entitled to refuse to complete.

Example

In *Wroth v Tyler* (1974) a husband with sole legal title contracted to sell the property. His wife registered an MHA charge and refused to remove it. The buyer sued the seller for damages for breach in failing to give vacant possession and was awarded very substantial damages, being the difference between the sale price and the greatly increased value of the property at the time of judgment.

A large award of damages could bankrupt a seller. Although the bankruptcy would not immediately extinguish the MHA right, the trustee in bankruptcy will be entitled to apply to the court for an order of sale and after 12 months the court must consider the creditors' interests as paramount: s.336, Insolvency Act 1986.

If the spouse had joined in the contract and had agreed to remove the entry, the buyer could sue the spouse for breach of contract if it is not removed, and could seek an order for specific performance.

You must not complete unless the MHA notice has already been removed or you receive an application form for its removal signed by the spouse.

9.6.4 Covenants and easements

If these bind the property then generally nothing can be done to remove them. Occasionally the person with the benefit of them will be prepared to relinquish their rights and enter into a deed of discharge.

If that person cannot be found, an alternative is to take out indemnity insurance. For a one-of premium, based on the value of the property, it is often possible to insure against the event of the person having the benefit of these rights seeking to enforce them.

Finally, in certain circumstances, eg. where restrictive covenants are obsolete, application may be made to the Lands Tribunal under s.84, LPA 1925, for their discharge or modification. This is a lengthy process which is rarely viable.

Generally though, covenants and easements are burdens on the property which should be disclosed by the seller and the sale made subject to them. The buyer must then decide whether or not to buy such a property.

9.6.5 Estate contracts

Sometimes an estate contract entry in the Register is, on investigation, found to be protecting a contract which no longer exists as the contract has been discharged. The seller should then secure its removal. If the entry is a 'live' entry the buyer will be bound by it.

Local land charges

9.6.6

The buyer will be subject to them. Although financial charges can be removed by the seller paying them off, other types cannot generally be removed.

Self-assessment questions

1   A seller of a registered title must deduce title in accordance with s.110, Land Registration Act 1925. What does this require of the seller?

2   What is the buyer's solicitor looking for when they investigate title?

3   When should a buyer's solicitor insist on the seller appointing a second trustee?

4   A mortgagee does not own the freehold title so how can they sell it to a buyer and why will the buyer take free from certain incumbrances which would have bound them had they bought from the mortgagor?

Chapter 10

Exchange of contracts

Preparation for exchange: buyer

10.1

Before exchanging contracts you must be certain that the:

- *Terms of the contract* are satisfactory;
- *Investigation of title* and the results of all the *pre-contract searches and enquiries* are satisfactory;
- *Finance* for the purchase has been organised;
- *Client understands* all three issues above, has *signed* their part of the contract and has given you *authority* to agree the completion date and to exchange contracts.

Approval of the draft contract

10.1.1

The draft contract must be considered to ensure that it accords with your client's instructions and that its terms are appropriate to protect the buyer's interest and do not place excessive obligations on the buyer. The following questions in particular must be addressed:

- Are the names and addresses of all *parties* correctly stated? Should anyone else be made a party to the contract, eg. another trustee?
- Is the *seller's capacity* correctly stated?
- Is the *property* correctly described, both as regards its physical description, including any plan, and the estate in it which is being sold?
- Is the *price* correctly stated? If chattels are being sold are they to be included in the price or is there to be a separate consideration? Is there a list of all chattels which are being sold and of all fixtures which are excluded from the sale?
- Are the terms regarding the *deposit*, the *rate of interest* and the *time for completion* acceptable?
- Are special conditions which bar *requisitions* after exchange acceptable? Special condition 2 of the Standard Agreement bars requisitions on the incumbrances (as defined in SC 3.1.2) and if the title has been fully deduced before exchange a special condition will probably bar all requisitions on title. If so, you must be sure that the title has been fully deduced, that you have fully examined it and that all requisitions previously made have been satisfactorily dealt with.

- *Special conditions*, especially those which modify the Standard Conditions, should be very carefully considered as they will invariably be for the seller's benefit.

Where amendments to the draft contract are negotiated and agreed they must be incorporated by you in *both* copies of the draft contract. You should then return one copy of the approved contract to the seller's solicitor.

10.1.2   Satisfactory investigations

The evidence of title must be satisfactory. This means not only being satisfied that the seller has the right to transfer the legal title but also being satisfied as to third party rights that the property enjoys or that incumber it. Specifically:

- Does the property have all *rights* necessary for its use and enjoyment, eg. rights of way to give access to the property for persons, vehicles and services? Will there be any liability to contribute to the maintenance of these facilities?

- Are the *covenants* and *easements* which burden the property a problem? Will they impede the use which the buyer intends to make of the property or possible future development? Will they involve the buyer in expense, eg. maintaining drains that run across the property or maintaining boundary walls and fences?

  Although positive covenants are generally only directly enforceable against the original covenantor, they will be indirectly enforceable against the buyer if there is an indemnity chain. Will the buyer be required to give an indemnity? Standard condition 4.5.3 provides that if after completion the seller will remain bound by any obligation affecting the property, the buyer is to covenant in the transfer to indemnify the seller against liability for any future breach of the obligation and to perform it from then on. Where a transferee enters into an indemnity covenant it will be noted in the Proprietorship Register so as to remind them of the need to obtain an indemnity when they come to sell.

  Note _____

  This helpful note is not entered by the Land Registry on a first registration. Consequently a first proprietor needs to look back at the conveyance to them to check whether they gave an indemnity and therefore need to take one from their successor.

- Are other *incumbrances* on the property going to be removed and, if so, is their removal assured? Are those which are irremovable acceptable to the buyer?

The results of all the other pre-contract searches and enquiries must be satisfactory, eg. does it matter to the buyer that the property does not have mains drainage, or that the neighbours are noisy, or that even a small extension will require specific planning permission and will not be covered by the General Development Order?

Finance   10.1.3

The *purchase* may be financed by:

- The *proceeds* of sale of an existing property;
- The client's own *savings*;
- *Borrowing*, which will invariably be secured by a charge on the property.

Before *exchanging contracts* to buy you must be sure that:

- A *binding contract* for the sale of the existing property already exists or will come into existence at the same time as the purchase contract and that the completion dates are consistent;
- Any *savings* will be readily available in time for completion;
- A satisfactory *mortgage offer* for the necessary amount has been made and accepted by the buyer. Are any of the conditions attached to the offer a problem, eg. is there the required NHBC cover? Will the funds be available when required?

As well as ensuring that the necessary finance will be available for completion you must also ensure that the *deposit* is available immediately. This may come from:

- The *deposit* on a related sale which has been paid over on an agency basis and can therefore be utilised;
- The client's own *savings*;
- A *bridging loan*.

  This is a temporary loan, generally from a bank, to bridge the gap until mortgage funds and/or the proceeds of a related sale are available. It must then be repaid. A bridging loan is very expensive for the client and you should try to avoid having to resort to one.

  Note _____

  To enable the client to obtain bridging finance, you will be required to give the bank an undertaking for its repayment.

Signing the contract: buyer or seller   10.1.4

Before your client signs their part of the contract, you should go though it with them to ensure that they understand its main terms. In particular, they must appreciate that once contracts have been exchanged they are fully bound and that if they fail to perform their contractual obligations they will be in breach of contract and liable to compensate the other side.

When acting for the *buyer* you must also go through the results of your investigation of title and the pre-contract searches and enquiries and draw to your client's attention any problems which have arisen. Ensure that your client understands all relevant issues and that all their queries and concerns have been answered.

Also ensure that the buyer understands the terms of any mortgage offer and the effect of a mortgage, and that they are satisfied with the results of the survey.

> *Note*
>
> It is advisable to put in writing your information and advice regarding problematical issues.

When you are certain that your client understands all the issues and wishes to proceed, get the client to sign their part of the contract. Witnessing of their signature is unnecessary.

> *Note*
>
> A solicitor does not have implied authority to sign a contract on a client's behalf but could be expressly authorised, preferably in writing, to do so.

The signed contract is then left with you with authority to agree the completion date, within the limits laid down by your client, and to exchange contracts. You must be certain that you have your client's authority to exchange. Although a solicitor has ostensible/apparent authority to exchange contracts, and therefore an exchange effected by you will bind your client, if you do not actually have authority you will be liable to your client. If you do have your client's authority to exchange, it is implied that you may do so by any method which the law recognises as constituting an exchange: *Domb v Isoz* (1980).

10.2   Methods of exchange

10.2.1   Statutory requirements

Section 2, Law of Property (Miscellaneous Provisions) Act 1989, requires contracts for the sale or other disposition of an interest in land to be:

- *In writing;*
- Incorporate all the expressly agreed *terms*; and
- Be *signed* by each party.

Section 2 specifically recognises the practice of exchanging contracts and provides that all the terms must be set out in each part but the parties may sign separate parts.

Methods of exchange   10.2.2

Exchange of contracts involves the physical transfer of each signed part to the other side. However, even before the physical transfer occurs, a solicitor may acknowledge that they are holding their client's signed part of the contract on behalf of the other side and this will constitute an exchange (*see* below).

An exchange may be made in various ways:

- *In person.*

  The solicitors meet and exchange their respective parts.

- By *post* or delivery to a *document exchange.*

  The contract comes into existence when the second part is posted: *see* SC 2.1.1. This creates uncertainty as who is to know which is the second part?

- By *telephone, telex* or *fax.*

  This involves agreeing with the other side to hold your client's signed part on their behalf and undertaking to forward it to the other side. The exchange takes place from the moment the agreement is made on the telephone: *see* SC 2.1.2. The whole process depends for its effectiveness on the fact that it is underpinned by solicitors' undertakings.

  Note _____

  The vast majority of exchanges are effected over the telephone. It is the only method which is practicable where there is a chain involved and all parties wish to exchange as simultaneously as possible.

The Law Society formulae   10.2.3

To facilitate exchange by telephone/telex/fax, the Law Society has drawn up three formulae which specify the obligations of the respective solicitors when effecting such exchanges. They are used in different factual situations.

- *Formula A* is used where one solicitor (usually the seller's) already holds both signed parts.
- *Formula B* is used where each solicitor holds their own

client's signed part of the contract. This is the most widely used formula.

- *Formula C* is specifically designed for use in chain transactions and is considerably more complex than the other two.

By referring to one or other of these formulae the solicitors incorporate them into their agreement and thereby determine the effect of their agreement and the terms of the undertakings which they impliedly give. (Details of the formulae are contained in the documents.)

10.2.4 Dating the contract

Immediately before agreeing the exchange, the completion date must be agreed and inserted in each part of the contract and, following exchange, the date of exchange must be inserted in each part.

10.3 Conditional contracts

Although it is undesirable, contracts may sometimes be exchanged subject to a condition, eg. subject to a satisfactory local search or subject to obtaining planning permission.

The terms of the condition must be specific otherwise the whole contract will be void for uncertainty, eg. 'subject to survey' or 'subject to mortgage' would be too vague. 'Subject to planning permission' may also be too vague unless it can be construed as impliedly referring to a planning application which is pending. Where a condition is imposed a time limit for its fulfilment may be specified but if not it must be fulfilled by the completion date.

If the condition is not fulfilled the contract comes to an end, both parties are released from it and the buyer is entitled to recover the deposit. However, where the condition has been imposed for the benefit of one party only, that party may choose to waive its non-fulfilment and keep the contract in existence, eg. the buyer may waive the fact that the hoped-for planning permission has not been granted.

Self-assessment questions

1 What amendments to the draft contract is the buyer's solicitor entitled to make?

2 What should the buyer's solicitor do about any irremovable incumbrances which are discovered pre-exchange?

3 What is the purpose of a deposit; how much will it be; where will the money come from and to whom should it be paid?

4   When does an exchange of contracts
    (a) by post
    (b) by telephone take effect?

Chapter 11

Exchange to completion

The effect of a binding contract | 11.1

From the moment that contracts are exchanged the parties are legally bound. A failure by either party to perform their obligations under the contract will constitute a breach entitling the other party to the usual contractual remedies (*see* Chapter 13). However, as with any other type of contract the parties may, by subsequent agreement, modify or terminate the contract.

> *Note*
>
> Any such subsequent agreement must comply with s.2, Law of Property (Miscellaneous Provisions) Act 1989.

Protecting the buyer's equitable title | 11.1.1

A binding contract for the sale of land does more than just create contractual rights and obligations. 'Equity regards that as done which ought to be done' and therefore from the moment of exchange the buyer has the equitable title This equitable right of the buyer is known as an *estate contract* (a term which includes options to purchase and rights of pre-emption).

For this equitable right to bind a later purchaser of the legal estate, it must be protected as a minor interest by entering a notice or caution on the Register. However, unless the buyer has reason to suspect that the seller may subsequently enter into a contract with another purchaser, it is not usual to protect the buyer's estate contract where completion is planned to take place within a normal period of time, eg. within four weeks. Where there will be an unusually long period between exchange and completion, the estate contract should be protected immediately and it is also advisable to register the contract if completion is delayed.

Any contract which includes an option or a right of pre-emption should always be protected straightaway.

The risk in the property | 11.1.2

At common law the risk passes with the equitable title. If the property increases or diminishes in value between exchange and completion, that change is for the buyer's account. The property is also at the buyer's risk so far as physical damage is concerned so that the buyer must still perform the contract at the full price although the property has been damaged. Even if the buildings standing on the land have been totally destroyed, the buyer cannot plead that the contract has been frustrated by the destruction of the subject matter as the land is still there, and that is the real subject matter of the contract.

As the buyer has the risk in the property the buyer needs to have insurance cover from the moment of exchange. The seller also needs to maintain insurance cover on the property following exchange because if for some reason completion never takes place the seller will retain the property. Consequently property is often insured by both parties.

Unless the buyer is allowed into possession before completion, the seller is liable, as a qualified trustee, to take reasonable care to keep the property in its contract condition. The buyer may therefore have redress if the damage to the property is the result of the seller's breach of duty, eg. if the seller vacated the property without making it secure.

11.1.3   Standard condition 5.1

This seeks to remove the need for the buyer to take out insurance from exchange of contracts and so to avoid double insurance. Standard condition 5.1 states that the seller retains the risk until *completion*.

Note

This refers only to the physical risk and the risk of a change in the value of the property is still with the buyer.

SC5.1.1 provides that the seller will transfer the property in the same physical state as it was in at the date of the contract (except for fair wear and tear), ie. it imposes an *absolute* contractual obligation on the seller which is clearly far more beneficial to the buyer than the seller's common law duty as trustee to take reasonable care.

If the property is damaged the buyer will still have to complete, unless 5.1.2 applies, but will be able to claim damages from the seller for breach of condition 5.1.1. Unfortunately, 5.1.3 provides that the seller is under no obligation to the buyer to insure the property and some solicitors therefore consider that it is still advisable for the buyer to have their own insurance cover and may choose to delete condition 5.1 altogether.

Standard condition 5.1.2 provides that if at any time

before completion the physical state of the property makes it unusable for its purpose at the date of the contract, then the *buyer* may rescind the contract. The *seller* may rescind where the property has become unusable for that purpose as a result of damage against which the seller could not reasonably have insured or which it is not legally possible for the seller to make good. This is a sort of *force majeure* clause. If the property is so badly damaged that it cannot be used then the parties are released from the contract. The buyer will be entitled to the return of their deposit but the seller will not be liable for any damages.

Standard condition 5.1.4 provides that s.47, Law of Property Act 1925 does not apply. Section 47 provides that in certain circumstances insurance money received by the seller is received on behalf of the buyer. It is not a very satisfactory section so far as protecting the buyer is concerned and most contracts of sale exclude it.

Occupation by the buyer   11.1.4

Although the seller holds the legal title on trust for the buyer, the seller is entitled to retain possession of the property until completion. They will be entitled to any income from the property and must bear all outgoings on it. Sometimes the buyer is allowed into occupation before completion.

It is important to distinguish between allowing a buyer into *occupation* and allowing the buyer *access* to the property. Buyers are often allowed to go in and out of the property to measure up for curtains, carpets etc, or to get estimates for work to be carried out, and even for work to be done, but this does not normally amount to the buyer entering into occupation. While each case will depend on the particular circumstances, a vital factor would seem to be whether or not the buyer is allowed to *retain the keys*. If the keys have to be returned to the seller or the seller's agent after the work has been done, the buyer only has *access*, they have not been allowed into occupation.

The effect of the buyer entering into occupation is dealt with fully in standard condition 5.2. At common law the status of the buyer in occupation is less clear-cut and it might be difficult for the seller to remove the buyer if the buyer fails to complete. Also at common law, a buyer who enters into possession is presumed to be accepting the seller's title. Standard condition 5.2.7 clearly negates this and preserves the buyer's right to question the seller's title and raise requisitions on it.

11.2   Requisitions on title

Traditionally the seller deduces title and the buyer raises requisitions after exchange of contracts. Standard condition 4.1 preserves this traditional approach and lays down a timetable for the raising and answering of requisitions.

If the seller refuses to answer a proper requisition the buyer can either rescind the contract or take out a vendor and purchase summons under s.49, LPA 1925 to compel an answer.

If the Protocol is adopted, title is deduced before exchange and it is usual in the case of registered titles for title to be deduced pre-contract even in cases where the Protocol is not being followed. Where title is to be deduced pre-contract the seller should ensure that the contract contains a special condition stating that this is being done and that the buyer is barred from raising requisitions once contracts have been exchanged.

In addition to true requisitions on title, there are also certain standard form requisitions which the buyer will always raise pre-completion. These standard form requisitions are primarily dealing with the arrangements for completion. In particular, they ask for details of the client account of the seller's solicitor, to which payment of the price is to be made, and whether any existing mortgage will be discharged prior to completion and a Form 53 provided, or whether an undertaking will be offered instead. If the buyer's solicitor wishes the seller's solicitor to act as agent on completion (*see* Chapter 12, para. 12.4), this is also requested.

11.3   Preparing documentation

In preparation for completion there are various documents that will need to be drafted.

11.3.1   The Land Registry transfer

Legal estates must be transferred by deed and for registered titles there are prescribed Land Registry forms. In the case of a transfer of the entirety of the land Form 19, or Form 19(JP) if there are joint purchasers, will be used.

The *transfer* contains:

- The *title number* and *description* of the property.
- The *date* of the transfer.
- *Consideration and receipt clause*. The Stamp Act 1891 requires the consideration to be accurately stated and it is on the basis of this figure that any stamp duty liability will be calculated. It is only the consideration for the

land which is stated. Where there is a separate consideration for chattels this is not mentioned.

Note

The receipt element of the clause is important in two respects. *First*, the fact that the transfer is drafted incorporating a receipt clause serves as authorisation to the buyer to pay the purchase price to the seller's solicitor, ie. the presence of the receipt clause holds out the seller's solicitor as authorised to receive the purchase money. *Second*, the receipt clause serves as a sufficient receipt to the buyer who does not therefore need to obtain a separate receipt. This is particularly important where the money is being received by trustees as the receipt by them of the purchase price activates the overreaching machinery.

- *Seller's name and address.*
- A statement of the *capacity* in which the seller transfers the property and the operative words 'hereby transfers'. The capacity in which the seller transfers will affect the implied covenants for title (*see* Chapter 13, para. 13.4.2).
- *Buyer's name and address.*
- The *description* of the property transferred as being all the property registered under the specified title number.
- An express *indemnity covenant*. This is included where the sale is subject to existing restrictive covenants and the contract requires the buyer to give an indemnity to the seller in respect of the seller's continuing liability on those covenants.
- *Co-owners* – where there is more than one purchaser there will be a statement as to whether the survivor can give a *valid receipt* or not. If the survivor can give a valid receipt it indicates that they are to hold beneficially as joint tenants. If not, that they will hold as tenants in common.

Note

The transfer does not define the extent of the beneficial interests of tenants in common. These should be specified in a separate declaration of trust.

- *Certificate of value*, if appropriate (*see* Chapter 5, para. 5.2).
- *Execution and attestation* – both parties must sign the transfer and their signatures must be witnessed.

Execution takes place by signing the document as a deed and by delivering it. Delivery means an act done so as to indicate an intention to be bound. Handing the document over to the other side clearly does this but there can be a delivery without physical transfer of the document.

At one time, authority for an agent to deliver a deed had itself to be given by deed. This was rarely done. Consequently, when a seller signed a transfer and handed it to their own solicitor in readiness for completion, it was regarded as already having been delivered, although the delivery was conditional on the buyer paying the purchase price. A conditional delivery is known as a *delivery in escrow*. Once a conditional delivery has taken place, it must await the performance of the condition and the seller cannot withdraw the document.

Section 1, Law of Property (Miscellaneous Provisions) Act 1989 provides that authority to deliver a document as a deed need no longer be given by deed. It is therefore now possible for the deed to be left with the solicitor with authority to deliver it on the client's behalf without immediately constituting a conditional delivery.

Note

The seller can now have second thoughts and instruct the solicitor not to hand it over to the buyer.

Traditionally, the transfer document is drafted by the buyer's solicitor, sent to the seller's solicitor for approval and, when approved, engrossed, ie. re-typed, by the buyer's solicitor. This process may be followed in the case of a deed of conveyance for an unregistered title but a land registry transfer, especially when it is one of the entirety of the title, is so straightforward that it is generally unnecessary to prepare a draft. The form is prepared by the buyer's solicitor, the buyer executes it and it is sent to the seller's solicitor for the seller to execute in readiness for completion.

11.3.2   The buyer's mortgage

If the mortgage is to an institutional mortgagee there will be no need to draft a mortgage deed as there will be a standard institution form to use. The solicitor acting for the mortgagee must ensure that before completion the mortgage deed has been completed and executed by the buyer.

In good time before completion, the mortgagee's solicitor must send the mortgagee a Report on Title confirming that the title has been investigated and is good to lend against. If there are any problems with the title, these must be drawn to the mortgagee's attention.

Generally at the same time as the mortgagee is sent the

Report on Title, the solicitor requisitions, ie. requests, the mortgage money. The buyer's solicitor will need to clear the cheque through their client account before the funds can be utilised and therefore the cheque needs to be obtained a few days before completion to allow time for clearance.

Note

The mortgagee will start charging interest on the mortgage advance from the date of the cheque. This means that the buyer will have to start paying interest on the mortgage money before completion has actually taken place. The reasons for this need to be carefully explained to the client well in advance.

If the mortgage is an *endowment* mortgage, the buyer's solicitor must ensure that before completion the life insurance policy has been taken out and that it is for the correct amount. If the mortgagee requires the benefit of the policy to be formally assigned, the solicitor must ensure that the buyer/mortgagor signs the necessary deed to assign the life policy to the mortgagee.

For an assignment of a life policy to take effect as a legal assignment the insurance company must be notified in writing of the assignment. The solicitor will therefore prepare two copies of a notice of assignment ready to send to the insurer's head office post-completion. One copy will be returned by the insurance company as its acknowledgement that the notice has been received.

The seller's mortgage: undertaking for Form 53   11.3.3

Where the seller has a mortgage on the property it will have to be discharged in order for the buyer to take free from it. The buyer is entitled to insist that this be done before completion so that on completion the seller hands over to the buyer Form 53 executed by the mortgagee.

This form is a receipt for the mortgage money and is lodged at the Land Registry to secure the removal from the register of the registered charge. In practice the seller usually needs the sale proceeds to redeem the mortgage and if the buyer insists on the seller redeeming the mortgage before completion the seller may have to raise bridging finance to do so. This will be expensive for the seller. Consequently, the seller generally asks if the buyer will be prepared to complete on the basis of a solicitor's undertaking.

In the undertaking the solicitor must only promise to do things which are within their control, ie. to send off the money to redeem the mortgage to the mortgagee and to send to the buyer the Form 53, if and when it is received from the mortgagee. The solicitor cannot guarantee that the mortgagee will actually issue the Form 53. However, where the mortgagee is an institutional mortgagee, it is most unlikely that on repayment of the outstanding balance it will not issue the necessary Form 53. Buyers' solicitors are therefore generally prepared to complete on the basis of a solicitor's undertaking in the Law Society's approved form where the mortgage is an institutional mortgage.

In the case of a private mortgage, there is a risk that the mortgagee may fail to issue the Form 53 and therefore a buyer's solicitor should not agree to complete on the basis of an undertaking.

Where there is more than one mortgage on the property, the buyer's solicitor must ensure that all the mortgages will be discharged before completion or that a satisfactory undertaking, which covers all the mortgages, will be given.

11.3.4   Statements of account

Both solicitors should, before completion, send to their respective clients Statements of Account. In the case of the *seller* it will show what will be left out of the proceeds of sale when all outstanding mortgages and the costs of the sale have been paid. In the case of the *buyer* it will show how much is needed in order to complete the purchase, ie. the outstanding purchase price plus all the costs of the purchase. It will then set out how that is to be funded, eg. the proceeds of a related sale, the mortgage money, plus any sum to be provided by the buyer. Where the buyer has to provide funds to enable completion to take place then, if these are being provided by cheque, time must be allowed for the cheque to clear. The buyer's solicitor must therefore make it clear to the client that the cheque is required several days before the contractual completion date.

The statement to the buyer is sometimes preceded by a completion statement, issued by the seller's solicitor to the buyer's solicitor, setting out the amount required to complete the transaction. In a simple freehold transaction this is frequently dispensed with as what is required is simply the balance of the purchase price, ie. the price less the deposit already paid on exchange.

Note

The seller's failure to supply a completion statement does not justify the buyer's failure to complete. The buyer must still complete on the basis of offering what is believed to be the correct amount: *Carne v Debono* (1988).

Pre-completion searches   11.4

In preparation for completion the buyer's solicitor will need
to make certain searches.

Search of the Land Register   11.4.1

A search will be made at the relevant District Land Registry on
Form 94A. This is done to discover whether any new entries
have been made since the date of issue of the office copies.

The buyer will expect the search certificate to come back
saying that there have been no adverse entries. If there are
new adverse entries this may justify the buyer in refusing to
complete or, at the very least, is likely to delay completion
while the entries are investigated. The official search certificate is not conclusive in the buyer's favour and if there are
entries which it fails to reveal the buyer will still be subject
to them, but will be entitled to an indemnity from the state
under s.83, LRA 1925.

The great advantage of the official search certificate for
the buyer is that it gives a priority period of 30 working
days. This means that provided the buyer completes and
registers the transaction within that period the buyer will
not be affected by any further entries made after the date of
the search.

Inspection of the property   11.4.2

There should ideally be a last minute inspection of the
property, eg. by the client, to check that there is no one in
occupation who might have an interest that would be
protected under s.70(1)(g), LRA 1925, and that no fixtures
have been removed.

Search of the Local Land Charges Register?   11.4.3

It is not usual to repeat this search unless there has been a
particularly long period of time between exchange and
completion, eg. something in excess of six months. Even
then the purpose of the search is simply for the buyer's
information and if there are new charges it will not justify
the buyer in refusing to complete. The risk of new local land
charges is on the buyer from the moment of exchange.

Search of Company's Register?   11.4.4

Where the seller is a company, a search of the company's
register is advisable. All charges, including floating charges,
created by a company must be protected by entry on the
Register of Title, otherwise the buyer will not be bound by
them even if they are registered at Companies House. A

company search will, however, reveal other information about the company such as whether it is in the process of being wound up.

11.4.5   Mortgagee's Searches

The solicitor acting for the buyer's mortgagee must ensure that the searches already discussed are made. For the mortgagee to have the benefit of the priority period given by the Form 94A search, the search must be done specifically on behalf of the mortgagee. It will then allow 30 working days for the buyer to register the transfer and for the mortgagee to register the charge, and *both* will be protected against any new entries during this period.

The mortgagee's solicitor must also do a bankruptcy search against the name(s) of the prospective mortgagor(s), ie. the buyer(s). This is a search in the index to the registers which are maintained under the Land Charges Act 1972. It is not a full search of all the registers but is limited to bankruptcy entries, ie. bankruptcy petitions, bankruptcy orders and deeds of arrangement with creditors. If any such entry appears against a buyer's name, the mortgagee must immediately be notified and the mortgage advance will not be made. There will then inevitably be a failure to complete by the buyer.

Self-assessment questions

1   If the property is damaged between exchange and completion what rights, if any, will the buyer have?

2   What is the difference between the contract of sale and the Land Registry transfer?

3   Why does the buyer's solicitor not always insist on the seller paying off their outstanding mortgage before completion and how can the buyer's solicitor ensure that the buyer will not then be bound by the seller's mortgage?

4   What is the purpose and effect of the Form 94A Land Registry search and why, when the buyer is buying with the aid of mortgage, must the search by done in the mortgagee's name?

Chapter 12

Completion and post-completion

Completion defined 12.1

Completion is the performance of the contract. The buyer pays the price and the seller performs their side of the contract by putting the buyer in a position to acquire title by applying for registration of the transfer.

Payment of the price 12.2

The buyer pays the price less any deposit already paid. If the deposit was paid over on an agency basis the seller will already have received it. If it was paid to a stakeholder, at completion the stakeholder can pay it to the seller without waiting to receive authorisation to do so from the buyer: *Hastingwood Property Ltd v Saunders Bearman Anselm* (1990).

By telegraphic transfer 12.2.1

The buyer's solicitor instructs their bank to make payment direct from their client account to the client account of the seller's solicitor. The standard requisitions on title will have obtained details of the bank and account number.

The transfer does not occur instantaneously and there can be a delay of several hours between the bank being instructed to make the transfer and the seller's solicitor's bank receiving it. This can cause problems in a chain situation where the seller's solicitor is relying on the proceeds of sale to finance a related purchase.

The Solicitors' Accounts Rules prohibit the use, even for a temporary period, of funds in the client account belonging to other clients. You must therefore wait to receive the sale proceeds before you can pay for your related purchase. To overcome this problem, you may arrange for a telegraphic transfer from your client account to be transmitted to the client account of the seller's solicitor but on the strict understanding that the money is to be held to your order. When your client's sale proceeds are actually received into your client account you can then release the funds already transmitted to the other side and so complete on the purchase.

By banker's draft or in cash 12.2.2

A banker's draft is a promise of payment by a bank and it is regarded as being as good as cash. This method of payment involves the buyer's solicitor collecting from the bank a draft payable to the seller's solicitor and delivering it by hand. It is only convenient to pay by this method if the seller's solicitor is located nearby and even then it will rarely be used in a chain transaction.

Payment in cash is subject to the same constraints and is therefore rarely used.

12.2.3 Payment for chattels

Where chattels are purchased for a separate consideration, a separate receipt must be obtained from the seller, as the receipt embodied in the transfer is only for the price paid for the land.

12.3 Performance by the seller

Before paying over the price the buyer's solicitor must check that the seller is able to perform their side of the contract. This involves checking that:

- The seller's solicitor holds the *land certificate*, or *charge certificate* if there is an outstanding mortgage. There should be as many charge certificates as there are outstanding mortgages;
- A *Form 53* signed by the mortgagee will be handed over in respect of each outstanding mortgage or, if the buyer has agreed to complete on the basis of an undertaking from the seller's solicitor, that an *undertaking* in the Law Society's approved form is available;
- The Land Registry *transfer* is properly executed;
- Other *documents* which the seller has promised to supply are available, eg. NHBC documents, other guarantees that go with the property, planning consents; and
- A *receipt for chattels* is available.

12.4 The completion process

What actually happens at completion?
- The *checks* listed in 12.2 are carried out;
- The *buyer pays* the price;
- The *transfer is dated* and *handed over* to the buyer's solicitor together with the other documents listed in 12.2.
- The *keys are handed over* or *authority given* to whoever holds them, eg. the estate agent, to release them.
- Where the buyer is entering into a new mortgage, the

mortgage deed is dated with the same date as the transfer and takes effect immediately.

The completion can be performed either by *personal attendance* or by *post*.

If by personal attendance someone, eg. a trainee solicitor, will be sent from the buyer's solicitor's office to the seller's solicitor's office to 'do the completion'. If the seller's solicitor is not nearby the buyer's solicitor may appoint another firm, in the same town as the seller's solicitor, as agent to do the completion. In both these situations, payment is likely to be made by banker's draft. In a chain transaction, completion by personal attendance is unusual even if the other solicitor is nearby.

A further possibility is that the seller's solicitor is appointed as agent to do the completion on the buyer's behalf as well as on the seller's behalf. This is known as completion by post and it is the most common method of completion. In this method, payment will be made by telegraphic transfer.

Note

It seems that the general prohibition on acting for both seller and buyer does not apply to this arrangement but the possibility of a conflict of interest should always be considered. If it exists this arrangement is to be avoided, eg. if the buyer's solicitor suspects that the seller's solicitor may not be in a position to hand over the requisite documents.

The Law Society's Code for Completion by Post 12.4.1

The Law Society has drawn up a code of practice for postal completions. The Code makes it clear that the buyer's solicitor must give precise instructions as to what the seller's solicitors is to do, eg. documents to be checked, documents to be forwarded. It specifies the obligations of the seller's solicitor and incorporates into the agency arrangement certain undertakings, eg. the seller's solicitor undertakes that they have authority from both the seller and the seller's mortgagee to receive the purchase money.

The Code itself states that is only applies if specifically adopted by the solicitors involved. However, if the Protocol is being followed, the Code will apply automatically unless otherwise agreed. Where the Protocol is not being followed, adoption of the Code is nevertheless usual and is provided for in the standard pre-completion requisitions.

The effect of completion 12.4.2

• As the title is already registered, legal title does not pass to the buyer on completion but only on registration of the transfer.

- The doctrine of merger operates (*see* Chapter 13) but probably not until the transfer is registered.

12.5   Post completion

Each solicitor should immediately inform their client that completion has taken place and then deal with other post completion matters.

12.5.1   Seller's solicitor

The seller's solicitor must do four things:

- If acting as the buyer's agent on completion, comply with the obligation embodied in the arrangement and *forward documents* to the buyer's solicitor.
- If an undertaking has been given for the *discharge of an outstanding mortgage*, comply with it by forwarding the necessary funds to the mortgagee and on receipt from the mortgagee of the executed Form 53 forward it to the buyer's solicitor.
- If the seller has obtained *bridging finance* in connection with a related purchase, honour the undertaking given to the bank. (Be sure that you have first deducted all items which you are authorised to deduct, eg. your fees, estate agent's commission.)
- Pay any *balance in the proceeds of sale* to the seller or in accordance with their instructions.

12.5.2   Buyer's solicitor: stamping the transfer

Within 30 days the buyer's solicitor must send the transfer to the Inland Revenue together with a client account cheque for the stamp duty. At the same time a completed Particulars Delivered (PD) form must be submitted. When the transfer is returned by the Inland Revenue it will bear embossed stamps showing the amount of duty which has been paid and a printed stamp showing that particulars have been delivered. The Land Registry will not accept the transfer for registration until it has been stamped.

If there is no *ad valorem* duty payable the PD form is not submitted to the Inland Revenue but is submitted instead to the Land Registry together with the application for registration.

12.5.3   Buyer's solicitor: registering the transfer

Within the 30 working day priority period granted by the

Form 94A search, application must be made to the Land Registry to register the transfer. The application is made on Form A4 and in most residential transactions the application is to do three things:

- Remove the seller's *discharged mortgage(s)* from the register;
- Register the buyer(s) as the new *proprietor(s)*;
- Register the new *charge(s)* created by the buyer.

The documents to be lodged with the A4 application will then be the:

- Charge Certificate(s);
- Form 53 for each discharged mortgage;
- Form 19 Transfer;
- Original mortgage deed and certified copy for each new mortgage; and
- Fee.

Note —————————————————————————————

There is no fee for removing a charge. The fee for registering a transfer depends on the amount of the consideration. There is a fee for registering a charge but if it is done at the same time as a transfer is registered, the additional fee is waived.

———————————————————————————————————

Where there are joint buyers Form A4 asks whether or not the survivor can give a receipt for capital monies arising. If the answer is 'No' the appropriate co-ownership restriction will be entered in the proprietorship register.

If the Land Registry has queries about the application it will raise requisitions. The buyer's solicitor must answer them, if necessary enlisting the help of the seller's solicitor.

Custody of documents   12.5.4

Eventually a land or charge certificate will be received from the Land Registry. It should be checked to ensure it records accurately the name(s) and address(es) of the new proprietor(s) and all other necessary entries, eg. the new charge and any co-ownership restriction. The charge certificate should be sent to the mortgagee together with the bankruptcy search result and other important documents affecting the property such as the NHBC guarantee and planning consents.

If there is no mortgage the land certificate and all other documents will be sent to the buyer with advice as to their safe-keeping.

Self-assessment questions

1 Your principal, the buyer's solicitor, tells you to go and do a completion. List three things you would expect to have to do.

2 What is the Law Society's code for completion by post?

3 What is the difference between AV and PD stamping and do all transfers have to be AV and PD stamped?

4 What is the effect of failing to register the transfer within 30 working days of the pre-completion Form 94A search?

Chapter 13

Remedies

Delayed completion 13.1

If completion does not take place at the contractually agreed time, the party responsible for the delay will be liable for breach of contract. Although the other party will not normally be entitled to terminate the contract – as time is not generally of the essence of the contract – they will be entitled to compensation.

Note

Standard condition 6.1.2 provides that if the money due on completion is received *after 2pm*, completion is regarded, for the purpose of calculating compensation, as taking place on the next working day. Thus, a liability for several days' interest will arise if completion was due to take place on the day before a bank holiday weekend.

The open contract approach 13.1.1

Regardless of who is responsible for the delay, the open contract rule seeks to put the parties in the position they would have been in had completion taken place on time. The *seller* is entitled to receive interest at the contract rate on the outstanding purchase price and the *buyer* is entitled to receive any income accruing from the property and is liable for all outgoings.

If the *seller* is the defaulting party:

- They must pay the buyer a fair rent if they remain in occupation; (In practice this will normally cancel out the buyer's liability to pay interest.)
- The buyer is entitled to elect to allow the seller to retain the income from the property (and therefore not pay rent) instead of the buyer paying interest;
- The buyer is entitled to elect to place the outstanding purchase price on deposit and pay over to the seller the interest it actually earns instead of paying interest at the contract rate. This option will generally only be available to a cash buyer as a buyer's mortgage funds or the proceeds of a related delayed sale will not be available to place on deposit.

If the *buyer* is the defaulting party, none of these options is open to the buyer.

In *addition* to these adjustments there can also be an ordinary common law claim for damages to compensate the innocent party for any loss resulting from the breach of contract.

13.1.2   Damages

The normal rules regarding remoteness of damage apply and the plaintiff is entitled to compensation for those consequences of the breach that were reasonably foreseeable: *Hadley v Baxendale* (1854) and *The Heron II* (1969).

Example

In *Raineri v Miles* (1981), the defendant contracted to sell their house in West London to the plaintiff and to buy another house from the third party. Completion was fixed for 12 July on both contracts. Late on 11 July the third party informed the defendant that due to difficulties with the finance for their own purchase, they would not be able to complete their sale to the defendant the following day. The defendant immediately notified the plaintiff but they had already vacated their house in the north of England and their furniture was on its way south. The defendant did not vacate on the 12th and the plaintiff had to rent temporary accommodation. The defendant did, however, help the plaintiff to mitigate their loss by providing storage for the furniture. On 11 August the defendant was able to complete on their purchase and consequently on their sale to the plaintiff. The plaintiff sued for damages to cover the accommodation costs. The defendant settled the claim and sought indemnity from the third party. The main issue was whether the defendant was in breach, given that their failure to complete on time was due to the default of the third party.

The House of Lords held that they were in breach and liable to the plaintiff and therefore entitled to be indemnified by the third party. A delay on one transaction is no excuse for failing to perform a related transaction on time.

Where it is the buyer who fails to complete on time a seller with a related purchase will be faced with either delaying their purchase or raising bridging finance to complete on time. Bridging finance is very expensive and therefore delaying the related purchase, even though it will involve liability to that seller, may be preferable.

Note

There is always a duty on the innocent party to mitigate their loss.

13.1.3   The standard conditions

The sale contract usually modifies the open contract rules

regarding the consequences of delay.

- *SC 6.3.1* provides that in a sale with vacant possession the apportionment of income and outgoings is to be made with effect from the date of actual completion and not the date when completion should have occurred.

- *SC 7.3.1* provides that it is the party in default who has to pay compensation/interest and not, as under the open contract, always the buyer.

- *SC 7.3.2* provides that the party whose period of default is the greater shall pay compensation calculated at the contract rate on the purchase price, or (where the buyer is the paying party) the purchase price less any deposit paid.

- *SC 7.3.3* makes it clear that a claim for damages for breach of contract can still be brought if the loss exceeds the fixed compensation provided for in SC 7.3.2.

Notice to complete   13.1.4

A notice to complete is a device for making *time of the essence*, ie. making the time for completion a condition of the contract. It sets a deadline and if completion does not take place by that date, the party who is *then* responsible for the failure to complete has committed a major breach, ie. a breach of condition. The other party may then elect to withdraw from the contract and in addition claim damages for non-completion. This threat to terminate the contract if completion does not take place by the deadline may well induce a dilatory party to complete.

Under the *open contract rule* a notice to complete can be served at any time *after* the contractual completion date and completion must then be within the specified time or if no time is specified within a reasonable time.

Special condition 6.8 provides that a notice to complete can be given at any time *on or after* the completion date and that completion must then be within ten working days. The party giving the notice must be ready, able and willing to complete. The notice makes time of the essence for *both* parties so that if the party serving the notice is later responsible for completion not taking place by the deadline, the party on whom the notice was served will then be the one entitled to terminate the contract and claim damages.

Note

SC 6.8.4 seeks to ensure that if the buyer fails to comply with a completion notice, the seller will have in hand the traditional 10% deposit which then can be forfeited.

If completion does not take place by the deadline the *innocent party* may:

- *Terminate* the contract and *claim damages* for non-performance;
- *Waive* the deadline and allow the other side extra time. If it is later decided to impose a further deadline, another notice to complete will be needed.
- Sue for *specific performance*.

13.1.5 Specific performance

A decree of specific performance can be applied for even before the contractual date for completion if there is reason to believe that the other party will not perform, but it is normally only sought after there has been some delay. Often a notice to complete is tried first and only if that fails to induce completion is specific sought.

Specific performance is primarily a buyer's remedy but a seller may seek it where it is believed that the buyer has the money to complete but is refusing to do so. It is an equitable, and therefore a *discretionary* remedy, and may be refused if, for example, the court considers that to award it would cause undue hardship to the defendant. Damages may be awarded in lieu of specific performance. If a decree of specific performance is not complied with, the plaintiff may ask the court to terminate the contract and award damages instead: *Johnson v Agnew* (1980).

13.2 Non-completion

A failure to complete will constitute a major breach and entitle the other party to terminate the contract where:

- There is a failure to complete on time and time is of the essence, either because it was made so originally or because a notice to complete has been served;
- The seller is unable to transfer what they contracted to transfer. This may be because they cannot show a good title, or because there was some major misdescription in the contract or the non-disclosure of some major incumbrance. (Where title is investigated pre-exchange there is little chance of this type of problem arising.)

The buyer can immediately terminate the contract and does not first have to serve a notice to complete, although in practice the buyer may allow the seller time to try to remedy the defect. If the buyer elects to complete despite the defect, they will be entitled to damages for the diminution in the value of the property and will therefore be entitled to a price reduction.

Where the contract is terminated both parties are discharged from further performance and the innocent party can also claim damages for non-performance.

Damages recoverable by a buyer   13.2.1

The normal rules of remoteness apply and the buyer can recover for the reasonably foreseeable consequences of the breach.

- A loss of a bargain is foreseeable, so in a rising market the buyer will recover the difference between the contract price and the increased value of the property.

- Wasted conveyancing costs are not recoverable as these would have been incurred anyway to acquire the bargain.

Note
If there is no claim for loss of bargain, wasted costs can be claimed.

- A claim for loss of profit, eg. on reselling or on developing the property, will only succeed if the seller knew of the intention to resell/develop.

- In a chain transaction a breach by a seller will probably result in the buyer breaking their related sale contract and incurring liability, at least for delay, to their buyer. This can normally be recovered, as in residential conveyancing the existence of a related transaction is generally known to all parties and the loss is therefore foreseeable.

  If the buyer completes, whether on time or belatedly, on their related sale they will need temporary accommodation until they can find another house to buy. The cost of this and the costs of the new purchase are recoverable: *Beard v Porter* (1948).

The buyer will also be entitled to the return of the deposit plus interest. SC 7.6.2 confirms this and SC 7.6.3 leaves untouched the common law claim for damages for breach.

Damages recoverable by a seller   13.2.2

Where non completion is due to the buyer's default the seller is entitled to retain the deposit and accrued interest irrespective of whether or not the seller has suffered any loss. The court does have a discretion under s.49(2), LPA 1925 to order its return but this is most unlikely to be exercised if the deposit is only the customary 10%.

If the seller claims damages the forfeited deposit must be

brought into account. It is therefore only where the seller's loss exceeds the amount of the deposit that the seller will need to claim damages.

- In a falling market the seller's loss of bargain will be the difference between the contract price and the decreased market value, which will be taken to be the price achieved on a resale provided it occurs within a reasonable time.

- Wasted conveyancing costs are not recoverable but the costs of the resale are.

Note

Wasted costs are recoverable if the seller does not claim for loss of bargain but then the deposit cannot be forfeited so such a claim is most unlikely.

- Where the seller has a related purchase, and the buyer knows this, then liability incurred to that seller will also be recoverable.

13.2.3   The date for assessing damages

As a general rule damages for breach of contract are assessed as at the date of breach and then carry interest from that date. In a number of conveyancing cases it has been recognised that this is not always appropriate.

Example

In *Wroth v Tyler* (1974), where specific performance was sought but the court awarded damages in lieu, the plaintiff was awarded the difference between the contract price of £6,000 and the market value at the date of judgment, which was £11,500.

In *Johnson v Agnew* (1980) specific performance was ordered but subsequently became impossible because the mortgagee took possession and sold the property. The buyer therefore asked for damages instead and the date on which the mortgagee contracted to sell was taken as the appropriate date. The House of Lords held that the general rule that damages should be assessed at the date of breach is not an inflexible rule and that the court has power to select such other date as is appropriate to avoid injustice to the innocent party.

13.3   Misrepresentation

A misrepresentation in the negotiations leading to the contract will, if it induces the contract, render it voidable. The fact that the misrepresentation may have become a term of the contract or that the contract may have been performed by completion taking place does not prevent the party misled seeking rescission: s.1, Misrepresentation Act 1967. If the misrepresentation was not fraudulent the court may refuse rescission and award damages in lieu: s.2(2), Misrepresentation Act 1967. A claim for damages may be brought under s.2(1) but will fail if the defendant can prove that they had reasonable grounds to believe and did believe up to the time the contract was made that the facts represented were true.

Section 3 provides that a contractual term which seeks to exclude or restrict liability for, or the remedies for, misrepresentation shall be ineffective unless it is reasonableness. Under s.11(1), Unfair Contract Terms Act 1977 the term must be fair and reasonable having regard to the circumstances which were, or ought reasonably to have been, known to or in the contemplation of the parties when the contract was made. SC 7.1.3 does seek to restrict the circumstances in which rescission can be obtained for negligent or innocent misrepresentation by providing that rescission is only possible where the property differs substantially from what the injured party had been led to expect. Its reasonableness has not been tested but it is probably acceptable.

Note

SC 7.1.3 also applies to misdescription and non-disclosure. These constitute a breach of contract which, if sufficiently serious, will entitle the innocent party to rescind, not in the sense of seeking restoration to the pre-contract position as in the case of misrepresentation, but in the sense of terminating/repudiating the contract for the future. It could be argued that if a misdescription or non-disclosure is fraudulent or reckless then, regardless of its seriousness, SC 7.1.3 makes termination possible, but this is almost certainly not so.

Post completion   13.4

The doctrine of merger   13.4.1

At completion, or possibly at registration in the case of registered titles, the contract merges in the transfer, ie. the contract is terminated to the extent that it is intended to be performed by the transfer. Consequently, an action for breach of contract cannot generally be brought post completion. Terms of the contract which are not performed by the transfer remain outstanding and can still be sued on, eg. a term that vacant possession will be given or a term that the seller will carry out certain repairs to the property. SC 7.4 confirms this.

It is generally believed that damages for late completion can still be claimed and there is also a long-standing rule that an express contractual term providing for damages for misdescription survives: *Palmer v Johnson* (1884). SC 7.1.2 is such an express term.

If, therefore, a material misdescription of the property only comes to light after completion, the buyer can still claim damages for breach of contract, but the same would not apply to a non-disclosure.

The merger rule only affects actions based on the contract and does not prevent actions on other grounds. Rescission for misrepresentation can still be claimed post completion by virtue of s.1, Misrepresentation Act 1967, as can damages under s.2(1). The restriction on rescission contained in SC 7.1.3, assuming it is reasonable, probably also survives, as it would be anomalous for it to operate to restrict a buyer's right to rescind pre-completion but not post-completion.

13.4.2   The covenants for title

A seller may transfer in various capacities: as beneficial owner, as trustee, as mortgagee, as personal representative or by order of the court. Depending on the capacity in which they act, certain covenants for title are implied in the transfer by s.76, LPA 1925.

A *beneficial owner* covenants that:

- They have a *good right to convey*;
- The buyer will have *quiet enjoyment free from incumbrances* other than those to which the sale was made subject; and that
- They will do anything further which is necessary for vesting the property in the buyer. This is known as a *covenant for further assurance*.

A seller transferring in the other capacities only covenants that they have not done, or permitted to be done, anything to incumber the property.

Even the beneficial owner covenants are not an extensive as may at first appear. This is because the 'quiet enjoyment free from incumbrances' covenant is not an absolute promise but is limited to defects and incumbrances arising from the acts or omissions of the seller and persons claiming through or under them, or through whom they derive title otherwise than by a purchase for value.

If, therefore, an incumbrance comes to light after completion, the seller will not be liable if it was created by a previous owner from whom the seller bought the property. The buyer may, however, be able to claim against the previous seller because the benefit of the implied covenant which they gave when selling runs with the land, but they may not be traceable. The implied covenants do not therefore provide a remedy for all post completion problems and there is particular controversy as to whether they apply at all to undisclosed overriding interests. However, action on implied covenants does occasionally succeed.

Example

In *Dunning & Sons Ltd v Sykes & Son Ltd* (1987), on a sale of part of the land comprised in the seller's title, the plan in the transfer included a small area of land which was no longer part of the seller's title as it had been the subject of a previous sale. There was therefore a discrepancy between the transfer plan and the verbal description of the property which referred to the register and consequently to a smaller area. The Court of Appeal held that the transfer plan should prevail as 'where parcels in a conveyancing document are described by reference to a plan attached to the document, the natural inference is that it was the intention that anyone concerned should see from the document alone, which means from the plan on it, what land the document was purporting to pass'. The seller was therefore held to be in breach of the implied covenant for title.

Self-assessment questions

1 What is the effect of either party being unable to complete on the contractually agreed date?

2 What is a notice to complete?

3 Why do sellers rarely need to sue buyers for damages for failure to complete?

4 When the seller is unable to transfer what they contracted to sell can the buyer:

(a) Withdraw from the contract?

(b) Recover their deposit?

(c) Recover their wasted conveyancing costs?

(d) Recover by way of damages an increase in the value of the property?

(e) Recover the cost of buying another property?

(f) Recover any damages they might have to pay to their buyer if they delay completing on their related sale?

(g) Recover accommodation and storage costs if they complete on a related sale and are therefore homeless?

(h) Recover the deposit which they had paid, and have now lost, on a new kitchen which they had ordered for their new home?

Chapter 14

Unregistered freeholds: deducing and investigating title

Deducing title

14.1

Where the title is unregistered there is no register you can consult to see who is the owner of the estate. Instead, ownership must be proved by tracing a chain of title back through the title deeds to a *good root of title*. The open contract rules require that this root be at least 15 years old.

> *Note*
>
> All references in this chapter are to the Law of Property Act 1925 unless otherwise stated.

A good root of title

14.1.1

There is no statutory definition of a good root of title but it is generally accepted that it must be a document which:

- Deals with the *whole estate* which is the subject of the sale;
- Contains an *adequate description* of the property;
- Contains *nothing to cast doubt* on the title.

Deals with the whole estate
This means that if you are dealing with the freehold title a document which deals only with the leasehold title or only with the beneficial interest will not be good enough. However, it does not mean that the root document cannot include other land which is not the subject of the sale.

> *Example*
>
> The seller may have bought the land from someone who did not part with the entirety of their property. To deduce title back for a sufficient period, the seller may have to trace title to a document which comprised more than is currently being sold.

Nor does it mean that there can only be one root involved in a sale.

> *Example*
>
> What is now being sold may in the past have consisted of two pieces of land which then came into common ownership. The seller may therefore have to trace title back along two chains of title.

The description of the property

Ideally, this should be a freestanding description which does not require reference to any other document. However, a root which describes the property by reference to a description in an earlier document will be acceptable if that earlier document is also provided.

Does not cast doubt on the title

The fact that the root refers to certain earlier incumbrances which effect the property does not cast doubt on the title, although details of those earlier incumbrances, eg. covenants, will have to be supplied with the root document.

What would cast doubt on the title would be if the root document said, for example, that the then seller could not prove title but only had title by adverse possession.

Acceptable roots

The most acceptable root of title is a *conveyance on sale*. A voluntary conveyance, ie. a conveyance by way of gift, or an assent by PRs to a beneficiary, may meet the three characteristics specified for a good root but will not be as acceptable as a conveyance on sale because a donee or assentee will not have investigated the title. On a sale, the buyer would have investigated the seller's title back for a further period of at least 15 years.

A mortgage is technically not a good root because it does not deal with the entire estate as the mortgagor retains the freehold title. It may, however, be used where you can be certain that the mortgagee would have investigated the title back for at least a further 15 years. This the mortgagee would have done if they were an institutional mortgagee (such as a bank or building society) and the mortgage was for a large amount relative to the value of the property, but this is probably impossible to ascertain.

14.1.2 The age of the root

The 15-year rule

Under the open contract rule as laid down in s.44 (as amended by s.23, LPA 1969) the root of title must be at least 15 years old but to find a document which satisfies this requirement it may be necessary to go back *much further* than 15 years.

The open contract rule is not normally modified by the terms of the contract. It would be most exceptional to find a buyer insisting on an older root of title.

Shorter roots

Sometimes the seller offers the buyer a shorter, ie. a younger, root. There are *specific risks* for a buyer in accepting a shorter root.

- The buyer will be fixed with *constructive notice of any incumbrances* that would have been discovered had title been investigated for the normal statutory period.

  This means that if an investigation of the title for the minimum 15-year period would have revealed certain third party rights, and if the enforceability of those rights depends on the doctrine of notice, eg. pre-1926 restrictive covenants, then the buyer will be bound by them.

- The buyer will not be entitled to compensation under s.25, LPA 1969 in respect of registered land charges which would have been discoverable had title been investigated for the normal statutory period.

Registered land charges

The weakness of the system of registration of land charges under the Land Charges Acts 1925 and 1972 is that charges are registered against the names of previous estate owners. A buyer therefore needs to know the names of previous estate owners to search against.

An investigation of title will reveal the names of previous estate owners back to the root of title and the buyer will therefore be able to make a land charges search against those names.

If land charges are registered against the names of pre-root estate owners the buyer will still be bound by those charges, but s.25, LPA 1969 provides for compensation to be paid to the buyer in these circumstances. This compensation will *not* be available, however, where the buyer's failure to discover a registered land charge was because the buyer accepted a root less than 15 years old and not because the charge was registered against a name hidden behind the normal minimum 15-year root.

Note

The non-availability of compensation under s.25 is more serious for a buyer than being fixed with constructive notice as there are many more third party rights whose enforceability depends on registration than there are third party rights whose enforceability depends on the old doctrine of notice.

The abstract of title   14.1.3

The chain of title from the root document to the present day is set out chronologically in an abstract of title.

The traditional abstract of title consists of a précis of the contents of the title deeds. Nowadays what is usually provided is a schedule setting out in chronological order the documents and events constituting the chain of title (an *epitome*) together with photocopies of the relevant documents.

Note

The term 'abstract' is often used to encompass both the traditional abstract and the more modern epitome plus copy documents and we will use it to cover both from now on.

At some stage, probably not until completion, the buyer will need to check the abstract against the original deeds to ensure its accuracy and to ensure that their investigation of title has therefore been based on accurate information.

14.1.4   Documents to be abstracted

The abstract will commence with the *root of title*.

This will be followed by any *pre-root documents*, or extracts from them, which need to be included.

Example

If the root describes the property by reference to a description and/or plan in an *earlier document*, that earlier description and/or plan must be abstracted. If the root refers to earlier covenants or easements, or if at the time of the root transaction there was a prior undischarged mortgage, the details of these *outstanding incumbrances* must be included. If the root document was executed pursuant to a previously granted power of attorney then the *power of attorney* must also be abstracted.

There will then follow in chronological order the documents which form the *links in the chain of title* from the root to the present day, eg. conveyances, grants of representation, assents and mortgages (including the present seller's mortgage(s), which will be discharged on completion).

Note

A legal mortgage is an essential link in the chain of title and even discharged mortgages must be abstracted. Thus, the abstract will show that at a certain date a mortgage was granted and then show that at a later date it was discharged.

Leases which have expired by passage of time do not need to be included but leases which have come to an end in other ways, eg. by surrender or forfeiture, must be abstracted.

Death (and *marriage*) *certificates* are documents of record and copies of them could be obtained by the buyer if they are given the relevant dates, but in practice sellers usually provide copies of any necessary certificates.

Central Land Charge Certificates obtained on the occasion of previous transactions relating to the property are generally kept with the title deeds. Although they are not title documents, and therefore do not have to be included in the abstract, sellers, as a matter of courtesy, will generally include any such certificates that they have. This may mean that pre-completion the buyer will not need to do their own search against those names in respect of which the seller has supplied search certificates (*see* Chapter 16, para. 16.4.1).

Investigation of title 14.2

The buyer will investigate the seller's title by:

- Examining the abstract of title;
- Carrying out certain pre-completion searches (*see* Chapter 16, para. 16.4);
- Verifying the title by checking the abstract against the original deeds.

Examining the abstract 14.2.1

The buyer must investigate the *chain of title* by checking that all the documents in the chain:

- Are *properly executed*;
- Are *properly stamped* (if they require stamping); and
- Form an *unbroken chain of title*, ie. the buyer must check for any missing or weak links in the chain. If any are found corrective action will be necessary. This can be a complex business, especially if previous conveyancing transactions have not been carried out as carefully as they might have been.

Stamping 14.2.2

It is the *seller's responsibility* to ensure that all title documents which required stamping at the time of their execution are properly stamped and the seller cannot contract out of this obligation.

An unstamped or incorrectly-stamped document is *not admissible* in evidence. It will *not* constitute a good root or link in a chain of title and will *not be accepted* by the Land Registry on any application for registration.

Late stamping may involve the seller in payment of a penalty to the Inland Revenue.

Note

In the past many conveyancing documents attracted stamp duty but over the years stamping requirements have been progressively abolished. It is beyond the scope of this companion to give details of these old stamp duties but remember that if you encounter a mortgage, or mortgage discharge, dated prior to 1 August 1971 it may have been subject to stamp duty.

An assent, a deed of appointment of a new trustee or a power of attorney pre-26 March 1985 should have been stamped with a fixed rate duty of 50p and a voluntary transfer, ie. deed of gift, prior to that date would have attracted *ad valorem* stamp duty payable on the value of the gift.

14.2.3   Requisitions on title

The buyer is entitled to raise queries on the title (*requisitions*) to ensure that they have full details of the title and of any incumbrances affecting it. If any defects in the title are discovered the seller will be required to rectify them. If they cannot be rectified and consequently the seller cannot prove a good title to the property, the buyer will be entitled not to proceed.

Barring requisitions

Section 45 provides that the buyer is not entitled to raise requisitions on pre-root root matters. There are however important *exceptions* to this rule and the buyer is entitled to require the seller to produce:

- Any *power of attorney* under which an abstracted document is executed;
- Any document creating or disposing of an *incumbrance* which still affected the property at the time of the root;
- Any *plan* referred to in the root document.

Requisitions may also be barred by *special conditions* in the contract. Where any aspect of the title has been shown to the buyer before contracts are exchanged, it is usual for the contract to provide that after exchange the buyer will not raise any requisitions on that matter, eg. if details of restrictive covenants binding the property have been fully disclosed in the draft contract. Where the *Protocol* is being followed and the entire title is deduced pre-exchange, a special condition should bar all requisitions post-exchange.

14.3   Sale by a sole seller

Where the title is owned by just one person the conveyance

by them alone will give the buyer legal title. However, if there is anyone else with a beneficial interest in the property the buyer will be bound by that interest if the buyer has notice of it and the buyer will be fixed with constructive notice of the beneficiary's right if the beneficiary is in occupation and their right could reasonably have been discovered from inspection of the property (the rule in *Hunt v Luck* (1902) and s.199).

Where such a beneficial interest exists the buyer must insist on the seller appointing a second trustee so that the buyer can pay the purchase money to at least two trustees and so overreach the beneficiary's interest.

Sale by a surviving co-owner   14.4

Where the title was owned by two or more persons but the others have died and there is now only one surviving co-owner, they will by virtue of the *right of survivorship* have sole legal title.

Whether or not the you should insist on the survivor appointing a second trustee depends on how the beneficial title was held. You must first look at the conveyance to the co-owners. This may specify how they held the beneficial title. If it says that they held for themselves as beneficial *joint tenants*, then provided that the joint tenancy was not severed before the first one died, the survivor will also have sole beneficial title and it will not be necessary to insist on the appointment of a second trustee.

The problem is how can you be sure that the beneficial joint tenancy has not been severed? The Law of Property (Joint Tenants) Act 1964 is specifically designed to protect a purchaser in this situation. It provides that a purchaser is entitled to assume that the joint tenancy has not, at the time of death, been severed if:

- There was *no memorandum of severance* endorsed on the conveyance to the joint tenants;
- There was no *bankruptcy entry* recorded at the Land Charges Registry against the names of either of the joint tenants;
- The surviving co-owner *conveys as beneficial owner* (alternatively the conveyance can contain a statement that the survivor was solely and beneficially entitled. This alternative will not generally be used when the survivor is the seller but will be used if the survivor's PRs are selling (*see* Chapter 18).

The buyer from a sole surviving co-owner must therefore:

- Check the *conveyance* to the co-owners to ensure that they held initially as beneficial joint tenants;
- Check that there is no *memorandum of severance* endorsed on that conveyance;
- Undertake a *bankruptcy search* against the names of the joint tenants; and
- Ensure that the survivor conveys as *beneficial owner*.

The buyer should insist on the appointment of a second trustee if:

- The requirements of the 1964 Act are not satisfied;
- The conveyance to the co-owners states that they held as beneficial tenants in common or does not state how they held beneficially;
- If there is any reason to suppose that they were holding not on trust for themselves but on trust for some other third party.

14.5   Sale by a mortgagee

There is no fundamental difference between a mortgagee's sale of a registered title and of an unregistered title. The existence of the power of sale, when it arises, when it becomes exercisable and the effect of its exercise are all exactly the same.

14.5.1   Second mortgages

Where there is more than one mortgage on the property the second mortgagee will probably (invariably in the case of an institutional mortgagee) have notified the first mortgagee of their existence. Nevertheless, a first mortgagee selling should always search the Land Charges Register to see if there is a second mortgagee to whom any surplus in the proceeds of sale should be handed. If they fail to do so and consequently hand the surplus back to the mortgagor, they would be liable to the second mortgagee to the extent of the latter's interest.

14.5.2   Equitable mortgages

An equitable mortgage of an unregistered title can be created by the deposit of title deeds with the creditor plus, as required by s.2, Law of Property (Miscellaneous Provisions) Act 1989, a written contract signed by both parties.

If this written memorandum of the arrangement (usually referred to as a *memorandum of deposit*) goes beyond the requirements of s.2 and is by deed, the equitable mortgagee will have a statutory power of sale but will not be able to convey the mortgagor's legal title to a buyer unless the mortgage deed contains either:

- A *trust clause* whereby the mortgagor acknowledges that they hold the legal title on trust for the mortgagee and will convey it in accordance with the direction of the mortgagee when required to do so; or

- An *irrevocable power of attorney clause* (*see* Chapter 18, para. 18.2.7) which would enable the mortgagee to convey the mortgagor's legal title as their agent.

Third party rights   14.6

Appropriate action must be taken when certain third party right are encountered.

Mortgages   14.6.1

Discharge

These can be discharged by the seller paying them off. A separate deed of discharge could then be executed but this is not normally done as s.115 provides that a receipt endorsed on the mortgage deed is equally effective. Such a receipt is known as a *statutory receipt*.

> *Note*
>
> Where the mortgagee is a building society, there is an alternative form of receipt which does not specify the name of the payer.

As with registered titles the discharge of the seller's mortgage may not actually take place prior to completion. The seller's solicitor may give an undertaking to forward the money to the mortgagee to discharge the mortgage and then to forward, when received from the mortgagee, the discharged mortgage deed.

> *Note*
>
> Where the mortgage is discharged pursuant to such an undertaking, it is important that the receipt on the mortgage deed should be dated on or before the date of the conveyance to the buyer so that events appear to have taken place in the correct sequence, ie. the seller's mortgage was discharged before the conveyance by the seller to the buyer.

Second mortgages

If there is a second mortgage on the property which has been protected by the entry of a C(i) land charge, the buyer will take free from it but should require the seller to secure its removal from the register and to hand over to the buyer at completion an application for its removal signed by the second mortgagee. This is to ensure that the Land Charges Register is not cluttered with obsolete entries.

14.6.2 Beneficial interests

The position for unregistered title is the same as that described in Chapter 9, para. 9.6.2 for registered titles.

14.6.3 MHA rights

A spouse's right of occupation under the Matrimonial Homes Act 1967 is registrable as a Class F land charge. If so protected the buyer will take subject to it. The only way that it can be removed is by the spouse who entered it applying to the Land Charges Registry for its removal.

The position is therefore very similar to that described in Chapter 9, para. 9.6.3 and the buyer must not complete unless the Class F charge has already been removed or the buyer receives an application for its removal signed by the spouse.

14.6.4 Covenants and easements

The position is the same as that described in Chapter 9, para. 9.6.4.

14.6.5 Estate contracts

These are registrable as Class C(iv) land charges and the position is the same as in Chapter 9, 9.6.4.

14.6.6 Local land charges

The position is exactly the same as in Chapter 9, para. 9.6.6.

Self-assessment questions

1. What is the difference between a root of title and an abstract of title?
2. Why is a conveyance on sale the best root of title?
3. A buyer from a surviving co-owner will need to examine the conveyance to the seller and the deceased. What two things will the buyer particularly look for?
4. Which of the following is it necessary to include in an abstract of title?

    (a) Pre-root documents.

    (b) Discharged mortgages.

    (c) Expired leases.

    (d) Old land charge certificates.

    (e) Death certificates.

    (f) The seller's mortgage which will be redeemed at completion and will not therefore bind the buyer.

Chapter 15

Unregistered freehold title: 1

Taking instructions

The main difference from taking instructions to sell a registered title (*see* Chapter 3) is that you ask the seller for the *title deeds* instead of for the land certificate. If the property is *mortgaged* the mortgagee will have possession of the title deeds. As there is only one set of title deeds they will be with the first mortgagee and any later mortgagee should have registered their mortgage as a C(i) Land Charge (*puisne* mortgage).

You will write to the mortgagee requesting the title deeds, giving the usual undertaking for their safe-keeping and return.

Drafting the contract

Before drafting the contract you must investigate the seller's title to:

- Ensure that the seller can *prove title*; and to
- Discover if there are any *incumbrances* which will bind a buyer and which therefore need to be disclosed in the draft contract.

The main *differences* between a contract for the sale of a registered freehold (*see* Chapter 7) and an unregistered freehold will be the:

- *Description* of the property (the particulars of sale);
- Need to specify a *root of title*;
- *Incumbrances* subject to which the property is sold.

The particulars of sale

This is the description of the property being sold. It may be a freestanding description which does not refer to any other document, for example:

The property known as 22 Station Road, Melbury, Northshire having a frontage to Station Road of 12 metres and a depth from Station Road of 30 metres on the western boundary and 32 metres on the eastern boundary.

Alternatively it may describe the property by reference to the subject matter of an earlier conveyance, for example:

The property known as 22 Station Road, Melbury, Northshire being the property comprised in a conveyance dated 2 May 1970 between

Jessica Evans (1) and Jeremy Hobbs and Elizabeth Hobbs (2).

The deed referred to in this second method will often be the holding deed, ie. the deed under which the seller obtained title. However, if that deed does not itself contain a free-standing description of the property but refers back to a description in an earlier deed, the earlier deed will have to be referred to.

Whenever the property is described by reference to a description in another document, that other document, or at least an extract from it containing the description of what was conveyed, must be supplied with the draft contract.

Note

Reference back to a description in the holding deed, or an earlier deed, should ensure that the seller does not contract to sell more than they actually own, but you should always check whether they have previously sold off some of what was conveyed to them, or whether they have subsequently acquired extra land which they now intend to sell.

A *plan* is not essential where the seller is selling the whole of the land. If a plan is used it should be carefully drawn to scale and of sufficient size to be of use. (Poorly drawn plans are a major problem in the conveyancing of unregistered titles.)

If there is a conflict between the verbal description of the property and the plan (in a contract or in a conveyance) the question of which should prevail will arise. If the property is stated to be 'more particularly delineated on the plan' then the plan prevails. If the plan is said to be 'for the purpose of identification only', then the verbal description will prevail. This does not mean that the plan can be ignored as it may supplement the verbal description. It is only if there is a conflict between the two that the words will prevail.

15.2.2   The root of title

The open contract rule requires the root of title to be at least *15 years old* and the contract does not generally vary this. If the seller does offer a shorter title, ie. a root of title which is less than 15 years old, there will be risks for the buyer if they accept it. (*See* Chapter 14.)

The contract must specify what instrument is being offered as the root of title and state the date and the names of the parties thereto. Generally the root offered will be a conveyance on sale. A copy of this document does not have to be provided with the contract unless:

- The *protocol* is being followed and title is being deduced pre-exchange; or

- It also contains *details of incumbrances* subject to which the property is sold (*see* below).

Incumbrances

Incumbrances subject to which the property is sold should be specified in special conditions, for example:

The property is sold subject to the covenants contained in a conveyance dated 24 September 1960 between Algernon Brian Baron and Christopher Edward Lloyd (1) and Jessica Evans (2).

A copy of these covenants must then be supplied with the draft contract. The special condition will normally go on to provide that the buyer will raise no requisitions on them, which means that all enquiries on the covenants must be raised by the buyer before contracts are exchanged.

Pre-contract searches and enquiries

Most of the pre-contract searches and enquiries will be exactly the same as for a registered title (*see* Chapter 8). Whether the buyer's solicitor does them or they are provided as part of the pre-contract package by the seller, will depend on whether or not the protocol is being followed. Remember that it is always the *buyer's solicitor* who needs to ensure that all necessary searches and enquiries are made and that the results and replies are satisfactory before the buyer exchanges contracts.

Thus the buyer's solicitor must make:

- Pre-contract enquiries of the seller;
- A local land charges search;
- Enquiries of the local authority;
- Special searches and enquiries as appropriate.

They must also ensure that there is a survey of the property to reveal its physical state.

Inspection of the property

The property must be inspected to:

- Check on what fixtures there are;
- Reveal any patent incumbrances which the seller is not obliged to disclose, eg. rights of way;
- Check on who is in occupation in case they have rights in respect of the property.

Rights of persons in occupation

In the case of both registered and unregistered titles an inspection to discover whether there are occupiers needs to be made but the rights of any such occupiers are protected differently under the two systems.

(a) *Registered titles.* If those in occupation (or in receipt of the rents or profits) at the time of the transfer have rights, those rights (with a few exceptions) will be protected as overriding interests under s.70(1)(g), LRA 1925.

(b) *Unregistered titles.* The inspection is to discover if there is anyone with rights, the enforceability of which depends on the *doctrine of notice.* The purchaser will be fixed with *constructive* notice of such rights if they would have come to the purchaser's knowledge if such enquiries and inspections had been made as ought reasonably to have been made: the Rule in *Hunt v Luck* (1902) and s.199, LPA 1925. If the rights of the occupier were capable of registration under the Land Charges Act but they have not been registered, they will be void against the buyer and notice is irrelevant: *Midland Bank Trust Co v Greene* (1981).

Under *s.70(1)(g)* the key to the protection afforded is *occupation.* Under the rule in *Hunt v Luck* the key to the protection is that the right is *reasonably discoverable from inspection.*

The differences between the forms of protection

Section 70(1)(g) Registered titles	The Rule in Hunt and Luck Unregistered titles
The occupier must be in occupation at completion.	Not applicable.
Occupation includes the receipt of rents and profits.	Not applicable.
Whatever rights in the land the occupier has will be protected, except MHA rights and rights of beneficiaries under a strict settlement.	Only rights whose enforceablity depends on the doctrine of notice are protected, eg. rights beneficiaries and rights acquired by virtue of the doctrine of promissory estoppel.
Neither the occupation nor the occupier's right need be reasonably discoverable.	The buyer is only fixed with notice of rights that are reasonably discoverable from inspection of the property.

15.3.2   Index map search

This is an extra search which must be made whenever the title is unregistered. It is made at the appropriate District Land Registry but it is not a search of the Register but of a separate index which the Land Registry keeps based on the ordnance survey maps. The search is made on Form 96 and the result will show whether any:

- *Title is registered* in a particular piece of land and if so the title number;

● *Caution* against first registration has been lodged.

Note

A caution against first registration must not be confused with a caution against dealing which is lodged where title is already registered in order to protect a minor interest which cannot be protected in any other way.

A caution against first registration is lodged where title is still unregistered. It entitles the cautioner to be notified whenever there is an application for first registration of title in that particular piece of land. The cautioner can then assert their claim to the land. They may be able to prevent its registration or limit the area of land included in the title or have the title registered subject to their right in the property.

Note

The index map search is the means by which any member of the public can discover the title number of a particular title and then apply for office copies of that title.

Land charges search: unregistered titles   15.3.3

The land charges search in the Central Register of Land Charges is primarily a pre-completion search (*see* Chapter 16).

At the pre-contract stage the buyer may not know the names of all previous estate owners to search against, and even if a full search were possible it would be necessary to repeat it pre-completion in order to obtain the benefit of the priority period. However, at the pre-exchange stage a search might be made against the seller's name. This should certainly be done in the case of a sole seller if there is any possibility of a spouse having registered a *class F charge,* or if there is reason to suspect that the seller may have created other charges, eg. other contracts regarding the land.

Deducing and investigating title   15.4

If the Protocol is being followed the abstract of title will be supplied and requisitions raised on it *before* exchange of contracts (*see* Chapter 14). Where the protocol is not adopted the abstract will be supplied and requisitions raised *after* exchange. This is the traditional procedure envisaged by SC 4.1.

The whole process of deducing and investigating title is more complex when the title is unregistered than when it is registered (*see* Chapters 9 and 14) and there is a greater likelihood of requisitions being raised. If it is not done until after exchange and problems are then discovered, it may take time to sort them out and completion may be delayed as a result. The problem might even entitle the buyer to withdraw from the contract. It therefore makes practical sense for title to be deduced pre-exchange – but this is not always done. The seller's solicitor may not be prepared to send the buyer a large bundle of copy documents and deal with all the requisitions until they are certain that the buyer is committed to proceeding with the purchase. Deducing title pre-exchange is, however, increasingly common, even where the Protocol is not being followed.

Note

As buyer's solicitor you should bear in mind that post-completion you will have to apply for first registration of title and that in order to obtain absolute title you will need to prove title to the satisfaction of the Land Registry. You must therefore be absolutely certain that all possible problems regarding the title are resolved.

15.5   Exchange of contracts

There is no difference between registered and unregistered titles (*see* Chapter 10).

Self-assessment questions

1   Are there any advantages/disadvantages in the contract describing the property to be sold by reference to the subject matter of an earlier conveyance?

2   Why should the contract never say that the property is 'for the purpose of identification only more particularly delineated on the attached plan'?

3   When will a buyer of an unregistered title be bound by the rights of those in occupation?

4   What is the difference between a caution against first registration and a caution against dealing and where is each one found?

Chapter 16

Unregistered freehold title: 2

The effect of a binding contract 16.1

The only difference here between registered and unregistered conveyancing is the mechanism for protecting the buyer's estate contract. It is registrable as a Class C(iv) land charge against the name of the seller in the Central Land Charges Register.

Requisitions on title 16.2

The position is the same as that described in Chapter 11, 11.2.

Preparing the documentation 16.3

Here there is a major difference between registered and unregistered conveyancing. Unregistered titles are conveyed by a *deed of conveyance*.

There is no prescribed form to be completed but there is an established structure for a deed of conveyance which must be followed.

Deed of conveyance 16.3.1

Commencement and date
This identifies the document as a deed of conveyance. The date will be left blank and only inserted when completion actually occurs.

The parties
The names and addresses of all parties to the deed are set out.

Normally there are just two parties, seller and buyer, but occasionally another party is also joined in the conveyance, eg. on a sale of part (*see* Chapter 19) which is mortgaged the seller's mortgagee will join in to release the part being sold from the mortgage.

In the case of a sub-sale where the seller is conveying direct to the sub-buyer the intermediate buyer/seller may join in to give a receipt for part of the purchase money.

Recitals
These are not essential but can be useful in explaining the background to the conveyance, ie. they can explain how the seller came to own the property and the reason for the

conveyance. Often they say no more than that the seller is seised of the estate in fee simple and has contracted to sell it. Such a recital is really superfluous.

Where a recital might be useful is in the case of a sale by a surviving beneficial joint tenant. A recital can then state that the property was conveyed to the joint tenants, record the death of one of them and state that the title is now solely and beneficially held by the survivor. Recitals are also valuable in sales by PRs (*see* Chapter 18, para. 18.1.3).

The testatum

In a traditional deed of conveyance this is the part which says 'now this deed witnesses as follows'. In more modern forms of conveyance, it is often omitted.

The consideration and receipt clause

This serves exactly the same purposes as the consideration and receipt clause in a land registry transfer (*see* Chapter 11, para. 11.3.1).

There must be a statement of the capacity in which the seller conveys the property and the operative words 'hereby conveys'.

The parcels clause

This is the physical description of the property being conveyed. It may be a freestanding description of the property or it may refer back to what was conveyed in an earlier deed of conveyance.

The description must be complete and accurate. It must accord with the terms of the contract and with what the seller is able to convey.

If there are any rights attached to the land, eg. if it has the benefit of a right of way over neighbouring property, the parcels clause will generally state that the property is sold together with the benefit of rights attached to the property (appurtenant rights). However even if it is not expressly mentioned, the buyer will still obtain the benefit of all rights that go with the land by virtue of s.62, LPA 1925.

If new rights are being created in the buyer's favour, these will need to be expressly stated, eg. new easements being granted to the buyer. This will not arise in the case of a sale of the entirety of the seller's land but only in the case of a sale of part (*see* Chapter 19).

Exceptions and reservations

Exceptions are things that already exist but which are not intended to pass to the buyer, eg. mines and minerals may be excepted from the conveyance.

Reservations are new rights created for the benefit of the seller out of the land conveyed, eg. new easements.

On a sale of the entirety of the seller's land the reservation of new easements will not occur but on a sale of part reservations will be usual (*see* Chapter 19, para. 19.1.4) and they will appear immediately after the parcels clause.

The habendum

This describes the estate conveyed and then specifies existing incumbrances, eg. it may say that the property is hereby conveyed subject to covenants 'contained or referred to' in a specified earlier deed of conveyance. This would mean that the present conveyance is stated to be subject not only to the covenants imposed by the earlier deed but also to even earlier ones referred to in that deed.

Co-ownership declaration of trust for sale

In the case of co-owners a trust for sale is implied by statute. However, where there is more than one buyer the conveyance may expressly state that the buyers will be holding on trust for sale and it may then specify their beneficial entitlement. For example, it may say that they are holding on trust for sale for themselves as beneficial joint tenants, or they are holding on trust for sale for themselves as tenants in common in equal shares, or as tenants in common in some other given shares.

This clause frequently goes on to provide that the trustees shall have all the powers of beneficial owners. This is inserted because trustees for sale have limited powers when it comes to mortgaging and granting leases over the property. If the trustees are themselves the beneficiaries this will not be a problem as they can, as beneficial owners, give themselves as trustees full powers to deal with the land but if they are holding for other beneficiaries their powers as trustees will be limited.

Declarations

On a sale of part there will usually be a declaration limiting or excluding the implied grant rules (*see* Chapter 19).

There may also be a declaration as to who owns which boundaries.

Express covenants

Where the land is being sold subject to existing covenants the contract will normally have provided for the buyer to given an indemnity to the seller if the seller will remain liable on the covenants after completion. The seller will remain liable on the covenants if they are either the original covenantor or if they have themselves given an indemnity to their predecessor in respect of the covenants.

Standard Condition 4.5.3 provides that the buyer will not only covenant to indemnify the seller against liability for future breaches but will also covenant to perform the covenants. As a result the seller will be able to take direct action against the buyer to prevent a breach of covenant and not merely claim an indemnity if they themselves are held liable for the breach.

On a sale of part there will usually be new covenants entered into pursuant to the terms of the contract for sale (*see* Chapter 19, para. 19.1.1).

Acknowledgement and undertaking

This applies on a sale of part where title deeds are retained by the seller (*see* Chapter 19, para. 19.3.4).

Certificate of value

This is included if appropriate (*see* Chapter 5, 15.2)

Schedules

These are particularly likely to be found on a sale of part where new easements are being granted and reserved and new covenants imposed. Rather than setting out the detail of the new covenants and easements in the body of the conveyance, it is often neater to set them out in schedules.

If one deed of conveyance is being used to convey several parcels of land it may also be convenient to set out the description of the different parcels in separate schedules.

Execution and attestation

The conveyance must be *signed as a deed* by all parties and their signatures witnessed: s.1, Law of Property (Miscellaneous Provisions) Act 1989.

Note

Unlike Land Registry transfers which must be executed by all parties, deeds of conveyance need only be executed by buyers if the buyers are doing something in the deed, ie. if they are entering into covenants, whether original covenants or merely an indemnity covenant, or if they are making a declaration of trust.

16.3.2   Transfer under rule 72

Where the conveyance will lead to an application for first registration of title, then instead of using a deed of conveyance you can use a document similar to a Land Registry transfer which follows the same structure. If the sale is a sale of the entirety of the seller's land and the property can be easily and succinctly described and there are not many incumbrances to be set out in the conveyance, then the Land Registry transfer format may be useful. However, for more complex conveyances the normal deed of conveyance for an unregistered title is preferable.

The mortgage deed   16.3.3

The same mortgage documents can be used for registered and unregistered titles as the operative words 'charge by way of legal mortgage' are applicable to both types of title.

Undertaking for discharge of the seller's mortgage   16.3.4

The seller's mortgage will normally be discharged by means of a receipt endorsed on the mortgage deed. A separate deed of discharge, although possible, is in practice virtually never encountered.

If completion is to be on the basis of a solicitor's undertaking the procedure will be virtually the same as that described in Chapter 11, para. 11.3.3 save that the undertaking will refer to the seller's solicitor forwarding the receipted mortgage deed rather than Form 53.

Even though the mortgage may not actually be discharged until after completion, it is important that the receipt should be dated no later than the date of completion.

Statements of account   16.3.5

These will be prepared in exactly the same way as is described in Chapter 11, para. 11.3.4.

Pre-completion searches   16.4

Here there are major differences between registered and unregistered conveyancing.

Central Land Charges search   16.4.1

The main pre-completion search where the title is unregistered is a land charges search at the Central Land Charges Registry.

Registrable incumbrances are registered against the name of the estate owner who created the incumbrance, so the buyer will need to search against the name of the seller and that of all previous known estate owners. Your examination of the abstract of title will have identified the names of previous estate owners back to the root document and there may even be references in the root or other abstracted documents to certain pre-root names. All known names should be searched against as any charges registered will bind the buyer.

There may however be certain pre-root estate owners' names that are not mentioned in the abstract of title and consequently the buyer's solicitor will not be able to search against those names. In this eventuality s.25, LPA 1969 provides for the buyer to be compensated out of state funds if they have investigated title for the normal statutory period but are nevertheless bound by a pre-root registration that they were unable to discover (*see* Chapter 14, para. 14.1.2).

The Central Land Charges search is not generally made in person but by means of an application for an official search.

The advantages of an official search are:

- The result is conclusive in favour of the buyer, ie. if the search certificate states that there is no entry against a particular name and this is incorrect, the buyer will take free from the registered land charge and it will be the chargee who will have to seek compensation from the state indemnity fund.

  In this respect the Central Land Charges search differs from both the Local Land Charges search and the District Land Registry search, which are not conclusive in the searcher's favour and the buyer will be bound even by entries that the search certificate fails to reveal although in such circumstances the buyer will be entitled to compensation from state funds. In other words, the enforceability of the entries and the entitlement to compensation are reversed.

- An official search carries with it the benefit of a 15 working day priority period. This means that provided the buyer completes within the priority period of the search they will not be bound by any new entries on the register subsequent to the date of the search.

- The official search certificate protects the buyer's solicitor who will not be liable for any loss arising from error in the certificate.

Making the search

Care must be exercised to ensure that the search is made against the correct version of all names. The definitive version of anyone's name is taken to be the version as it appears in the title deeds. A search in the incorrect version of a person's name will not be conclusive in the buyer's favour. It is similarly important when registering a charge at the Land Charges Department to ensure that the charge is registered against the correct version of the estate owner's name, otherwise the registration will give no protection to the chargee against someone who does search in the correct version of the name.

Note

Registration in an incorrect version of a name will still protect the chargee against someone who doesn't search at all or who searches in the incorrect version of the estate owner's name: *see Oak Co-operative Building Society v Blackburn* (1968).

In order to narrow down the search, the form enables you to specify the years of ownership of the names specified and the county in which the land is situated. For example, if you are buying land in Devon which was owned by someone called John Smith between 1960 and 1966 you will, by narrowing down the search, ensure that you do not get a reply which shows every entry against any John Smith who has owned land anywhere in the county since 1925.

The search is actually a search in the index to the various registers that are kept under the Land Charges Act 1972 (previously 1925). The certificate will simply indicate that, say, a C(i) or a D(ii) was registered on a certain date but will not give details of the entry. Further details of any entry revealed by the search can be obtained by applying to the Land Charges Department for an office copy of the entry.

The entries revealed by the search should not surprise the buyer. They should all have been disclosed by the seller or known to the buyer at the time of contracting. Any charges registered will bind the buyer and if the buyer did not contract to buy subject to them then the seller is in breach of contract. It will depend on the seriousness of the breach as to whether the buyer is entitled only to damages or is also entitled to refuse to complete.

Sometimes the search will reveal old obsolete entries, eg. C(i) entries in respect of mortgages that have already been discharged or C(iv) entries in respect of contracts that have already been performed. In such cases the buyer should require the seller to try to secure the removal of these obsolete entries.

Relying on previous land charges searches
A buyer will always have to search against the seller's name but may not need to search against the names of all previous estate owners. With the title deeds there may be old search certificates which were obtained by prospective purchasers – buyers, mortgagees, lessees – prior to their acquisition of the

property. Provided that the transaction in contemplation of which the previous search was made was completed within the priority period of the search, the then purchaser would have taken free from any subsequent entry and likewise subsequent purchasers will take free from that entry.

Example

- Property conveyed to A.
- A contracts to sell to B.
- B does land charges search against A which reveals no subsisting entries.
- A's spouse later registers a Class F land charge.
- Completion of the A to B sale takes place within 15 working days of B's search.
- B is therefore not bound by the spouse's Class F charge.
- Years later, B contracts to sell to you and supplies you with the search certificate for B's search against A.
- You do not need to do a fresh search against A. You are buying from someone who is not bound by the entry and so you will not be bound by it either.

The same principles will apply to search certificates obtained prior to transactions further back in the title. To rely on an old search certificate you must be certain that:

- The search was correctly made, ie. against the correct version of the estate owner's names for the correct period of ownership and specifying the correct county; and
- The transaction in contemplation of which the search was made was completed within the priority period of the search.

If these points are not satisfied then you must do a fresh land charges search against the previous estate owner's name and this is very cheap and quick to do.

16.4.2   Inspection of the property

As with registered titles, you should ensure that shortly before completion an inspection is made of the property to see if there is any third party in occupation. (The rules for determining whether any such third party's interest will bind the buyer are considered in Chapter 15.)

16.4.3   Search of the Local Land Charges Register?

The position is the same as that described in Chapter 11, para. 11.4.3.

Company search   16.4.4

Any charges created by a company over its assets must be registered at Companies House otherwise the charge will be void against, *inter alia*, a liquidator of the company: s.399(1), Companies Act 1985. Thus, any fixed or floating charge created by a company over land which it owns requires registration at Companies House.

Prior to 1970, if a company created a fixed charge over land and the charge was registered at Companies House it was unnecessary for it to be registered under the Land Charges Act as well.

Note
_____

Floating charges are *not* registrable under the Land Charges Act.
_____

In the case of an unregistered title it is therefore necessary for the buyer to make a search at Companies House to discover:

- Any pre-1970 fixed charge that might not have been registered under the Land Charges Act;
- Any floating charge whenever created.

The search will also reveal the objects of the company, whether the company has been removed from the register and whether any resolution for winding up the company has been passed.

A company search *must* be made whenever the present seller is a company and whenever a company owned the land prior to 1970.

Whether it is necessary to make a search against a company that owned the land between 1970 and the present seller is a moot point. Any *fixed charge* created by such an owner would have required registration under the Land Charges Act if the mortgagee did not obtain the title deeds and any *floating charge* will no longer affect the land after it has been disposed of by the company as the whole essence of a floating charge is that the charge is only over the property of the company *for the time being* and it leaves the company free to deal with the property prior to the charge crystallising. Nevertheless many people take the view that a company search should be done against *any* company that previously owned the property.

Where the present seller is a company and the essential company search reveals a floating charge which covers the land in question, the buyer must be certain that the floating charge has not crystallised. To do this the buyer's solicitor needs to obtain a *certificate of non-crystallisation*. This should be obtained from the chargee. Often the buyer's solicitor is offered a certificate or letter of non-crystallisation issued by the company itself. This is *not* sufficient. The certificate/letter should come from the company's chargee.

> *Note*
>
> There is no official search mechanism for making a company search. It has to be done by somebody physically going to Companies House in either London or Cardiff. There are firms that specialise in providing this service and the buyer's solicitor will normally instruct such a firm to make the search. The search should be done as close as possible to completion as it does not carry the benefit of any priority period.

16.4.5   Mortgagee's searches

The solicitor acting for the buyer's mortgagee must ensure that the various searches already discussed are made. Unlike the Land Registry search application form which has to specify on whose behalf this search is made, and where it is important to make the search on behalf of the mortgagee and not the buyer, the application for a land charges search does not specify for whom the search is made. Thus, both the buyer and the buyer's mortgagee can rely on it and obtain the benefit of the priority period.

The mortgagee's solicitor must also search at the Land Charges Registry against the names of the prospective mortgagors, ie. the buyers. Whether this should be a full land charges search or a 'bankruptcy-only' search, as in the case of registered titles, is another moot point. The traditional view is that it should be a full land charges search in the indexes to all five registers that are maintained under the Land Charges Act. In practice solicitors generally only do a 'bankruptcy-only' search and with compulsory registration, and the consequent need to register the title post-completion, this is sufficient.

Self-assessment questions

1   On a sale of whole what are the three main differences between a deed of conveyance and a land registry transfer?

2   Will a buyer be bound by land charges which are registered:

(a) against the names of pre-root owners;

(b) after the buyer has made their search?

3   Why does the land charges search only give a 15-working day priority period whereas the land registry search gives a priority period of 30-working days?

4   When copies of old land charge search certificates are
    provided as part of the abstract of title, can the buyer's
    solicitor rely on them or will they need to make fresh
    searches against the same names?

Chapter 17

Unregistered freehold title : 3

Completion 17.1

There is no fundamental difference between the completion of the sale of an unregistered freehold title and of a registered freehold title. In both cases the buyer's obligation is to pay the balance of the purchase price and the seller's obligation is to hand over the executed transfer document and other relevant documentation.

Payment will be made in the same way whether title is registered or unregistered.

Verifying the title 17.1.1

The buyer's solicitor will so far have based their investigation of the seller's title on the abstract supplied by the seller's solicitor. Before paying over the price the title must be verified, ie. the abstract must be checked against the original title deeds held by the seller's solicitor to ensure that the abstract is accurate.

Note

This process does not apply to registered titles as the buyer receives office copies of the entries on the register and then updates that information by the means of a Land Registry search, and the information in those documents is authoritative as to the state of the title.

Where the abstract takes the usual form of an epitome and copy documents the process of verification is somewhat easier than where a précis form of abstract has been supplied. In the latter case the originals will have to be very closely read to ensure that nothing important was omitted from the précis.

Where there is a long and complex title to be verified it is questionable whether the use of the Law Society's code for completion by post is appropriate. If it is used the seller's solicitor must be given very precise instructions as to exactly what documents are to be verified.

Note

The checking of the abstract against the originals before paying over the price is necessary even where the original title deeds are going to be handed over by the seller's solicitor.

17.1.2   Documents to be handed over

The documentation to be handed over on a sale of an unregistered freehold will be different from that required where the title is registered, as the table below shows.

Registered	Unregistered
1 Land Registry transfer.	Deed of conveyance (or Rule 72 transfer).
2 Land/charge certificate. (There will be as many charge certificates as there are outstanding mortgages.)	All the title deeds including pre-root deeds and the seller's mortgage deed(s).
3 If the seller is not identical with the registered proprietor who appears in the certificate, other documents to link the proprietor with the seller must be handed over, eg. where a surviving co-owner is selling, the death certificate of the other proprietor; where PRs are selling, the grant of representation (*see* further Chapter 18).	These documents will form part of the bundle of title deeds.
4 Form 53 for each outstanding mortgage.	The mortgage deed(s) must be receipted.
5 Miscellaneous documents promised by the seller, eg. NHBC guarantees; planning consents. Receipt for chattels paid for separately.	

Note _____.

With unregistered as with registered titles the evidence of the discharge of any outstanding mortgages may not be available at completion. Completion may take place on the basis of a solicitor's undertaking to forward the funds to the mortgagee to redeem the mortgage and then forward the evidence of discharge when received from the mortgagee. In the case of an unregistered title this will be the receipted mortgage deed.

17.1.3   The passing of the legal title

There is a fundamental difference here between registered and unregistered titles.

Where the title is *registered*, the buyer does not obtain legal title until the transfer is registered. Although there is no fixed time limit specified for registration, the application should be made within 30-working days of the Form 94 pre-completion search. This is because the priority period conferred by that search will expire and the buyer will then be subject to new entries placed on the register between the date of the search and the date of their application for registration.

With *unregistered* titles the legal title passes to the buyer on completion but first registration of title is compulsory whenever there is a conveyance on sale of the freehold: s.123, LRA 1925. The application for first registration must be made within *two months* of completion otherwise the legal title that vested in the buyer at completion will revert to the seller. The seller will then hold the legal title on trust for the buyer.

An application may be made to the Land Registry for late registration and if the application is not excessively late it may be accepted. If not, there will have to be a fresh (confirmatory) conveyance from the seller to the buyer. This the seller cannot refuse to do as the seller is already holding the legal title on trust for the buyer. The buyer does not have to pay again for the property but any costs incurred by the seller in this process will have to be paid by the buyer.

Post-completion   17.2

Seller's solicitor   17.2.1

If an undertaking was given for the discharge of any outstanding mortgage, this must be complied with. You will need to send to the mortgagee not only the funds required to discharge the mortgage but also the mortgage deed itself (which will have been obtained with the other title deeds from the mortgagee at the outset of the transaction) so that the mortgagee can endorse on it the statutory receipt.

Buyer's solicitor: stamping   17.2.2

The requirements are exactly the same as for a Land Registry transfer, ie. AV duty at 1% of the consideration unless the conveyance contains a certificate of value and PD stamping to show delivery of the particulars delivered form to the Inland Revenue.

You must submit the deed of conveyance to the Inland Revenue for AV and PD stamping before the application for first registration of title is made. If there is no AV duty payable then the Land Registry can deal with PD stamping and the particulars delivered form will therefore be lodged at the District Land Registry at the same time as the application for first registration.

17.2.3   Buyer's solicitor: first registration of title

The application for first registration of a freehold title is made on Form 1B. The solicitor making the application certifies that they have examined the title and are satisfied with it and that all incumbrances are being declared. The Land Registry will then examine the title itself and decide on the basis of that examination whether to grant the applicant absolute, possessory or qualified title.

Documents to be produced

All the documents relating to the seller's title and to this particular transaction leading to the application for first registration must be produced, specifically:

- The *root of title* and *all deeds* comprising links in the chain of title down to the present seller (including the seller's mortgage(s) with receipt(s) endorsed thereon).
- The *contract of sale*, the *property information form* and all *searches and enquiries* made in connection with this transaction, eg. Local Land Charges search, enquiries at the local authority, Central Land Charges searches.
- *Requisitions on title* and the *replies* to them.
- The *deed of conveyance* (or Rule 72 transfer) plus a certified copy.
- The buyer's new *mortgage* (if any) plus a certified copy.

All these documents are listed on Form A13 which you submit in triplicate together with the original documents, the Form 1B application form and the appropriate fee.

On receipt of the application the Land Registry checks the documents received against the A13 list and returns one copy of the list as evidence of receipt. When the registration is complete and the Land Registry issues the appropriate land / charge certificate, a second copy of the form A13 will be returned to you showing which documents are being returned and which have been retained by the Land Registry. The third copy of the list is retained permanently by the Land Registry.

Requisitions on title

In examining the application for first registration the Land Registry may raise various requisitions on the title. The buyer's solicitor will have to answer these satisfactorily if the client is to obtain absolute title. It is therefore vital that you have throughout the transaction obtained all the information necessary to prepare to answer any Land Registry requisitions which may arise.

If necessary you can refer to the seller's solicitor for assistance in answering the Land Registry requisitions but whether or not the seller's solicitor has an *obligation* to assist is a grey area. Where the seller has conveyed as beneficial owner, then the covenant for further assurance probably applies but the position in other cases is less certain. If in the course of the conveyancing transaction you encounter problems which you suspect may lead the Land Registry to raise requisitions, you should ensure that you obtain from the seller's solicitor an undertaking to assist in dealing with any Land Registry queries.

The pre-registration deeds   17.2.4

It is always difficult to know what should be done with the pre-registration title deeds. Now that the title has been registered they no longer constitute the estate owner's proof of title and are therefore largely superfluous.

There are, however, two particular situations in which the old deeds still have a role to play.

1 *Indemnity covenant.* The conveyance to the buyer may have contained an indemnity covenant which the buyer entered into in respect of existing covenants. When the buyer comes to sell they will therefore need to take an indemnity from their buyer. However, the fact that the buyer (the first registered proprietor) gave an indemnity will not be indicated on the register. The solicitor acting on such an occasion will therefore need to look back at the conveyance to the first proprietor, ie. the conveyance leading to first registration, to see if an indemnity was given and therefore whether one should be taken in the subsequent transfer.

Note

If, in the subsequent transfer, the buyer gives an indemnity then the Land Registry will make a note of that on the proprietorship register. It is an anomaly of the land registration system that such a note is made where an indemnity is included in a transfer but not where it is included in the conveyance leading to first registration.

2 *General boundaries rule.* The Land Registry operates a general boundaries rule. This means that the filed plan only gives a general indication of the boundaries of the property and does not indicate who has responsibility for the various boundaries. The title deeds may contain more detailed information as to the boundaries and responsibility for them and so it can sometimes be useful to look back at the pre-registration deeds if there is a boundary dispute relating to property.

17.3   Remedies

The remedies for delayed completion, non-completion, breach and misrepresentation are the same as those described in Chapter 13 relating to registered titles.

17.3.1   Post-completion

The position is basically the same as that explained in Chapter 13 *except* that there is a further remedy which may be available to a buyer under s.25, LPA 1969. This may provide compensation where post-completion the buyer discovers that they are bound by a charge registered under the Land Charges Act which their pre-completion search failed to reveal because they did not search against the name against which the charge was registered.

Section 25 deals with the problem that arises because the seller only has to deduce title back to a good root of title which is at least 15 years old. Consequently the buyer may not discover the names of pre-root owners (unless they are referred to in the root or subsequent deeds) and therefore no central Land Charges search will be made against those names. However, if there are any charges registered against the names of those estate owners the buyer will be bound by them. This is obviously very hard on the buyer and s.25 accordingly provides that in such circumstances the buyer will be entitled to seek compensation from state funds.

This compensation is only available if the buyer has investigated title for the normal statutory period. If a root less than 15 years old has been accepted by the buyer, then their failure to discover certain pre-root names will be due to their own acceptance of a short title and not to the operation of the 15-year rule and they will not be entitled to compensation in respect of entries they would have discovered had they not accepted a short title.

Note

Section 25 does not apply to provide compensation for a lessee who is granted a lease out of an unregistered freehold as it is not the operation of the 15-year rule for roots of title that prevents the lessee discovering the names of certain estate owners to search against but the operation of the open contract rule that a lessee is not entitled to see evidence of the freehold title (*see* Chapter 22).

Self-assessment questions

1   How does an application for first registration differ from

an application to register a transfer of an already registered title as regards:

(a) The time limit (if any) for registering;

(b) The purpose of the documents which accompany the application for registration?

2   What are Land Registry requisitions?

3   If you are selling for a client who is the first registered proprietor, why may you need to look back at the conveyance by which they acquired legal title?

4   In what circumstances will a buyer be entitled to compensation under s.25, LPA 1969?

Chapter 18

Special dispositions

Dispositions by personal representatives 18.1

Legal title will only pass to personal representatives where a sole or last surviving proprietor/estate owner dies.

Proof of the PR's title 18.1.1

To become registered as proprietors of a *registered title*, the PRs will need to produce to the Land Registry a *grant of representation*. However, the PRs will not hold the legal title for long but will either sell the property or assent to its vesting in the beneficiary. This they can do without ever themselves being registered as proprietors.

In the case of an *unregistered title* the abstract will recite the death of the estate owner and the grant of representation. A copy of the grant must be supplied.

Note _____

A copy of the death certificate is not necessary as the grant is itself proof of death.

Assents by PRs 18.1.2

Where PRs transfer title to a beneficiary they do so by means of an assent. This must be in writing but need not be by deed and is therefore an *exception* to the normal rule that a legal estate can only be created or transferred by deed.

Registered titles
In the case of a registered title the assent must be in a prescribed Land Registry form.

An assentee applying to the Land Registry to become the new proprietor must lodge:

- The deceased's *land certificate;*
- A certified copy of the *grant of representation;*
- The *assent.*

An assentee can, however, dispose of the title without ever being registered as proprietor. The buyer from an assentee will have to lodge at the Land Registry the above three documents *plus* the transfer to themselves from the assentee.

Unregistered titles
In the case of an unregistered title the buyer from an assentee will similarly need to see both the grant of representation to the

PRs and the assent from the PRs to the beneficiary, as they are both essential links in the chain of title.

Memorandum

An assentee is entitled to require the PRs to endorse on the grant of representation a memorandum recording the granting of the assent: s.36(5), Administration of Estates Act 1925. This the assentee should insist on in order to safeguard their position in the event of a subsequent sale by the PRs of the same property.

PR as beneficiary

Where a PR is also a beneficiary then if they are intending to dispose of the property as beneficial owner there must be an assent from themselves as PR to themselves as the beneficiary. Similarly, if PRs are also trustees of any trusts created by the will or intestacy then before they can dispose of the property as trustees, there must be an assent from themselves as PRs to themselves as trustees: *Re King's Will Trust* (1964). An assent will, of course, not be necessary if the PRs are disposing of the property in their capacity as PRs.

18.1.3 Sales by personal representatives

All proving PRs must be party to any transfer/conveyance but it is unnecessary for there to be more than one PR. A sole PR, acting as PR, can give a valid receipt for the proceeds of sale and the buyer will take free from the interest of the beneficiaries in the estate: s.27(2), LPA 1925.

There are various other statutory provisions which protect buyers.

1   The sale will be valid even though it was not necessary for the PRs to realise the property in order to pay the debts of the estate: s.36(8), AEA 1925.

2   Where the PRs have assented to a beneficiary who then sells the buyer is entitled to assume that the PRs have assented in favour of the correct person: s.36(7), AEA 1925.

3   'A statement in writing by a personal representative that he has not given or made an assent or conveyance in respect of a legal estate, shall, in favour of purchaser, but without prejudice to any previous disposition, made in favour of another purchaser deriving title mediately or immediately under the personal representative, be sufficient evidence that an assent or conveyance has not been given or made in respect of the legal estate to which the statement relates, unless notice of a previous assent or conveyance affecting that estate has been placed upon or annexed to the probate or administration.': s.36(6), AEA 1925.

Section 36(6) is very important because it enables a purchaser from PRs to obtain the legal title even though the PRs have previously assented the property to a beneficiary. The beneficiary will lose the legal title and the purchaser from the PRs will obtain it.

The operation of s.36

To obtain the protection of s.36 a buyer from PRs must:

- Check the *original grant of representation* to see whether there is endorsed on it a *memorandum* of any earlier assent or conveyance by the PRs.

- Check that the *conveyance* to them by the PRs contains a statement by the PRs that they have not previously assented or conveyed the property to anyone else. (Such a statement will be made in the recitals part of the conveyance and is generally known as a 's.36(6) statement'.)

Provided there is no memorandum on the grant of a previous disposition and provided that the PRs have given the buyer the s.36(6) statement, the buyer will obtain legal title unless there has been a previous disposition in favour of another purchaser, who may be a purchaser directly or indirectly from the PRs.

Example

- PRs assent to X.

- Memorandum of the assent is endorsed on the grant of representation.

- PRs later convey to Y, a purchaser, giving the s.36(6) statement.

- Y will not obtain legal title. The memo on the grant safeguards X's title. If the memo had not been placed on the grant X would lose the legal title and Y would obtain it.

If there had been an earlier disposition to a purchaser, Y would not obtain legal title even if a memorandum of the earlier purchase had not been endorsed on the grant. It makes no difference whether the earlier purchase was from the PRs directly or from an assentee from the PRs.

- PRs assent to X.

- No memo is placed on the grant.

- X sells to Z.

- PRs later sell and convey to Y giving the s.36(6) statement.

- Y will not obtain legal title because Z is an earlier purchaser obtaining title mediately, ie. indirectly, from the PRs.

The existence of s.36(6) should not be taken to indicate that PRs are in the habit of dealing twice with the same property, but it is something that may occur accidentally. In such a situation s.36(6) seeks to regulate the conflicting claims of the first and second parties.

Section 36(6) would seem to be capable of applying to both registered and unregistered titles. However, where the title is registered, an assentee who fails to get a memorandum of the assent endorsed on the grant but who nevertheless immediately registers the disposition to them and so becomes the registered proprietor, will not be in danger of losing the legal title to a later purchaser from the PRs because the register is conclusive.

18.1.4   PRs and beneficial joint tenancies

Where co-owners hold for themselves as beneficial joint tenants then the last surviving co-owner will have sole legal and beneficial title. On their death the sole legal and beneficial title will pass to their PRs.

Unregistered titles

A purchaser from the PRs must have regard to the provisions of the Law of Property (Joint Tenants) Act 1964. This Act applies only to *unregistered titles*. (It is covered in Chapter 14, para. 14.4. Revise that section before reading further.)

Example

- Conveyance to A and B as beneficial joint tenants.
- A dies.
- B therefore has sole legal and beneficial title.
- B dies.
- Grant of representation to B's estate to X and Y.
- X and Y are now selling as PRs.

To obtain the protection of the 1964 Act and to be sure of obtaining a good title, the buyer from the PRs will need to:

- Investigate the *title* of A and B back to a good root at least 15 years old;
- Check that the conveyance to A and B is not endorsed with any *memorandum of severance*;
- Do a *bankruptcy search* against the names of A and B to ensure that there was no bankruptcy entry against either of them;
- Obtain a copy of A's *death certificate*;
- Obtain a copy of the *grant of representation* to B's estate;
- Obtain in the *conveyance* from the PRs a statement that B

was solely and beneficially entitled at the date of death. (Such a statement would normally appear in the recitals.)

Note —————————————————————————————

If B had been selling a statement that they were solely and beneficially entitled would not have been necessary as B could simply have conveyed in the capacity of beneficial owner. X and Y will be conveying as personal representatives and therefore the statement is necessary for the 1964 Act to protect the buyer.

Registered titles

In a similar situation where the title is *registered* the buyer will need to:

- Check by means of up-to-date office copies that A and B were the *registered proprietors* and there was *no co-ownership restriction* entered on the proprietorship register before A's death;

- Obtain a copy of A's *death certificate*;

- Obtain a copy of the *grant of representation* to B's estate in favour of X and Y.

PRs and tenancies in common   18.1.5

If A and B had held as beneficial tenants in common, then on A's death B would have sole legal title but would hold the legal title on trust for themselves and for A's estate. If a new trustee has not been appointed, then when B dies the legal title will pass to B's personal representatives who will likewise hold the legal estate on trust, partly for B's estate and partly for A's estate.

Generally it is only necessary to have one PR but in this situation a buyer should not buy from a sole PR. (The position is in fact quite complex and goes beyond the scope of this course.)

Dispositions by attorneys   18.2

A seller (or buyer) may act through an agent. An agent who is to sign a deed on another's behalf must be appointed by deed. The deed of appointment containing the agent's authority/mandate to act is called a *power of attorney*. The person granting the power (the principal) is known as the donor and the person to whom the power is granted (the agent) is the donee/attorney.

General and specific powers   18.2.1

A *general power* entitles the attorney to do anything that the donor could themselves have done. A simple form of general power of attorney is provided for by s.10 of the Powers of Attorney Act 1971 and is set out in the schedule to the Act.

A *specific power* entitles the attorney to do specific things on the donor's behalf. It will require special drafting.

18.2.2   Trustee's powers

A trustee can delegate trustee functions but not by means of a general power. The power must be specific and for a period not exceeding 12 months. It must be witnessed and a trustee cannot appoint their sole co-trustee (unless a trust corporation) as attorney: s.25, Trustee Act 1925 and s.9, Powers of Attorney Act 1971.

Co-owners hold as trustees for sale and PRs are also trustees. Both are therefore subject to these requirements.

18.2.3   Revocation of authority

The attorney's acts will only bind the donor if:

- The attorney is acting within the *scope of their authority* – this can be checked by examining the power; and
- The authority has *not been revoked*.

Revocation will occur if the donor:

- *Revokes* the power (unless it is an irrevocable security power, *see* 18.2.7);
- *Dies*;
- Becomes *bankrupt*;
- Becomes mentally incapable of looking after their affairs (unless it is an enduring power, *see* 18.2.8).

If the attorney's authority has been revoked then *prima facie* a buyer dealing with the attorney will not obtain title from the seller.

18.2.4   Protection of buyers and other purchasers

Protection available
Section 5(2) of the PAA 1971 provides that if a purchaser has no knowledge of the revocation the transaction shall be as valid as if the power has still been in existence.

Knowledge of an event which causes revocation constitutes knowledge of the revocation, eg. if you know the donor is dead you are conclusively presumed to know that the effect of that is to revoke the donee's authority.

Section 5(4) goes further in protecting later purchasers by providing that in favour of a later purchaser a *lack of knowledge* on the part of the person who dealt with the attorney will be conclusively presumed if:

(a) The transaction between that person and the attorney was completed within 12 months of the power coming into operation; *or*

(b) That person makes a statutory declaration before or within three months after the completion of the purchase (ie. the later purchase) that they did not at the material time know of the revocation of the power.

Section 5(4) is not designed to protect the person dealing directly with the attorney; their protection is s.5(2). However, the Land Registry also applies the conclusive presumption in s.5(4)(a) in favour of such a person. Only where the power is utilised more than 12 months after it was granted does the Land Registry require the person who dealt with the attorney to lodge, with their application for registration, a statutory declaration as to their lack of knowledge of any revocation.

Buyer's actions

A buyer from a seller acting through an attorney must:

- See the *power of attorney* or a certified copy of it to ensure that it covers the transaction in question and that if the seller is a trustee that the power of attorney is a trustee power;

- Be *unaware of the revocation* of the attorney's authority;

- If the power is being exercised more than 12 months after it was granted (trustee powers cannot be granted for more than 12 months anyway), then a *statutory declaration of lack of knowledge* is lodged at the Land Registry with their application for registration (whether it is an application for first registration or an application to register a dealing) together with a *certified copy of the power of attorney*.

A buyer of an *unregistered title* who, on examination of the abstract, sees that there was at some stage in the past a disposition by an attorney must:

- See the *power of attorney* or a certified copy to ensure that it covers the transaction in question, and that if the seller was a trustee that the power was a trustee power;

- Check whether the *power was utilised within 12 months* of it being granted, if so the later buyer is protected by s.5(4)(a);

- If the power is utilised more than 12 months after it was granted then check whether there is a *statutory declaration of lack of knowledge* made by the person who dealt with the attorney. This must be made before or within three months of the disposition by that person;

- If the three month time limit has expired the subsequent buyer will still get a good title if the person who dealt with the attorney *did not have knowledge of any revocation* and therefore obtained a good title from the attorney by virtue of s.5(2);

- If that person's knowledge at the relevant time cannot be ascertained, eg. because they are dead, then you must investigate whether at the time the power was utilised the *power was in fact still in existence*, eg. get a statutory declaration from the attorney, or better still from the donor, that the power was still in existence at the time it was utilised.

18.2.5 Execution of deeds by attorneys

The donor of the power is the seller and is the party to the deed. The attorney merely executes the deed on the donor's behalf.

Section 7 of the PAA 1971 provides that the attorney may either sign in their own name as attorney for the donor, eg. 'Amanda Smith as Attorney for John Ball', or sign in the donor's name, eg. 'John Ball by his attorney Amanda Smith'. There is no difference in effect.

18.2.6 Proof of a power of attorney

Section 3 of the PAA 1971 provides that an instrument creating a power of attorney may be proved by means of a copy certified as a true and complete copy of the original by the donor of the power or by a solicitor or stock broker. Where the power consists of more than one page, each page must be certified as a true and complete copy of the original.

The power may also be proved by means of a certified copy of a certified copy.

18.2.7 Irrevocable security powers

An irrevocable security power is a power granted to a creditor as part of their security for the donor's indebtedness. If it is expressed to be irrevocable it cannot be revoked by the donor so long as the debt exists. For example, an equitable mortgage may give the mortgagee an irrevocable power to enable the mortgagee to sell the mortgagor's legal title and thereby realise the security.

Irrevocable security powers are regulated by s.4, PAA 1971.

18.2.8 Enduring powers of attorney

An enduring power is a special kind of power of attorney which will not be revoked by the donor's subsequent mental incapacity. There are detailed provisions as to the form and effect of such powers under the Enduring Powers of Attorney Act 1985. (A detailed consideration of them goes beyond the scope of this companion.)

Dispositions by companies

A corporation in an artificial legal person and its powers will be prescribed in its constituent documents. In the case of a trading company the powers will be contained in the objects clause of the memorandum of association, although a company registered since the Companies Act 1989 may have an objects clause which merely states that it is a 'general commercial company'. The company should not act *ultra vires*, ie. beyond those powers.

> *Note*
>
> Although the *ultra vires* rule has been abolished in relation to transactions with third parties, it still applies within the company and the members of a company can seek to prevent a proposed *ultra vires* transaction.

If you are acting for a company which is buying land, or lending money to someone else on the security of land, you should check the memorandum of association to ensure that it provides for these activities. On any application to the Land Registry to register the company as the proprietor of the legal title, or of a charge over the land, you will be required to certify that the company has the necessary powers. If the application is made by someone other than a solicitor or licensed conveyancer, the Land Registry will actually want to see a copy of the memorandum of association to ensure that the company has the necessary powers.

However, when *buying* from a company you will have the protection of s.35(1), Companies Act 1985 (as amended by s.108, Companies Act 1989). This provides that the validity of an act done by a company shall not be called into question on the grounds of lack of capacity by reason of anything in the company's memorandum. A third party dealing with the company does not, therefore, have to be concerned as to whether or not a particular transaction falls within the company's powers.

Powers of directors to bind the company

The company acts through agents and the normal rule of the law of agency is that an agent's acts will only bind the principal if the agent acts within the scope of their authority.

However, s.35A of the Companies Act 1985 provides that 'In favour of a person dealing with a company in good faith, the power of the board of directors to bind the company, or authorise others to do so, shall be deemed to be free of any limitation under the company's constitution.' Furthermore, s.35B provides that 'a party to a transaction with a company is not bound to enquire as to whether it is permitted by the company's memorandum or as to any limitation in the powers of the board of directors to bind the company or authorise others to do so.'

18.3.2   Execution of deeds

Section 1 of the Law of Property (Miscellaneous Provisions) Act 1989 abolished the need for deeds executed by individuals to be sealed.

Section 36A of the Companies Act 1985 (inserted by s.130, Companies Act 1989) provides that a company need not have a common seal and that a document signed by a director and the secretary of a company, or by two directors of a company, and expressed (in whatever form of words) to be executed by the company has the same effect as if executed under the common seal of the company.

A company that has a common seal can still execute a deed in the old way provided for by s.74, LPA 1925, ie. by affixing the seal in the presence of and attested (witnessed) by its clerk, secretary or other permanent officer or their deputy and a member of the board of directors.

Thus, in favour of a purchaser, a deed will be duly executed by a company if it is executed in accordance with either s.74, LPA 1925 *or* s.36A, Companies Act 1985.

18.4   Voidable dispositions

A voidable disposition is one that can be set aside by certain persons who choose to avoid the disposition.

18.4.1   Dispositions by trustees to themselves

Trustees must not dispose of trust property to themselves unless:

- The trust instrument authorises it; or
- It is sanctioned by the court; or
- All the beneficiaries are of full age and (preferably with the benefit of legal advice) authorise the transaction.

In all other cases the transaction will be *voidable by the beneficiaries*, even though it was at full market value.

There is no time limit on the beneficiaries setting the transaction aside although if they are of full age and know of the transaction and do nothing they will probably be taken to have confirmed it.

These principles apply to personal representatives as they hold the estate on trust for the beneficiaries.

Example

If Peter and Rosa (PRs) transfer property comprised in the estate to Rosa, the beneficiaries may set the transaction aside. However, if the deceased had contracted to sell the property to Rosa, the PRs in transferring the property to her are merely performing a contractual obligation of the estate and that cannot be set aside. A sale by Peter and Rosa to Rosa's husband or other relative is probably not voidable by the beneficiaries provided it was at full value but the position is not free from doubt and such a transaction is not recommended.

Dispositions affected by undue influence 18.4.2

Where the relationship between buyer and seller is such that one party is in a position of trust/confidence/influence in relation to the other then a transaction between them may be voidable for undue influence.

There are certain (fiduciary) relationships where undue influence will be presumed unless proved otherwise. They include solicitor–client, doctor–patient, minister of religion–member of congregation, trustee–beneficiary, parent/guardian–child/ward. The husband–wife relationship is *not* one where undue influence will be presumed but is one where undue influence may be proved to have existed on the facts in relation to a particular transaction.

Where the parties are in a relationship where undue influence will be presumed or might be proved to have existed, the vulnerable party must receive separate legal advice.

Note

This is a case where even though the transaction falls within one of the situations mentioned in Rule 6(2) of the Solicitor's Practice Rules, the same solicitor should *definitely not* act for both parties.

Transaction at an undervalue 18.5

There is a danger that such transactions may be set aside if the person making the disposition is later declared bankrupt.

18.5.1   Definition

Section 339 of the Insolvency Act 1986 defines transactions at an undervalue as:

● Gifts;

● Transactions in consideration of marriage;

● Transactions for a consideration which is significantly of lesser value than that provided by the debtor.

18.5.2   Setting aside the transaction

Within two years

The trustee in bankruptcy may set the transaction aside if it was entered into within two years prior to the presentation of the petition: s.339.

Between two and five years

If it was entered into between two and five years prior to the petition it may still be set aside if the person making the disposition was *insolvent* at the time or *became insolvent in consequence of the transaction:* s.339.

More than five years

If it was entered into *more than five years* previously it may only be set aside if the purpose of the transaction was to put *assets beyond the reach of creditors* or otherwise prejudice such persons – a transaction defrauding creditors under s.423.

18.5.3   Protection of third parties

The Act provides protection (ss.342 and 425) for those who later acquire the property 'in good faith and for value without notice of the relevant circumstances', ie. the circumstances in which an order under ss.339 or 423 could be made. However, in the case of dispositions within the previous two years, there are no particular circumstances to be satisfied before the transaction can be set aside and therefore no relevant circumstances of which a later purchaser can be without notice. It is therefore unsafe to buy property which is *known* to have been the subject of a transaction at an undervalue within the previous two years. If the donor becomes bankrupt it can be set aside.

In the case of transactions within the previous two to five years you should ensure that you get a statutory declaration of solvency sworn by the person who disposed of the property at an undervalue.

The fact that there has been a previous disposition by way of gift will, in the case of an unregistered title, be apparent from the abstract of title. Where the title is registered the register *may* state that a particular transaction was by way of gift and so warn a later purchaser of the possibility that it might be set aside.

However, in the case of transactions at an undervalue, other then by way of gift, a later purchaser will probably be totally unaware that the transaction was at an undervalue and therefore will be protected.

Miscellaneous dispositions   18.6

There are many other people who are in a special position when it comes to buying or, more particularly, selling land. It is beyond the scope of this companion to consider all of them but you should nevertheless be aware that:

- A minor, ie. anyone under 18 years of age, cannot hold a legal estate in land and that any purported transfer to a minor can only given the minor a beneficial interest and not legal title;
- Special steps will need to taken if you are buying from:
  - a charity;
  - a person who is a patient under the Mental Health Act 1983;
  - a tenant for life under a strict settlement.

Dispositions other than sales   18.7

The focus of this companion has been on sales. We have concentrated on ensuring that the buyer, and consequently the buyer's mortgagee, will obtain a good title and on the incumbrances that may burden that title.

The principles and processes involved are, however, equally applicable to a situation where an existing owner is creating a new mortgage. In such a case the owner/mortgagor is in a similar position to a seller and the mortgagee is in a similar position to a buyer. The solicitor acting for the mortgagee will therefore need to carry out the same investigations of title, searches and enquiries as if acting for a buyer.

The various statutory provisions which protect buyers, eg. provisions regarding overreaching, s.5, Powers of Attorney Act 1971; s.36, Administration of Estates Act 1925; s.4, Land Charges Act 1972, protect 'purchasers', a term which includes mortgagees and also lessees. A new lessee is therefore also in the position of a buyer and in acting for a lessee you will consequently do more or less the same as you would do when you are acting for a buyer of a freehold (*see* Chapter 22).

18.8 Auction sales

So far we have assumed that the sale is by private treaty, which means that until contracts are exchanged the buyer's solicitor has an opportunity to negotiate changes to the draft contract and to make various searches and enquiries.

At a sale by public auction the various bids constitute offers and the auctioneer accepts the highest bid by banging the hammer and the parties are then legally bound.

Note

Auction sales are *not* subject to the requirements of s.2, Law of Property (Miscellaneous Provisions) Act 1989 and therefore the contract does not have to be in writing.

Before the auction takes place the draft contract will be available for inspection but bidders will be unable to negotiate changes to it. They must ensure that they carry out and are happy with all their pre-contract searches and enquiries before they participate in the auction.

Self-assessment questions

1 What is a s.36(6) statement? Where is it made and what is its effect?

2 Where an abstract of title includes a disposition by an attorney, why must the present buyer:

(a) See a copy of the power of attorney;

(b) Check when the power was granted?

3 If you are buying from a company do you need to check that the transfer/conveyance by the company has the company's seal affixed to it?

4 Why may it be dangerous to buy land from someone who received it as a gift?

Chapter 19

Sales of part

Creation of new covenants and easements   19.1

This section applies to both registered and unregistered titles.

Note _____

You should make sure that you have a sound knowledge and understand of covenants and easements from the pre-course primer before reading this chapter.)

_____

On a sale of part of the seller's land new covenants and easements will generally be created. You will need to take instructions from the seller as to what covenants and easements are to be provided for in the draft contract and from the buyer as to whether those provided for are acceptable and whether any others need to be negotiated.

New covenants   19.1.1

These are frequently imposed on the part sold for the benefit of the seller's retained land. If the buyer is in a strong negotiating position, the seller may also enter into covenants for the benefit of the parts sold.

A special condition in the contract will provide that 'The buyer shall in the transfer enter into a covenant in the following terms...'. The condition will then set out the exact wording of the covenant which is to be included in the transfer. To ensure that the burden and the benefit of the covenant will run with the respective estates, the wording will generally state that the covenant is imposed '... for the benefit of the seller's retained land and each and every part of it.' and that it is imposed '... with the intent that it shall bind the land transferred into whoever's hands it may come.'

Note _____

If existing covenants affecting the seller's land were imposed using a similar form of words, on a sale of part, the part sold, as well as the part retained, will be bound by the existing covenants.

_____

Grant of new easements   19.1.2

A special condition will provide for the transfer to include an express grant of easements to the buyer. Even though certain easements might be impliedly granted in the buyer's favour by virtue of the operation of s.62, LPA 1925 or the rule in *Wheeldon v Burrows*, it is not desirable for either party to rely on the implied grant rules because the extent of easements thereby granted might be a matter of dispute. When an easement is expressly granted its scope can be clearly stated, eg. the route of a right of way can be marked on a plan.

19.1.3 Preventing new easements being granted by implication

The implied grant rules may result in easements being granted to the buyer that the seller does not intend the buyer to have. They constitute a trap for the unwary seller and the seller's solicitor should ensure that the contract provides for them to be excluded, or at least limited.

Standard Condition 3.3.2 provides that the buyer will have no right of light or air over the retained land but this only limits the implied grant rules to prevent implied easements of light and air arising. If the seller wishes to exclude implied easements entirely, a *special condition* will be necessary to provide that the buyer shall have no rights whatsoever over the retained land other than those expressly granted.

It is not sufficient for the contract alone to limit or exclude the implied grant rules because they will operate on the transfer/conveyance. The contractual provision must therefore be followed up with a *declaration in the transfer/conveyance* that the buyer shall have no right of light or air over the retained land.

19.1.4 Reservation of new easements

Any easement to be created in the seller's favour must be specifically provided for by special condition and expressly reserved in the transfer/conveyance. Section 62, LPA 1925 and the rule in *Wheeldon v Burrows* (1879) do not operate in a seller's favour to create implied reservations. However SC 3.3.2 provides '... the seller and the buyer will each have the rights over the land of the other which they would have had if they were two separate buyers to whom the seller had made simultaneous transfers of the property and the retained land.' This provision has the effect of entitling the seller to reserve *Wheeldon v Burrows*-type easements, ie. the seller is to be treated as if they were themselves a buyer of part in whose favour the rule in *Schwann v Cotton* (1916) would apply.

SC 3.3.3 provides that either party may require that the transfer contains appropriate terms, and if the seller wishes to have the benefit of the reservation provided for by SC

3.3.2 the transfer/conveyance must contain an express reservation of such easements as would fall within the rule in *Wheeldon v Burrows*.

Procedures: registered title   19.2

Where the seller is disposing of part of a registered title the procedures to be followed will differ slightly from those described in earlier chapters dealing with a sale of the entirety of a registered title.

Description of the property   19.2.1

Both the contract and the transfer will make it clear by referring to the title number that what is being sold is part of registered title but there must also be a specific *description* of the part being sold, including a plan. The plan must show clearly the part being sold and the part retained, and the route of any easements being created over either property.

> *Note*
>
> Plans in land registry transfers must be signed by the transferor and by or on behalf of the transferee. Indeed, in both registered or unregistered conveyancing, it is advisable to follow this practice whenever a plan is used.

Discharge of seller's mortgage   19.2.2

Where the entire property is mortgaged it will be necessary to get the mortgagee to release the part being sold from the mortgage. It will be a matter for negotiation between the seller and their mortgagee as to whether the mortgagee is prepared to release part of their security. Some reduction in the outstanding debt may be required. At completion the buyer must receive from the seller a Form 53 (or a satisfactory undertaking for a Form 53) relating to the part sold.

Pre-completion search   19.2.3

The Form 94A Land Registry Search is a search in respect of the whole of the land comprised in a particular title. A slightly different form – Form 94B – is used to search in respect of part only of the title. The application must normally be accompanied by a plan in duplicate showing the precise extent of the land to be searched.

Form of the transfer   19.2.4

This will contain the covenants and easements provided for by the contract and a declaration to limit or exclude the operation of the implied grant rules.

19.2.5   Placing the seller's land certificate on deposit

The seller will not wish to hand over their Land Certificate to the buyer at completion but the certificate will need to be produced to the Land Registry for the transfer to be registered. Prior to completion the seller will therefore place the Land Certificate on deposit at the Land Registry and obtain for it a deposit number which will be advised to the buyer on completion.

Where the property is mortgaged the Land Certificate will already be at the Land Registry but the mortgagee will have a charge certificate. When the seller arranges with their mortgagee for the release of the part being sold from the mortgage they must also arrange for the mortgagee to place the charge certificate on deposit at the Land Registry.

19.2.6   Registration of the transfer

Following completion the transfer must be registered within the 30-working day priority period of the Form 94B search. When applying for registration you will quote the deposit number so that the Registry can locate the seller's Land Certificate or the Charge Certificate.

The buyer will be registered as the first proprietor of a new title. Easements reserved by the seller and covenants entered into by the buyer will be entered in the Charges Register and any easements granted for the benefit of the part sold will be noted in the Property Register. A new Land Certificate will be issued to the buyer. The seller's title will be amended to show the removal from it of the land sold and to record easements and covenants affecting the retained land. The amended Land Certificate will then be returned to the seller (or amended Charge Certificate to the seller's mortgagee).

19.3   Procedures: unregistered title

This section considers the differences between the steps to be taken on a sale of part and those described in Chapters 15–17.

19.3.1   Description of the property

In both the contract and the conveyance, the land sold and the land retained should be precisely defined and a plan should always be used.

19.3.2   Discharge of the seller's mortgage

The mortgagee's release of the part sold is effected by the mortgagee joining in the conveyance of part to release that part from the mortgage and not by a separate document (as in the case of a Form 53).

The deed of conveyance

The deed will contain the easements and covenants provided for by the contract and a declaration to limit or exclude the operation of the implied grant rules.

Although the present deed of conveyance will be handed to the buyer at completion, the earlier deeds will be retained by the seller as they remain the seller's proof of title to the retained land. The conveyance will include a list of these retained title deeds and an acknowledgement, and possibly an undertaking, in respect of them.

Acknowledgements and undertakings

Under the open contract rules a buyer is entitled to receive a statutory acknowledgement and undertaking in respect of documents of title which are retained and not handed over to the buyer.

'Statutory acknowledgement and undertaking' means an acknowledgement and undertaking in accordance with s.64, LPA 1925. The *acknowledgement* is an acknowledgement of the buyer's right to inspect the originals and to receive (at the buyer's expense) copies of them. The *undertaking* is an undertaking for safe custody of the deeds.

Note

Traditionally, someone who holds the deeds in a fiduciary capacity only gives an acknowledgement for production and does not give an undertaking for safe custody. Consequently a seller who conveys as trustee will not give an undertaking for safe custody.

An acknowledgement and/or undertaking can only be given by someone who is in *possession* of the deeds. Therefore, if the retained land is mortgaged – the title deeds will here be in the possession of the mortgagee – the seller cannot give an acknowledgement or undertaking and the open contract rules do not require the seller/mortgagor to obtain an acknowledgement for production from the mortgagee. (An undertaking for safe custody would not be given anyway as a mortgagee holds the deeds as a fiduciary.)

The benefit and burden of acknowledgements and undertakings run respectively with the land sold and with the title deeds. If a mortgagee does give an acknowledgement for production it will therefore bind the seller/mortgagor when they redeem the mortgage and recover the title deeds.

However, the mortgagee will not have given any undertaking for safe custody and therefore the seller will not be bound by any such undertaking unless they themselves give an undertaking when they recover the deeds. This is most unlikely.

SC 4.5.4 provides that 'In relation to every document of title which the buyer does not receive on completion the buyer is to have the benefit of (a) a written acknowledgement of his right to its production and (b) a written undertaking for its safe custody (except where it is held by a mortgagee or by someone in a fiduciary capacity).'

This means that the seller must arrange for the buyer to have the benefit of an acknowledgement for production from the mortgagee. It does not, however, require the seller to give an undertaking for safe custody when they subsequently discharge the mortgage and recover the title deeds. If the buyer thinks that this is necessary it needs to be provided for by special condition.

Note

The importance of acknowledgements and undertakings is diminishing. Post-completion the buyer of part will have to register title to that part and if absolute title is granted there will be no need for the buyer, at any time in the future, to resort to the original title deeds.

19.3.5   Marking the abstract and recording sales off

At completion the buyer's solicitor will, as in the sale of the whole, verify the title by checking the abstract of title against the original title deeds. As regards those deeds which the seller is retaining, the abstract will need to be marked to show that it has been examined against the originals. Each page of the abstract must be noted to say that it has been examined against the original and to state when, where and by whom this was done. This marked (examined) abstract is now the buyer's proof of title. It needs to be in good order as when the buyer applies for first registration of title this will be the proof which is presented to the Land Registry.

The seller's retained land will remain an unregistered title (unless the seller applies for voluntary registration) until it is itself sold. It is important that the retained title deeds should record the fact that part of the land has been sold off. This is done by means of a *memorandum* endorsed on the holding deed (the deed under which the seller acquired title). The memorandum will generally be quite brief. It will state the date and parties to the sale off and describe the part sold but will not give all the terms of the conveyance, ie. it will not detail all the easements and covenants provided for. It is therefore advisable that the seller should take, and keep with the title deeds, a certified copy of the conveyance of part.

Registration of title   19.3.6

Post-completion the buyer must apply for first registration of title to the part bought within two months. The application will be on Form 1B but the evidence of title lodged will be a marked abstract rather than the original title deeds.

Self-assessment questions

1 How can the buyer of part of the seller's land take free from the seller's mortgage?

2 Why must the seller of part of a registered title place the land/charge certificate on deposit at the Land Registry?

3 Why must the buyer of part of an unregistered title ensure that at completion they obtain a marked abstract of the seller's title?

4 When will the seller of part of an unregistered title give both an acknowledgement for production and an undertaking for safe custody?

Chapter 20

Estate conveyancing

Introduction   20.1

It is usual to sell houses on estates freehold but in some parts of the country they are sold leasehold.

Essentially, the sale of a house on an estate is a sale of part of the land belonging to the seller. All the matters which need to be considered where there is a sale of just one part are therefore relevant, eg. consideration needs to be given to necessary *easements*, desirable *covenants*, etc.

The *difference* between selling a house on an estate and a sale of part of the land (*see* Chapter 19) is that, on an estate, the sale of a house will be only one of a number of sales of part. Thus, it would be neither efficient nor sensible to consider each house individually – the estate as a whole needs to be taken into account.

For this reason, there is a high degree of conformity in the documentation used for each sale of a house on an estate. Indeed, there may be a strategy for the estate which needs to be followed for each property, eg. that the front gardens will all be open plan. Also, the mechanism for selling the properties needs to be as streamlined as possible to cut down on costs.

It is normal, therefore, for the seller's solicitor to prepare and send to the buyer's solicitor at the outset a large package of documents very similar to the documents sent to a buyer under the Transaction Scheme embodied in the National Conveyancing Protocol.

You need to bear in mind that although estate conveyancing has its own peculiarities and requirements, it is essentially the sale of a freehold property and the normal rules and methods for buying and selling will apply. This chapter will highlight the *differences*. If no mention of a particular matter is made, assume there is no difference between estate conveyancing and normal freehold conveyancing on the point.

Seller   20.2

Title   20.2.1

The seller will need to deduce title to the property to the various buyers. If the property is unregistered this will mean finding a good root of title at least 15 years old and deducing all title from that time to the present day. If the title is registered, office copies of the title will normally be provided. Once the estate layout has been prepared it can be deposited at the Land Registry. This makes the buyer's solicitor's task of undertaking Land Registry searches before completion easier as the description of the plot being bought can be made with reference to the deposited layout plan.

Land Registry Form 102 is also important in estate conveyancing. A file pan of an estates can be large and complicated, particularly if it was originally several pieces of land each with its own rights and burdens. To simplify deducing title in these circumstances, the seller can supply Form 102 instead of a file plan. This form verifies that the plot being sold is contained within the seller's title.

It is far simpler (and usually cheaper) to deduce registered title rather than unregistered. Thus, if title to the estate itself is currently unregistered, you would do well to consider applying for voluntary registration so that registered title can be deduced to buyers.

Note

Because of the time it takes to obtain first registration, voluntary registration is something that you will need to consider very early in the selling process. Once buyers have been found for properties on the estate, it is likely to be too late.

Whatever type of title being sold, you need to check it thoroughly. If it contains any flaws these will either need to be remedied or dealt with by way of a *special condition* in the contract barring requisitions.

If the title contains *covenants* which the current development will break, these too need to be dealt with. The alternatives available to solve this problem are covered in Chapter 9, para. 9.6.4.

20.2.2 Contract

The contract will need to contain all the usual clauses for selling either registered or unregistered title, which ever it may be, eg. parties, property, price, deposit, etc. There will, however, be the following additional matters to consider.

Seller's register of title

If the title being sold is registered, the fact that part of the title has been sold will need to be noted on the seller's register of title.

To do this the seller's certificate must be deposited at the

Land Registry. The Land Registry will provide a 'deposit number' which must be given to the buyer at completion and then quoted by the buyer to the Land Registry when registering the transaction.

The contract will need a special condition providing that the certificate will be deposited and the deposit number given to the seller.

Sale before completion of the property

It is very common for plots to be sold on estates before the property is completed. In these circumstances, the contract will need to contain detailed clauses concerning the *completion* of the building of the property and the *obligations* on the seller to complete this work to a reasonable standard.

There will be no fixed date for completion if the property is in the course of construction. Instead, the contract will provide for completion to take place within a specified period after the buyer has been served with notice that the property is completed. The normal period of notice is 14 days, but this is negotiable.

Note

It is unreasonable for a seller to become committed to completing a property by a specific date as so much of the building process is liable to the effects of unknown variables such as weather.

Services

The contract will also need to refer to the seller's obligations with regard to services to the property, for example drainage, roadways and landscaping gardens, and state that these will be completed to a satisfactory standard – again with no deadline.

NHBC cover

If the property is to have the benefit of NHBC cover this will be stated in the contract and a contractual obligation imposed that the necessary documentation will be available on completion.

Note

It is unlikely that any house on an estate will be easily marketable without this cover.

Form of transfer

Because of the need for conformity between the houses on an estate, the seller's solicitor would normally draft the conveyance or transfer to be used on the sale of each house, and this would be annexed to the contract. The contract would then provide, by way of special condition, that upon completion the buyer would accept a transfer in the form of the conveyance or Land Registry transfer annexed to the contract. Thus, any negotiation to be carried out in relation to the contents of the conveyance or transfer (the purchase deed) takes place at the pre-contract stage.

Note

Most solicitors acting for sellers of houses on estates are unwilling to accept variations to the standard form of transfer and make this clear when sending out preliminary documentation to the buyer's solicitor.

20.2.3 Transfer

As the sale will be a sale of part transaction, the contract and purchase deed will almost certainly need to contain new *easements* (both granted and reserved) and new *covenants*.

You must give careful consideration to the requirements of each house on the estate, and the estate as a whole, to ensure that each property is granted:

- The easements it requires over neighbouring properties;
- That those neighbouring properties have reserved to them the easements they require over their neighbouring properties; and
- That the character of the estate is preserved by the imposition of certain covenants, eg. leaving the front gardens open plan.

Once the estate is fully sold the seller will not retain any land which is to have the benefit of the covenants given by purchasers of the individual properties and it is therefore common to find the benefit of these covenants being made to run with the land through the mechanism of a building scheme. This enables the owners of each plot on the estate to enforce restrictive covenants imposed on their neighbours.

On the practicalities of drafting a transfer for the sale of a house on an estate, it is normal that the transfer would refer to the house or plot number only as the property being sold. The rights being granted and reserved and the covenants being imposed would be contained in schedules to the transfer. This is merely the standard method of drafting such documents, commonly used but not obligatory.

What is *essential* is that you consider these points and that they are covered, specifically, in the contract and purchase deed.

Documents provided with the contract   20.2.4

With the contract, you will normally send a large bundle of documents containing other information concerning the property to be sold, analogous to the documentation sent out under the transaction scheme, with the aim of putting the buyers in a position to exchange contracts at an early stage.

A property information form will be sent, and possibly also the result of the local search (local land charges search and enquiries of the local authority).

If the property is already constructed and has the benefit of an NHBC documentation, this too will be forwarded.

Roads and drainage

On most estates, almost the last thing to be completed will be the roads. This applies to a lesser extent to the drains. No one buying a house on the estate will want to have their property abutting a private road. While it remains private, they will be liable for its upkeep.

Note

Liability to contribute is based on the *frontage* of the property abutting the road, not on the size of the plot!

If the local authority decides to 'adopt' the road as a public highway, ie. bring it up to their required standards and maintain it thereafter at the public expense, all properties abutting that road will have to contribute towards the cost – which can run into thousands of pounds. The decision on whether or not to adopt a private road is made by the local authority, sometimes against the wishes of the property owners. Thus, it is better to have the estate roads adopted at the outset to avoid cost of this kind later. However, until the roads are completed, no local authority will adopt them.

Buyers therefore need to be protected against the possibility that the roads will not be completed, and this is done by a combination of two documents.

1 An *agreement* under s.38, Highways Act 1980 entered into by the local authority and the builder under which the builder agrees that they will construct the roads, pavements, street lighting, etc to the standards required by the local authority. The local authority, for their part, agree that once this has been done they will adopt the roads and thereafter maintain them at the public expense.

2 A *bond* supporting the agreement between the builder and the local authority. This is to cover the position that might arise if the builder was to become insolvent and therefore become unable to complete their part of the agree-

ment. The parties to such a bond are the builder, the local authority and, normally, a bank. In the bond the bank states that if circumstances arise whereby the builders are unable to complete the roadways to the required standards, it will provide finance to enable either the local authority or another construction body to complete the works. This finance will have a fixed upper limit.

When both these documents are in place, a buyer can be assured that the road outside their house will eventually become an adopted road, at no expense to them.

Exactly the same principles apply to *drainage to a main sewer* under s.104, Water Industry Act 1991 and agreements and bonds also need to be seen in respect of these.

> *Note*
>
> In order to be able to provide these to a buyer's solicitor, the seller will need to have negotiated and put in place these agreements and bonds at an early date in the preparation for selling the estate, ideally long before buyers are sought.

20.3   Buyer

On receipt of the substantial bundle of documents forwarded by the seller's solicitor, you will need to consider in detail both the contract and transfer.

20.3.1   Contract

The normal contract terms, eg. parties, price, etc, need checking as do any special conditions dealing with faulty title. These are dealt with in the same way as on an ordinary freehold sale. In addition, the detailed terms of the contract dealing specifically with the problems of a house on an estate, need to be considered. For example:

- Are the terms dealing with construction of the property adequate?
- Although no specific deadline for completing the building work will be given, are the sellers at least obliged to construct the property within a reasonable time?
- Are the other terms relating to completion of the estate in general – roads, landscaping, etc – adequate and reasonable?
- Do they meet your client's requirements/expectations?

20.3.2   Transfer

The *easements* granted and reserved in the transfer and the *covenants* imposed all need to be carefully considered to see that they give the buyer adequate protection and impose nothing too onerous.

Note —————————————————————————————

As the transfer is to be incorporated in the contract, there will be no opportunity for varying it once contracts have been exchanged, so this is the stage at which you need to negotiate its form and content.

Searches and enquiries   20.3.3

The information given on the *property information* form needs to be carefully looked at and all the *supporting documentation* on such matters as NHBC, road and drainage agreements, planning permission and building regulation consents, carefully read.

Note —————————————————————————————

The mere fact of their existence does not mean that they are adequate for your client's requirements. They all have to be checked to ensure that they do provide the cover needed.

You may also wish to consider submitting *additional enquiries* to the seller's solicitor relating specifically to properties on the estate, eg. when it is anticipated the roads will be finished, perhaps on the likely provision of public transport and/or shops on the estate; the list can become extensive.

If a *local search* has been provided by the seller's solicitor this will need to be checked, eg. how old is it? If no such search has been provided, you will need to carry out this search and ensure the result is satisfactory before exchange of contracts.

Other searches may be appropriate to the property being purchased. You will need to make these unless they have been provided as part of the pre-exchange package by the seller's solicitor. Examples are *mining* and *commons registration searches*, and a *public index map search* if the title being deduced is unregistered.

Title will normally have been deduced at the pre-contract stage in estate conveyancing. Whatever title has been deduced will need to be investigated in the usual way and any requisitions arising out of this investigation made at this stage.

Exchange and after   20.3.4

Once both seller and buyer are satisfied with the form of the contract (incorporating the transfer), and the buyer's solicitor is satisfied with the results of all searches and enquiries, and the buyer has the necessary mortgage offer (if required), exchange can take place. This occurs in precisely the same way as an exchange on a normal freehold sale.

Where the property being purchased is still in the course of construction, there is likely to be a considerable time between exchange of contracts and completion. In such circumstances, the buyer's solicitor must consider protecting the contract. The contract constitutes an *estate contract* which can be protected by the registration of a C(iv) *land charge* (where seller's title is unregistered) or a *notice* or *caution* against the seller's title (where it is registered).

20.3.5   Completion and post-completion

If the house is finished at the time of exchange of contracts, the contract will have provided for a fixed completion date and completion will take place in the normal way.

If the house is still being built, completion will take place once the buyer has been served with notice that it has been finished. Once this notice has been served, the buyer's solicitor will need to carry out the normal pre-completion searches, obtain any required advance cheque from the mortgagee, and notify the client of the completion date which has now become fixed. Completion will then take place in the same way as a normal freehold purchase.

After completion, the buyer's solicitor will need to take the same steps to protect the buyer's (and the mortgagee's) interest as on the purchase of part of land (*see* Chapter 19, para. 19.2.6).

The only additional point to consider is that if the seller's title is registered, their certificate of title will need to be deposited at the Land Registry so that a note of this sale of part of that land can be made against it. The sellers will have deposited their title and received a deposit number from the Land Registry which will need to be quoted in the buyer's application for registration. The contract will have provided for this (*see* above 20.2.2).

Self-assessment questions

1 What is Form 102, and what function does it perform?

2 Make a list of the documents you would expect to send out to a prospective buyer's solicitor with the contract.

3 What post-completion steps are necessary if the land is:

   (a) registered;

   (b) unregistered?

4 Look at the standard Property Information Form and
   consider what additional information a client might
   want if buying on a new estate. Draft appropriate enquiries and then consider how you would view them if
   you were acting for the builder/seller.

Chapter 21

Leasehold conveyancing

Introduction

When purchasing or selling a long residential lease the *similarities* between leasehold and freehold conveyancing exceed the differences: the 'Transaction' scheme can still apply; the same searches and enquiries need to be made before exchange (with the addition of some extra enquiries relating specifically to the leasehold nature of the property); instructions need to be taken; and the client kept informed. This and the following chapters will therefore emphasise the areas where leasehold conveyancing *differs* from freehold. Where no mention is made of any difference, you can assume that the procedure will be exactly the same as in a freehold transaction.

> *Note*
>
> A solicitor will *not* normally act for both tenant and landlord in a transaction, as such a situation is governed by Solicitors' Practice Rules 6(1) and 6(2). Acting for a tenant and a mortgagee is treated in the same way as acting for buyer and mortgagee in a freehold transaction.

Advantages of selling leasehold

In spite of what has been said above, leasehold conveyancing is still more complex than freehold conveyancing. As complexity normally increases cost, which most people seek to avoid, there must be good reasons for deciding to opt for selling a lease. The common advantages are as follows.,

Rent

A lease will contain an obligation on the tenant to pay rent to the landlord throughout the term of the lease, in addition to the capital sum (premium) which is paid when the lease is granted. In a long residential lease, however, this rent (called the 'ground rent') is usually an insignificant or nominal sum in relation to the other outgoings the property will have. Receiving this relatively small sum is not likely to be the deciding factor in considering whether or not to sell a lease.

Continuing interest

The landlord will remain the owner of the superior title. 'Superior title' is the title above the lease being sold. Commonly this is the freehold title, and this manual will treat all leases as if they had been granted by the freeholder (or, to use another phrase often found, 'out of the freehold title').

You need to be aware, however, that superior title may be more than just the freehold, for example, the lease being granted may be granted out of a head lease, which has itself been granted out of the freehold. Superior title in this case would be that head lease and the freehold, ie. superior title will encompass all preceding titles back to and including the freehold. (*See* Figure 21.1 for an example of how this might work in practice.)

When the fixed term of a lease comes to an end, the landlord will be able to sell the freehold, free of the lease, or grant another lease out of that freehold. Ownership of this superior title is called ownership of the *reversion*. A landlord therefore has a continuing interest in the property by virtue

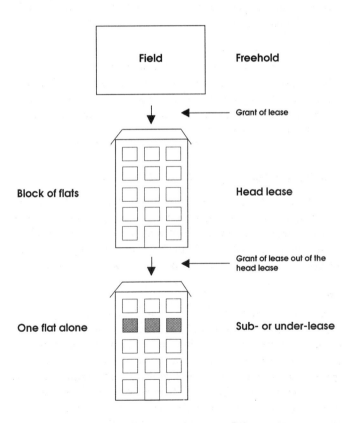

Superior title to the block of flats is the freehold. Superior title to the flat will be the head lease (of the whole block, built on the original field) *and* the freehold. Title to the flat will be the sub- or under-lease of that one flat.

Figure 21.1

of this ownership. The reversion is worth something, and can itself be sold. Any sale of the freehold reversion will, of course, be subject to the existing lease and the value of the reversion will depend on the terms of the lease, eg. on how long the lease has left to run and therefore when the freehold reversion will fall into possession.

Enforcing covenants

21.2.3

Perhaps the most important reason for granting a lease rather than selling the freehold lies in the area of enforceability of covenants. Where property is sold leasehold, the burden of both positive and restrictive covenants can be made to run with the lease and/or the reversion. For this to be effective, the covenants must *touch and concern the land*, and there must be *privity of estate* between the party in breach and the party seeking to enforce, in other words the parties should be within a *landlord and tenant relationship*.

The burden of *positive* covenants cannot be made to run with the land in freehold conveyancing, except in extremely limited circumstances, so the sale of the property by means of a lease enables a seller who wishes to be able to impose positive covenants against successors in title to the original purchaser to do so easily. This is a great advantage for such sellers. In addition, the sanctions against any tenant breaching such a covenant are greater than the penalties incurred by breach of a freehold covenant (*see* para. 21.4.9).

The grant of a long lease of a house

21.3

When you are instructed to sell a property by means of a long lease rather than by selling the freehold you need to consider certain preliminary matters.

Taking instructions

21.3.1

Detailed instructions will be needed from the client on exactly what the lease is to contain.

How *long* a lease is to be granted? It would be unusual for a residential long lease to be less than 99 years. Such leases are therefore normally granted for this length or longer. The *rent* which is to be paid has to be decided, and whether or not any restriction is to be put upon the *use* of the property, eg. is its use to be strictly limited to residential purposes?

Note

Your client may need guidance on what is and what is not acceptable in a lease if it is to be saleable and part of your job is to give this guidance.

21.3.2   Investigating title

The seller's title will need to be investigated by the seller's solicitor. The title may contain restrictions which would impede the granting of the lease which is being contemplated, and if this is the case the mode of sale will need re-thinking or the restriction will need removal (*see* Chapter 9, para. 9.6.4).

Further, any prudent buyer of the lease will want to have the sellers title fully deduced, and it is important for the seller's solicitor to know that this can be done. Any flaws in the seller's title must be dealt with in the contract of sale in the same way as in freehold sales (*see* Chapter 8).

21.3.3   Mortgagee's consent

If the seller/landlord's title is mortgaged, then it is almost certain that the mortgage terms will require that the mortgagee gives consent before any lease is granted out of the title over which they hold a mortgage. This is because the granting of a long lease severely diminishes the value of the reversion, which is of course the mortgagee's security.

21.4   Drafting the lease

This is carried out by the landlord's solicitor and submitted to the proposed tenant's solicitor for approval. Only after all its terms have been approved can it be used.

Much of the contents of a lease corresponds closely with the contents of a conveyance of unregistered freehold land but it is not, of course, the same thing. Leases normally contain the following clauses.

21.4.1   Commencement, date and parties

These will be the same as for a conveyance, save that the wording will be 'a Lease dated ... ' and not 'a Conveyance dated ... '.

21.4.2   Payment of premium and receipt

This is analogous to the consideration and receipt clause in a conveyance.

21.4.3   Operative words

These will read 'hereby leases' instead of the words 'hereby conveys' which you would find in a conveyance.

21.4.4   Parcels

This will be the description of the property, including any easements which it is intended will benefit the property, or which will be reserved by the landlord to benefit adjoining property.

Term   21.4.5

This clause will state the length of the lease and when the lease is to commence. Note that this may be the date the lease is executed, or another date, for example one of the usual 'quarter days' (25 December, 25 March, 24 June, 29 September).

Rent   21.4.6

The rent payable will be stated in this clause, with details of when it should be paid and whether that payment is to be in advance or in arrears. There may also be provision for the rent to be increased in the future, either by a fixed amount or by review procedures which will take into account prevailing market trends.

Express covenants   21.4.7

There are a number of express covenants contained in *most* leases. They are both positive and negative.

To pay rent

The first of these is the covenant to pay rent. This is not the same thing as the last 'rent clause', which just states what should be paid and when. This clause *imposes an obligation* on the tenant to pay. It will be binding even if the landlord is in breach of repairing obligations under the lease and it is not unusual to see the obligation to pay rent continuing even if the premises are damaged or destroyed. To avoid paying rent in the latter circumstance the lease will need to contain a clause suspending rent at such times. It is also common for rent to be payable whether demanded or not.

To repair

A lease will also include a covenant to repair. Either the landlord or the tenant must be responsible for the good repair of the property, and the lease will specify which of them it is.

The *exception* to the rule that this is a matter for the parties to the lease to agree at its outset is the case of a lease of a dwelling for less than seven years. Here ss.11–14, Landlord and Tenant Act 1985 provide that certain items (structure, exterior, gas water electricity and sanitary installations and space and water heating) cannot be made the tenant's responsibility. The landlord therefore has to maintain and repair these items in property let on such a lease, unless the permission of the court has been granted to opt the lease out of the Act. (Both parties need to apply for such permission before the lease starts.)

Prohibitive covenants

Covenants which are effectively prohibitions are often found in leases. They take the form of 'absolute' or 'qualified' prohibitions. The former will say, for example 'not to make any alterations or improvements to the property'. The latter will say, for example 'not to use the property other than as a private residence *without the landlord's consent'*.

As a general rule, a *qualified prohibition* imposes an obligation on the landlord not to unreasonably withhold consent. This is provided by the Landlord and Tenant Act 1927. Some leases specifically state the landlord has such an obligation but even those Leases which do not so state will have that obligation imposed on the landlord by this statute.

Not to make alterations or improvements This is often present to protect the landlord's ongoing interest in the property. It can be an absolute or qualified prohibition. If it is qualified s.19(2), Landlord and Tenant Act 1927 provides that the landlord's consent cannot be unreasonably withheld.

Covenant restricting user This Covenant is another ensuring that landlords are able to protect their security by restricting the use to which a property is put. Such a covenant can again be either an absolute prohibition against a change from a specified use of the property, or a qualified prohibition. Unlike a covenant not to make alterations or improvements, s.19(3), Landlord and Tenant Act 1927 applies to such covenants if they are qualified and in this case there is *no* implied proviso that consent is not to be unreasonably withheld. In other words the landlord can withhold consent to change of use for any reason whatsoever. The landlord cannot, however, ask to be paid for granting consent. (This is an exception to the general rule.)

Insurance

The property must be insured and the lease must state who is to insure it to avoid the possibilities of the property being doubly insured, or left uninsured.

The landlord may want to insure the property and recover the premiums from the tenants. In this case the tenant's interest will need to be recorded on the policy. Alternatively, it may be made the tenant's obligation to insure. The landlord may then stipulate the terms of such insurance, and even require such insurance to be taken out through the landlord's agency.

Notice of dealings to landlord

Because of the continuing interest the landlord has in the property which is being let, most landlords require to be given notice of any change of ownership or mortgaging of the leased property. A lease requiring new tenants/mortgagees to notify the landlord of these dealings is usually accompanied by the requirement to pay a fee to the landlord for registering such notices in their own records.

Quiet enjoyment

This ensures the tenant has full use of the leased property without interference from the landlord (except as maybe provided for in the lease, for example access for repairs).

Covenant not to assign or underlet

21.4.8

Such a covenant would prevent the lease being sold to anyone else, or another lease being granted out of it and would therefore mean that in practice ownership of the property could never pass from the original tenant. Clearly this would be unacceptable in a long lease of residential property and a general bar against assignment or underletting is very unusual in the long lease of a house or flat. You would not accept the grant of a long lease containing such a covenant.

What is more likely is a qualified prohibition against assignment or underletting. A qualified prohibition against assignment is also rare in residential leases, although a prohibition against underletting part of the property is very common in order to avoid residential properties being split further.

Where there is such a qualified covenant, the following statutory provisions apply:

Requesting payment for consent

The landlord cannot request payment for giving consent: s.144, Law of Property Act 1925.

Withholding or delaying consent

Consent cannot be unreasonably withheld: s.19(1), Landlord and Tenant Act 1927. Here thought needs to be given as to what might be unreasonable withholding of consent. It is likely to be unreasonable if the grounds given for refusal do not affect the landlord and tenant relationship. The most common reasonable grounds for refusal is where a proposed new tenant is unable to provide good references.

If a tenant is refused the right to assign a lease on what they consider to be unreasonable grounds, ie. grounds which do not affect the landlord and tenant relationship, they have a number of options.

- They can *apply to the court* for a declaration that the withholding of consent was unreasonable. If this is granted then the assignment can proceed irrespective of any continued opposition from the landlord.

- They may be entitled to *damages* under Landlord and Tenant Act 1988, which places a statutory duty on a landlord to provide either consent to assignment or reasons for refusal of consent to a tenant within a reasonable time of consent being requested. Breach of this duty may cause the tenant loss, eg. the tenant loses the person interested in taking an assignment, and this loss makes the landlord liable to the tenant for damages.

21.4.9   Forfeiture (or re-entry)

This is a very effective weapon against tenants who breach covenants. When a lease is forfeited it ceases to exist.

Note

No such clause is implied by law. Thus, for a landlord to have the right to forfeit, the right must be expressly reserved in the lease.

Business leases often contain a clause whereby the lease is forfeited if the tenant becomes insolvent (known somewhat inaccurately as a 'forfeiture for bankruptcy' clause). Any such clause in a *residential lease* is *absolutely unacceptable*. This is because of its effect on mortgageability, a vital requirement for residential property. A lender takes a mortgage over the leasehold title as security. If that title disappears because the lease ends due to forfeiture, their security also disappears. If it disappears due to the insolvency of the tenant, then the cause of their loss of security is the very situation they tried to protect themselves against by taking security (in the form of a mortgage) in the first place.

A forfeiture for bankruptcy clause in a residential lease would therefore make the property almost unmarketable as most buyers need a mortgage to fund their purchase. If it could be sold it would be for a very low price.

Forfeiture can also be a landlord's remedy for breach of other tenant's covenants, eg. paying rent or repairing.

It is possible for the court to grant a tenant relief against forfeiture, but details of how and when this may apply are beyond the scope of this companion.

21.4.10   Certificate of value

Ad valorem stamp duty is payable on the premium paid for the grant of a new lease in just the same way as it is payable on the consideration shown in a conveyance or transfer of freehold land. This can only be avoided if the premium is less than the stamp duty limit (currently £60,000) and the lease contains a certificate of value, which in the case of a lease reads as follows:

It is hereby certified that the transaction hereby effected does not form part of a larger transaction or of a series of transactions in respect of which the amount or value or the aggregate amount or value of the consideration other than rent exceeds £60,000.

Stamp duty is also payable on the rent, whatever the premium paid. This is based on the length of the term and the amount of the rent and is calculated with the use of tables provided by the Inland Revenue. Stamp duty on the rent element of a lease is *only* paid upon the grant of the lease. When a lease is subsequently assigned stamp duty is simply paid on the sum shown as being paid for the assignment.

Production to the Inland Revenue   21.4.11

Leases for more than seven years need to be produced to the Inland Revenue (PD'd).

Self-assessment questions

1   Once a lease has been granted, what, if anything, does a landlord have left to sell?

2   State two circumstances which would lead you to advise a client to sell a lease rather than the freehold of their property.

3   By what means, if any, can a landlord prevent a tenant changing:

   (a) the external appearance;

   (b) the internal layout;

   (c) the use of the property?

4   List the clauses you would find unacceptable in a lease of residential property.

Chapter 22

Grant of a long lease

The draft contract

The contract is drafted by the landlord's solicitor and will often use the agreement incorporating the Standard Conditions of Sale (Second Edition) discussed in Chapter 7. Incorporated into the contract will be the draft lease (as agreed between the parties) and a condition of the contract will state that upon completion a lease in the form annexed to the contract will be granted to the buyer.

The contract will be completed as follows:

- *Agreement date:* inserted on exchange.
- *Seller and buyer.*
- *Property:* a description of the property being sold, eg. 15 Acacia Avenue, ... , *and* details of the lease, eg. 'upon completion the buyer will be granted by the seller a lease for x years at a yearly rent of £y the lease to take the form of the draft lease annexed to this contract'.
- *Root of title/title number:* will relate to the seller's title.
- *Incumbrances:* this will state any incumbrances on the seller's title (as if that title was being sold) 'together with those contained in the draft lease annexed'.

The other clauses in the contract will be completed in the same way as if the property to be sold was freehold.

Deducing title

A prudent buyer/tenant will want to see that the seller/landlord has good title to the freehold out of which the lease is to be granted. What has to be deduced to a buyer/tenant depends upon whether the landlord's title is registered or unregistered and whether the open contract rules or the Standard Conditions of Sale are being applied.

If a lease is to be granted for more than 21 years, the leasehold title will need to be registered following completion of the purchase and, in order to obtain absolute leasehold title, the tenant will need to satisfy the Registrar on all superior titles. The tenant must therefore be able to prove the landlord's superior title in exactly the same detail as if *that* title itself were being registered.

Types of registered leasehold title

As *absolute leasehold title* is the only readily saleable form of leasehold title. Therefore a purchaser will want to ensure that the contract provides for sufficient title to be deduced by the landlord to enable the property to be registered with title absolute.

There are two specific problems with good leasehold title:

- There is no guarantee that the lease has been validly granted;
- The leasehold title will be subject to all incumbrances contained on the freehold title although the tenant will not know about them if the freehold title has not been deduced in full.

If the Registrar cannot be satisfied on all superior titles then only *good leasehold titles* can be granted to the buyer/tenant. Although such a title is not totally unmortgageable, it is not very acceptable as security and it is therefore more difficult to find a lender prepared to take a charge over it. This severely affects the marketability of the property.

Where the superior title is unregistered
The open contract rule. Under an open contract the landlord is not obliged to deduce title to the freehold at all: s.44(2), Law of Property Act 1925.

Because of the need for registration following completion, no sensible buyer, or their solicitor, would accept this, especially if they are paying a substantial premium to buy the lease. The contract must therefore contain a clause requiring the seller to deduce *all* superior titles.

Standard Condition 8.2.4. This provides that where a new lease of over 21 years is being granted, ie. one requiring registration following completion, title must be deduced to a buyer to enable them to register their new title with absolute leasehold title. Even if the standard conditions of sale are not being used, such a clause should be incorporated in any contract where a lease of more than 21 years is being granted, in order to protect the buyer's position, and ensure the future saleability of the lease.

Where the superior title is registered
The open contract rule. Section 110, Land Registration Act 1925 does not apply to the granting of a lease and a buyer therefore has no right to see copies of the landlord's title. However, now that the register of titles is open to public inspection, there is nothing to prevent a buyer/tenant obtaining office copies of the seller's title for themselves.

Standard condition 8.2.4 (see above). This applies equally to the grant of a lease out of registered title.

Where a lease for more than 21 years is being granted out of registered title, it will be registered with its own title number following completion. Nevertheless, a note will still need to be made of the grant of the lease against the landlord's freehold title and, in order for this to be done, the landlord will need to deposit their Land Certificate with the Land Registry.

It must be a condition of the contract that the landlord will do this, and supply the deposit number – which will be given to the landlord by the Land Registry once the Certificate is deposited – to the buyer so that this number can be incorporated in the buyer's application to register the lease.

In the same way that the seller of a freehold must disclose incumbrances affecting the title when a freehold is sold, the seller when granting a lease must disclose in the contract any such incumbrances affecting the freehold.

Consideration of the draft contract   22.1.2

The buyer/tenant's solicitor will need to ensure that the lease which is to be granted, and registered following completion, will provide a good and marketable title, both for the buyer and their mortgagee, if any. The same attention must be paid to matters such as deposit, rate of interest, time for completion, etc in a sale of a lease as would be given to freehold sale contract.

Because this sale is more complex, special attention will therefore need to be paid to other items such as the title to be deduced. If for any reason, SC 8.2.4 has been excluded from the contract, or if the contract is governed by the open contract rules, this will be because the landlord either *cannot*, or *will not*, deduce sufficient title to the buyer to enable them to register with absolute leasehold title following completion.

Because of the short-comings of good leasehold title, the buyer's solicitor should make every effort to ensure that the contract contains an obligation on the landlord to deduce all superior title, ie. a clause such as SC 8.2.4.

Note

If this cannot be achieved, then both the buyer and their mortgagee (if any) must be informed that only good leasehold title will be granted on completion, and the consequences to them of this. Your advice is likely to be that the sale should not proceed, but the decision will be theirs.

As the draft lease will form part of the contract, obviously the terms and conditions of it will need to be considered too (*see* Chapter 21). Once contracts have been exchanged, no amendments will be possible.

22.1.3   Insurance arrangements

As discussed in Chapter 21, the lease will make provision for the property to be insured. Anyone lending money on the security of this new lease will also want to see that the insurance arrangements are adequate, and some mortgagees require that insurance be effected through their own agency. This may be in direct conflict with the proposed terms of the lease if it provides for the landlord to insure and some negotiating will need to be done to ensure that these conflicting interests are resolved before contracts can be exchanged, ie. either the landlord or the mortgagee must give way.

22.1.4   Mortgagee's consent

Where the landlord's title is mortgaged, the mortgagee's consent will almost certainly be needed before a lease can be granted (*see* Chapter 21, para. 21.2.3).

The contract will therefore need to contain a special condition requiring the seller/landlord to obtain this consent and, on completion, to provide evidence that this has been done.

22.2   Exchanging contracts and investigating title

22.2.1   Preparing for exchange: the buyer

The same points arise here as apply in a freehold purchase (*see* Chapter 10).

- The draft contract (incorporating the draft lease) must be approved.
- All usual pre-contract searches and enquiries must have been returned, and their results satisfactory.
- If the seller/landlord's title has been deduced at this sage, then a full investigation of it must have been made to your satisfaction.
- Your client must have their finance arranged in full to enable them to complete the transaction on the proposed date.

22.2.2   Buyer and seller

Both parties need to sign the contract before exchange and you must inform your client of its significance and terms (*see* Chapter 10, where the points detailed apply equally here).

Methods of exchange are exactly the same as for a sale of freehold property (*see* Chapter 10, para. 10.2).

Investigating title

This may be done before or after exchange, as in freehold conveyancing. It is even more common, however, in sales of leases for title to be deduced and investigated *before* exchange.

Just as the seller/landlord's solicitor will need to deduce title to the freehold as if the freehold itself were being sold, the buyer/tenant's solicitor will need to investigate that title accordingly. The same rules will therefore apply to investigating title in this situation as apply when purchasing the freehold (*see* Chapter 14).

This assumes that SC 8.2.4 (or similar) is applied and that the landlord is deducing title sufficient to enable the buyer to register with absolute leasehold title following completion. If any lesser title is being deduced, then the buyer's solicitor will have to apply the same rules for investigating title to whatever documentary evidence the landlord has provided.

Preparing for completion

Engrossing the lease

A perfect version of the agreed form of the lease is prepared in duplicate. (This is known as engrossing the lease.) It will take exactly the same form as the draft which was previously agreed and annexed to the contract.

It will be prepared by the seller's solicitor, which is the opposite of the situation in freehold, where the buyer's solicitor prepares the transfer/conveyance.

If the Standard Conditions are being used SC 8.2.6 deals with the time limit for engrossing and delivery of the lease to the buyer – at least five working days before the completion date.

The two copies of the lease are called the lease and counter-part.

Execution

Both lease and counter-part have to be executed as *deeds*. The lease is executed by the landlord/seller and the counter-part by the tenant/buyer. The same rules apply to their execution as apply to the execution of a transfer or conveyance of a freehold title.

Following their execution both lease and counter-part can be delivered to the other party in escrow, in the same way as deeds can be delivered in escrow in freehold conveyancing.

Note ——————————————————————

In practice it is rare for the lease but more common for the counter-part to be delivered in this way.

22.3.3   Pre-completion searches

The buyer/tenant's solicitor will need to carry out pre-completion searches.

Whether the title being deduced is registered or unregistered, pre-completion inspection of the property is always advisable for the same reasons as one would carry out an inspection in freehold conveyancing.

Unregistered titles

Where the title is unregistered the buyer's solicitor will need to carry out land charges searches against the estate owners of the superior title. Land charges searches must therefore be carried out against the landlord and all previous estate owners of the freehold, for the period of their ownership, unless satisfactory searches against their names have already been provided.

Registered titles

If the lease is being granted out of a registered title then the usual Form 94A land registry search must be carried out against the superior title. This is done on behalf of the buyer if no new mortgage is involved, or on behalf of their prospective mortgagee where the purchase of the lease will be with the aid of mortgage finance.

Again, there is no difference between the situation here and that in freehold conveyancing as regards the searches and method of searching undertaken.

22.4   Completion

22.4.1   Documents

The lease and counter-part are *exchanged* so that each party has an identical copy of the lease, executed by the other. The tenant holds the original lease and the landlord holds the counter-part, which they retain for their own records.

If the freehold title is *unregistered*, the buyer/tenant's solicitor will need to see all the original documents of title and mark the abstract or epitome as having been so examined in the same way and for the same reasons as apply to a sale of part (*see* Chapter 19, para. 19.3.5).

If the freehold title is *registered* the tenant should receive the deposit number of the landlord's certificate of title at the

Land Registry. If this is not available at completion, an undertaking for it to be forwarded as soon as the deposit number is received from the Land Registry must be given in its place.

> *Note*
> _____
>
> The contract will need to have provided for the abstract of title or deposit number to be given.

The tenant must receive the consent of the landlord's mortgagee if the landlord's title is mortgaged and the mortgage terms require such consent.

Purchase monies   23.4.2

The landlord will receive the balance of the purchase money (premium), together with any apportioned ground rent if the ground rent is to be paid in advance.

> *Example*
> _____
>
> Consider a lease which requires ground rent of £100 per annum to be paid in advance on the usual quarter days; this will mean £25 being paid on each. Completion of the grant of the lease takes place on 30 June. Rent has to be paid for the period from 30 June to the next quarter day (29 September) which is 60 days. The rent per day is $100 \div 365 = 274 \times 60 = £16.44$. This sum is the apportioned ground rent payable on completion. (Other sums paid or payable in advance are apportioned by the same method.)

Post completion stages   22.5

Stamping   22.5.1

The lease itself will need to be stamped with *ad valorem* duty on the premium and on the rent (*see* Chapter 5). The counter-part lease needs to be stamped with a fixed duty of 50p and the landlord's solicitor will need to ensure that this is done. Leases for seven years or more also require PD stamping to show that a particulars delivered form has been completed.

Registration   22.5.2

If the term of the lease exceeds 21 years it will need to be registered under its own title number to comply with the provisions of the Land Registration Act 1925.

First registration
If the landlord's title is *unregistered*, the registration of this

lease will constitute a first registration and will therefore need to be applied for within two months of completion or the legal title which passed to the tenant when the lease was granted on completion will revert to the seller/landlord. This is the same principal as in freehold conveyancing.

Application to register will be made on Land Registry Form 2B and the following documents will need to be sent to the Land Registry:

- The original lease, duly stamped;
- A certified copy of the lease;
- Evidence of the freehold title – this will be a marked abstract of the freehold title;
- If the property has been mortgaged, the original mortgage duly executed and a certified copy of it;
- The fee.

Dispositionary lease

If the landlord's title is *registered* then this is not a first registration. It is a *disposition* of registered land and until the lease is registered the tenant will not have legal title.

The application for registration must be submitted within the priority period of the Land Registry search taken out against the landlord's title before completion, ie. within 30 working days of the search date, otherwise the tenant will be bound by any new entries that might be made against the freehold title. The application will be on Form 3B and must be accompanied by all the documents listed above save that evidence of title will take the form of the landlord's title number and the deposit of the certificate of that title.

The grant of the lease will also need to be noted against the landlord's title. This is done by the Land Registry when the application to register the new lease is dealt with. It can only be done if they receive the deposit number of the landlord's certificate of title. The note provides notice to any purchaser of the freehold title that a lease has been granted out of it and they therefore buy subject to it.

Note

A purchaser of the freehold title *may* be bound by the tenant's interest even if such a note has not been entered. This is because the tenant will have an overriding interest under s.70(1)(g), Land Registration Act 1925 if s/he is *in occupation* at the time of the freehold sale.

22.5.3   **Notice to landlord**

If the lease contains a clause requiring notice to be given to the landlord whenever the lease is mortgaged, notice of any new mortgage must be served on the landlord and any fee required under the lease paid.

The normal method used for this is for a notice in duplicate to be prepared by the tenant's solicitor and sent to the landlord or their solicitor (as the lease requires) in duplicate with a request that one copy of the notice be receipted and returned. This receipted duplicate is then kept with the deeds as evidence that this covenant in the lease has been complied with and the other copy is retained by the landlord as a record.

Custody of the deeds and documents   22.5.4

Once registration of the lease has been completed and the Land or Charge Certificate and the original lease have been returned to the tenant's solicitor, all the deeds and documents (the Land or Charge Certificate, lease and all other documents which will be needed in any sale, for example NHBC documentation, damp proof guarantees and the like) will need to be stored somewhere for safe keeping. If there is a mortgage they must be sent to the mortgagee.

If the property is not mortgaged, the client's instructions must be sought as to where they want them stored.

Self-assessment questions

1 What is the difference between residue and reversion?
2 What title does a seller have to deduce when granting a new lease using the standard conditions of sale?
3 What pre-completion searches are needed if the title from which the lease is granted is:

   (a) unregistered;

   (b) registered?
4 What post-completion steps are needed and what are the time limits for these? Is your answer the same whether the superior title is registered or unregistered? If not, in what respects does it differ?

Chapter 23

Special problems relating to flats

Introduction

A flat is normally one of a number of flats in a block or house. In such a situation each individual flat in the block will be the subject of a lease to a particular tenant but there will be parts of the block which are not included in any of the leases, eg. the staircase, the roof, the foundations, the garden, etc. Any part not let to a tenant as their flat will be included in what are called the 'common parts'. The responsibility for maintenance of these parts will not be vested in any individual tenant but will be the responsibility of the landlord. The cost of fulfilling this obligation is not, however, paid by the landlord. Instead, any maintenance expenditure will be reimbursed to the landlord by the tenants via the service charge.

In a block of flats you would expect to find that each lease is on identical terms except for the description of the flat itself and the parties to the lease. A flat lease will take the general form shown in Chapter 21. The extra matters which need to be dealt with in a flat lease are:

- Parcels;
- Easements;
- Tenant's covenants;
- Enforceability of covenants;
- Landlord's covenants;
- Management company;
- Insurance;
- Statutory provisions for service charge levying.

Parcels

Because of the need to know what has been leased to the tenant – and is therefore the tenant's responsibility – and what has been included in the common parts – and is therefore the landlord's responsibility – this clause needs to be particularly detailed and accurate. It will have a direct bearing on the extent of the repairing obligations of both the landlord and the tenant. It is also advisable to have a good plan incorporated in the lease, to assist in this accurate identification.

23.3   Easements

Careful thought needs to be given to the rights the flat owner will need for such things as access and the passage of services over neighbouring flats and the common parts. Also, your client may need the right to enter other flats in an emergency, eg. an overflowing washing machine, or in order to fulfil repairing obligations. These rights need to be specifically granted. It is almost certain that other flats in the block will need reciprocal rights over the flat being sold and these need to be specifically reserved. The landlord will need to reserve a right of access to carry out repairs either to the flat or the structure of the block. This right is usually subject to giving reasonable notice to the flat owner. In cases of emergency, the need to give notice is waived.

In addition to these rights, each flat will need to grant, and have reserved for it, rights of support and protection to and from all the other parts of the block.

23.4   Tenant's covenants

Leases always contain far more covenants than those imposed upon freehold owners. Some of these covenants will be *restrictive*, eg. against nuisance, display of advertisements, the keeping of pets, the carrying out of alterations, etc, but the tenant will also be bound by a number of *positive* covenants, eg. to repair and maintain the flat, to pay rent and service charges.

23.4.1   Enforceability of covenants

Each lease of a flat in a block will contain the same covenants but there is no privity of estate between the individual tenants. This can cause problems. A typical example would be where a lease contains an obligation not to keep pets but one of the flat owners is keeping a dog which is proving to be a nuisance to the others. Each flat owner knows that this constitutes a breach of the lease because all leases in the block contain the same prohibition but, without privity, they cannot take direct action against the neighbour with the troublesome dog.

There are two solutions to this problem, and any lease must contain one or the other or it will be unmortgageable. A lease must contain a clause allowing 'mutual enforceability of covenants' so that tenants have some way of forcing neighbouring tenants to abide by the covenants in their leases.

Enforcement by the landlord
The first method is for each lease of a flat in the block to contain

a clause requiring the landlord to enforce the covenants against recalcitrant tenants at the request of another tenant. This can be achieved because the landlord has privity of estate with each tenant and if the landlord were to refuse to take action when requested to do so, the landlord would be in breach of covenant to the tenant requesting action.

Such a clause is normally accompanied by a requirement for the requesting tenant to *indemnify* the landlord against any costs incurred by the landlord in such enforcement.

Letting scheme
The second method is to create a letting scheme (similar to a building scheme in freehold land) which enables covenants to be enforced between tenants without recourse to the landlord. This is less commonly found.

Landlord's covenants 23.5

The most important landlord's covenant will be to deal with the maintenance and repair of the common parts and structure.

If the landlord has decided when setting up the scheme of leases in the block to provide services, this covenant also needs to make it clear that the *landlord* is to provide services Examples of services might be, garden maintenance, cleaning and lighting of the common parts.

The landlord will also covenant for *quiet enjoyment* in the usual way.

If the method of dealing with the enforceability of covenants outlined in 23.4.1 above is adopted, the landlord will also covenant to require each tenant to observe the covenants contained in the lease of their property.

The landlord can include in the leases a right to employ managing agents to carry out the landlord's obligations, particularly with regard to repair, maintenance and services. The cost of employing agents in this way will form part of the service charge payable by the tenants.

Management company 23.6

A landlord will often not wish to retain any obligations concerning the block once the flats are all sold. They may be unwilling to be responsible for the common parts or any services to tenants. In this situation landlords often divest themselves of these responsibilities through a management company.

Under this system one of two things can happen:

- Three-party leases;
- The freehold is vested in the management company.

23.6.1   Three-party leases

The leases are drawn up in such a way that there are three parties to each of them: the landlord, the management company and the tenant. All the covenants which would normally impose obligations upon the landlord are instead entered into by the management company, and usually the only duty remaining on the landlord is that of receiving rent!

The tenants are often made the shareholders in the management company and thereby have a direct say in the maintenance of the block.

23.6.2   Freehold vested in the management company

In this situation the tenants are again the shareholders in the management company but the freehold of the block is vested in that company, not in the landlord, the landlord bowing out of the picture altogether. The result for the tenants is essentially the same; they have a direct say in the running of their block.

In either situation, where the tenants are shareholders in a management company, their share in the management company must be transferred to the new owner when a tenant sells their flat. This will be important where the management company is *limited by shares*. If it is *limited by guarantee* then there will be no share to be transferred. For this reason, management companies limited by guarantee are more popular.

23.7   Insurance

The usual problem of who should take out insurance on a leasehold property also arises in connection with blocks of flats. It is almost invariably the case that the entire building is covered by a 'block' policy, on which each tenant's interest is noted.

Any mortgagee of an individual flat will need to ensure that the insurance is adequate. They may be happy with the 'block' policy or may prefer to have their own separate insurance. The dangers of double insurance will need to be pointed out to those who choose the latter course and it is their solicitor's duty to do this.

23.8   Statutory provisions for service charges

It is a common complaint among flat owners that they do

not get a fair deal where services charges are concerned. This problem is particularly acute when major works are undertaken to a block, eg. painting the outside, general refurbishment, roof repairs, and the costs thereby imposed on the tenants are high. Tenants often feel they have too little control in these matters.

In an attempt to improve the situation, ss.18–30, Landlord and Tenant Act 1985 made special provisions to protect tenants.

Payment required in advance   23.8.1

It is not unusual for a landlord to set up a 'sinking fund' by which each tenant contributes (through their service charge payments) some money each year towards a fund which is not immediately expended on current maintenance. This fund builds up with the intention of it being used in the future to cover the expenses of major works, the cost of which, payable in one go, might be beyond the tenants' pockets.

If such sums are requested in advance by a landlord, under the Act the sums requested must be reasonable. For example, the request of a large sum payable in advance to cover the cost of future expenditure and maintenance would be unreasonable on a brand new block, where one would expect maintenance costs to be low for several years.

Payment for work already carried out   23.8.2

The Act provides that the work must have been completed to a satisfactory standard, or the tenant is not obliged to pay towards it.

Payment of large sums   23.8.3

Sometimes, there is no alternative to charging the tenants large sums for expensive work, eg. when no sinking fund has been maintained. The third provision deals with this.

Where such works will incur expenditure above a prescribed limit, the landlord must obtain *two estimates* for the work. The current prescribed limit is £25 multiplied by the number of flats in the building, or £500, whichever is the greater.

One of the estimates must be from someone unconnected with the landlord and each tenant is entitled to make observations to the landlord on the estimate, to which the landlord must then pay regard.

Further information   23.8.4

The last provision allows a tenant to ask for further service charge information, which they are entitled to receive from the landlord. They are also entitled to ask that it be certified by a qualified accountant unconnected with the landlord.

Self-assessment questions

1 Draft a parcels clause for a middle flat in a block of three (ground, 1st and 2nd floor).

2 What rights, eg. access, services, will that flat need over the other two flats and how many of them will need to be reciprocated? List them.

3 Why does a flat lease need mutual enforceability of covenants?

4 What are the alternative methods of ensuring that a block of flats is looked after satisfactorily? Which would you prefer if you were:

(a) a tenant;

(b) the landlord?

Chapter 24

The assignment of a registered lease

Introduction

24.1

Where title to leasehold property has been registered, the assignment of the lease is basically a sale of registered land. The steps to be taken in the transaction are, therefore, almost identical to the steps to be taken in purchasing freehold registered land. There are, however, some *extra* matters that need to be considered because the property is leasehold.

> *Note*
>
> Throughout this and the next chapter, this companion will refer to 'sellers' and 'buyers'. 'Seller' means the *assignor* of the lease and 'buyer' means the *assignee* of the lease.

If no mention is made of a particular stage of the freehold conveyancing process (for example pre-exchange searches), assume that the procedure for leasehold land is identical to the freehold procedure. In order, the stages are:

- Taking Instructions;
- Drafting the contract and deducing the title;
- Making pre-contract searches and enquiries;
- Approving the contract;
- Investigating title;
- Preparing the purchase deed;
- Preparing for completion;
- Making pre-completion searches;
- Completion;
- Post completion.

Taking instructions

24.2

Consent to assignment

24.2.1

The seller's solicitor will need to take additional instructions from their client because of the provisions of the lease.

The lease may contain a *qualified prohibition* against assignment, eg. the lease cannot be assigned without the consent in writing of the landlord. If so, the landlord's requirements regarding the information to be provided before they will give consent must be ascertained at the earliest possible stage and complied with.

Note

No money can be charged by the landlord for giving such consent although the landlord's legal fees are usually payable by the tenant.

The consent should be available before exchange of contracts as the standard conditions (SC 8.3) stipulates that where such consent is required by the lease the seller will use all reasonable efforts to obtain it by completion or rescission will be available to both parties. To exchange contracts in the hope that it will be forthcoming by that time would be foolhardy, and if all reasonable efforts have not been made the seller will be liable for breach of contract and for all reasonable damages.

24.2.2 Other documents

The following items will also have to be provided to the buyer's solicitor and therefore need to be obtained from the seller:

- A receipt for the last ground rent payable;
- Details of insurance covering the property;
- Details of the last three years service charge accounts (where payable and assuming the property is at least three years old).

If the client is unable to provide these from their own records, copies must be obtained from the landlord, or managing agent, or management company. As no prudent buyer will exchange contracts for the purchase of the property until all these items have been provided, it is important that they are collated at an early stage in the transaction. They must therefore be asked for when taking instructions.

24.3 Drafting the contract and deducing title

This is done by the *seller's solicitor*.

In addition to the usual description of the property being sold, the description will also need to make reference to the number of years unexpired on the lease (the residue of the term).

A copy of the lease will be sent to the buyer's solicitor with the draft contract.

Deducing title

Where title is registered, the rules are the same as in freehold conveyancing. The open contract rule relies upon s.110, Land Registration Act 1925 and the standard conditions of sale improve upon that section by requiring the provision of office copies as opposed to mere copies of the entries on the register. The reference to 'evidence of matters as to which the register is not conclusive' will mean the lease in this context.

Title may be registered with absolute, good leasehold or possessory leasehold title.

If the title is absolute, the only evidence of title a buyer can (or would want to) require are office copies of the entries on the register and the lease.

If the title is less than absolute, ie. good leasehold or possessory, neither the open contract rule nor the standard conditions of sale entitle the buyer to anything more than this. However, if a seller is in possession of any evidence of the superior title a buyer will certainly want to see it, in the hope that it may be sufficient to enable them to upgrade the title. In such cases the seller's solicitor has to think carefully about what superior title (if any) the seller can deduce and make it quite clear to the buyer by means of a special condition in the contract that this is all that will be available.

Making pre-contract searches and enquiries

The property information form contains additional enquiries relating specifically to leasehold properties. The buyer's solicitor will want to see that satisfactory replies have been given to all these and that documentary evidence that will support statements has been provided before contracts are exchanged, eg. regarding service charge amounts.

The lease may contain a qualified (or absolute) *prohibition* against additions or alterations to the property. If so, information should be sought by the buyer's solicitor on whether any additions or alterations have been made since the lease was granted and, if so, evidence of the landlord's consent will need to be shown by the seller.

Other searches and enquiries will be the same as those for a freehold purchase.

Approving the contract

The buyer's solicitor will need to consider all the terms of the contract, as in freehold conveyancing.

The terms of the lease will also need careful consideration.

When taking an assignment of an existing lease it is extremely *unlikely* that a buyer's solicitor will seek amendments to that lease. Amendments simply improving upon the general structure, wording, style, etc of a lease, once it has already been granted, are not necessary or appropriate – the lease may not be perfect in your opinion, but changing leases is rare.

Sometimes a lease must be changed, however, because it contains a wholly unacceptable clause. A good example is a *forfeiture for bankruptcy clause*. In such circumstances a *deed of variation* will be needed to alter the lease. This has to be agreed between the current tenant (the seller) and the landlord before exchange of contracts and executed by them before completion. The landlord may or may not agree to do this. If they do not, the buyer will probably not proceed with the purchase.

If the title is anything less than absolute, the buyer's solicitor may want to insist upon a special condition in the contract requiring the seller to deduce the *superior* title which can then be forwarded to the Registrar with an application for the title to be upgraded. No application for upgrading good leasehold title to absolute can be made without supplying sufficient evidence to satisfy the Registrar on all superior titles.

Whether or not a seller's solicitor is able to agree such a special condition will entirely depend upon the title evidence they have available. Even if a seller is unable to supply sufficient evidence of title to enable upgrading to take place, if they have any title evidence relating to the superior title, it is in the buyer's interest to inspect whatever title can be provided. Again, a special condition will need to be inserted into the contract to enable the buyer to do this.

If such evidence cannot be given then the client and any prospective mortgagee need to be warned of the implications of less than absolute title.

24.6 Investigating title

Where the title is absolute, the procedure is identical to that in freehold conveyancing.

Where the title is less than absolute, whatever superior title the seller is able to provide must be investigated in the same way as if that title itself were being purchased. For example, if the superior title were unregistered freehold, you would adopt the same procedure as if you were buying the unregistered freehold title and you would look at all the documents supplied and raise any necessary requisitions on them.

Preparing the purchase deed   24.7

This will be a Land Registry Form 19 (or Form 19 JP if there are joint purchasers). This is prepared in exactly the same way as in freehold conveyancing with one additional concern relating to SC 8.1.4 which reads:

The transfer is to record that no covenant implied by statute makes the seller liable to the buyer for any breach of the lease term about the condition of the property. This applies even if the seller is to transfer as beneficial owner.

This relates to the implied covenants for title (*see* Chapter 13, para. 13.4.2). Where someone conveys a lease as beneficial owner they impliedly covenant that the lease is valid and subsisting and that all the lessee's covenants in the lease have been complied with up to the time of the conveyance. The seller does not want to make any such implied promise as to compliance with the repairing obligations in the lease. The buyer is to take the property as they see it – *caveat emptor*. SC 8.1.4 is therefore inserted in order to negate the implied covenants for title.

Where the contract incorporates the standard conditions of sale the subsequent transfer to the buyer will need to contain a clause reflecting the provisions of SC 8.1.4.

Preparing for completion   24.8

In addition to the normal preparations for the sale of registered freehold land, there will be other things to consider.

Seller's solicitor   24.8.1

You will need to:

- Prepare a *completion statement* which takes account additionally of any apportionment of ground rent, service charges, etc which are payable on the property;
- Ensure that *receipts* for all sums claimed in that statement are available to be handed over on completion;
- Ensure the landlord's duly executed *consent* is available by completion, if this is needed.

Buyer's solicitor   24.8.2

The completion statement containing the apportionments needs to be carefully checked.

Making pre-completion searches   24.9

If the title is absolute the searches will be identical to those undertaken for freehold registered land.

If the title is less than absolute and any superior title has been deduced, searches will need to be carried out in relation to that title, ie. if it is registered – Land Registry searches, if it is unregistered – Land Charges searches against known estate owners for the period of their ownership.

24.10   Completion

24.10.I   What the buyer must receive

On completion the buyer must receive:

- *Land certificate* (or charge certificate if the property is mortgaged);
- If the property is mortgaged, *Form 53* (or a satisfactory undertaking in respect of the same and the handing over of a duly completed Form 53 at a later date);
- *Transfer*, duly executed;
- Original *lease*;
- Duplicate *notices of assignment* relating to past transactions, if appropriate.
- The original of the *ground rent receipt* (or, at the very least, be able to inspect it).

Note

When a landlord has issued a clear ground rent receipt, it raises the presumption that the landlord has accepted that all the covenants in the lease have been complied with: s.42(2), Law of Property Act 1925. This protects the buyer as far as possible against action by the landlord for forfeiture for non-compliance by the seller with leasehold covenants.

24.10.2   Other documents

In *some cases* the buyer must also receive:

- The *landlord's consent* – where the lease provides that this is required before it can be assigned. Evidence of consent takes the form of a duly executed *licence to assign*.
- Evidence of *service charge payments* where these are payable under the lease. Either the receipts must be handed over or the originals made available for inspection.
- Originals of whatever *superior title* has been deduced if the title is less than absolute. You must inspect and mark your abstract or epitome of that title as having been so examined.
- The *share certificate* and a *transfer* of the share if the property has the benefit of a share in a residents' company (if the company is limited by shares and not by guarantee).

Post completion   24.11

Transfer document   24.11.1

The transfer document will need to be stamped.

Note

It is the transfer document itself, not the lease, which is stamped in this way following an assignment of an existing lease.

If the original lease term is seven years or more, the transfer will also need to be stamped and therefore the PD form must be completed. If the price being paid for the property exceeds the *ad valorem* stamp duty limit (currently £60,000) then *ad valorem* stamp duty will need to be paid on that consideration at the rate of 1%.

Land Registry   24.11.2

As this is registered land, the dealing has to be submitted for registration in precisely the same way and using the same forms as if this were registered freehold. The lease itself is only submitted to the Land Registry when the lease is registered for the first time, and it will not need to be sent when the application is only to register a transfer of the lease.

Notice to the landlord   24.11.3

If the lease contains a clause requiring notice to be given to the landlord of any assignment (and/or mortgage), this must be done.

Custody of documents   24.11.4

Once the:

- *Registration* of the transaction has been completed at the Land Registry;
- The *land or charge certificate* has been checked by the buyer's solicitor; and
- The landlord has returned duplicates of the *notices* served in accordance with the terms of the lease;

these items, together with the:

- *Lease*; and
- All other *documents relating to the property* which will be needed on any future sale;

have to be held somewhere for *safe custody*.

If the property is not mortgaged, you need to take instructions from the client concerning the destination of the deeds. If it is mortgaged, the deeds are sent to the mortgagee.

Self-assessment questions

1   List the searches and enquiries you would make throughout the transaction if the title being sold were absolute.
2   What is a licence to assign and when would you need it?
3   Why is a ground rent receipt needed?
4   When is a notice of assignment given, and by whom?
5   What document is sent for stamping after completion and on what is *ad valorem* duty paid?

Chapter 25

The assignment of an unregistered lease

Introduction   25.1

The stages involved in the assignment of an unregistered lease are the same as those involved in the assignment of a registered lease:

- Taking Instructions;
- Drafting the contract and deducing the title;
- Making pre-contract searches and enquiries;
- Approving the contract;
- Investigating title;
- Preparing the purchase deed;
- Preparing for completion;
- Making pre-completion searches;
- Completion;
- Post completion.

Taking instructions   25.2

The instructions that the seller's solicitor takes from the client when selling unregistered leasehold are no different from the points that need to be considered where the title is already registered (*see* Chapter 24, para. 24.2).

Drafting the contract and deducing title   25.3

The contract is drafted by the seller's solicitor.

Particulars of the lease   25.3.1

Particulars of the lease, and reference to the number of years outstanding on it, are the same as in registered leasehold title.

Deducing title   25.3.2

The open contact rule

Conditions relating to what title has to be shown will be different where the title is unregistered.

The open contract rule, which is unaltered by the Standard Conditions of Sale, provides that if the title to the lease is unregistered, a buyer is entitled to see the lease itself and all assignments and other dispositions, eg. assents to beneficiaries, under which it has been held during the 15 years prior to the contract date. If the lease has not been in existence as long as 15 years, a buyer will be entitled to see all the assignments and other dispositions of the lease that have taken place. Under the open contract rule the buyer is not entitled to see any superior title.

If, as is very likely, the term still to run on the lease exceeds 21 years, the buyer will need to apply for *first registration* of the lease following completion. The buyer will want to register the lease with absolute leasehold title as anything inferior is considerably less marketable. In order to obtain absolute leasehold title the buyer will need to satisfy the Registrar on all superior title. It is clear, therefore, that the unaltered open contract rule will be *wholly unacceptable* to a buyer in this position.

Special conditions

For this reason, every buyer will want to see a special condition providing for *deduction of title* to enable them to register with absolute leasehold title. If a seller is able to deduce title in this way, the contract should be drafted with such a condition in it.

If, however, the seller is not in a position to deduce all *superior title* in this way, then this also should be made clear by a special condition in the contract, detailing what title (if any) the seller is able to deduce and making it clear that no further requisitions or objections will be allowed from the buyer on this point.

25.4   Making pre-contract searches and enquiries

These will be the same as where the lease is registered (*see* Chapter 24, para. 24.4) with the addition of a public index map search.

25.5   Approving the draft contract

The points which need to be considered here are the same as where the lease being sold is registered, with the exception of the conditions relating to deducing title (*see* para. 25.3.2).

A buyer will need to seek the best possible evidence of superior title which, in effect, means having deduced to the buyer the superior title in exactly the same way as if that title itself were being purchased. Anything less than this is likely to mean that the application for first registration will result in less than absolute title being granted.

If such title cannot be deduced and the grant of an inferior class of title is predictable, the client and any prospective mortgagee must be fully informed of the consequences of this.

Investigating title   25.6

Whatever title has been deduced to the buyer it will need to be investigated in exactly the same way as if it were that title itself being purchased. If the lease being purchased was granted out of the freehold, then the freehold title needs to be investigated using the same procedures as apply to the purchase of freehold land.

In addition, changes in ownership of the lease being purchased will need to be examined, again applying the same principles and procedures as those applying in freehold land.

If the lease being sold is not the first to have been granted out of the freehold, and has itself been granted out of a lease, then that 'superior' lease, and all changes in ownership of it for the past 15 years (if possible) will need to be investigated in the same way.

Note

The rules for investigating title and the principles you apply will be familiar, but the investigation will need to be more extensive in respect of unregistered leasehold land as there will be more 'levels' of title to be checked.

Preparing the purchase deed   25.7

This will take the form of a deed of assignment. The clauses to be contained in an assignment reflect very closely those contained in a conveyance with the following differences.

Recitals clause   25.7.1

The recitals clause will refer to the lease and the various assignments and other dispositions that have been made of it, tracing its history from the original grant of the lease to the present day. The fact that there has been an agreement between the parties for the sale of the lease will be recited and, if the lease requires a licence to assign from the landlord, this will also be stated in the recitals clause.

Habendum clause   25.7.2

The habendum clause will need to refer to the years still to run on the lease and state that the unexpired term will now vest in the buyer.

25.7.3   SC 8.1.4

A clause to implement SC 8.1.4 (if incorporated in the contract) will be needed in the transfer in exactly the same way as if the title were registered (*see* Chapter 24, para. 24.7).

25.7.4   Indemnity covenants

Section 77, Law of Property Act 1925 provides that on the assignment of a lease for value the assignee impliedly covenants to pay the rent, to observe and perform the covenants in the lease and to indemnify the assignor against non-observance or non-performance of those covenants.

Because of the effect of s.77, no specific indemnity covenants need to be stated in an assignment of a lease for value, but if the assignment is dealt with in any other way, eg. a gift, and the assignor requires these covenants, they will need to be specifically stated.

> *Note*
>
> In the transfer of a registered lease such a covenant is never necessary because s.24, LRA implies it whether value is given or not.

25.8   Preparing for completion

The same considerations apply here as where the title to the lease is unregistered (*see* Chapter 24, para. 24.8).

25.9   Making pre-completion searches

Central land charges searches will need to be made against the owner of the lease and, if they are different (for example, on a sale by a mortgagee), the seller and also against the landlord at the time of the sale. Land charges searches will also need to be made against previous owners of the lease whose names have been revealed during the deduction and investigation of title procedure for the period of their ownership.

Where the freehold title has been deduced, land charges searches will also need to be carried out against the names of previous estate owners of the freehold title for the period of their ownership.

Thus, the principles used to decide which names should be searched against are the same as in freehold conveyancing, but the searches are likely to be against considerably more names because the title being sold is leasehold.

Completion   25.10

What the buyer must receive   25.10.1
The buyer must receive:

- The *original lease*;
- All *assignments* and other dispositions of that lease;
- The *assignment in favour of the buyer*, duly executed;
- If the property is mortgaged, the *receipted mortgage deed* or a *satisfactory undertaking* to supply it later;
- Duplicate *notices of assignment* if the lease requires this;
- Where the superior title has been deduced, the buyer's solicitor must inspect the originals at completion and prepare a *marked abstract* of the superior title.
- The original of the *ground rent receipt* (or, at the very least, be able to inspect it).

Other documents   25.10.2
These are as detailed in Chapter 24, para. 24.10.2 – which you should revise now.

Post completion   25.11

The assignment   25.11.1
The assignment itself will need to be stamped. The principles to be applied in stamping of an assignment are the same as applied to the stamping of a transfer (*see* Chapter 24, para. 24.11.1).

Land Registry   25.11.2
Unless there are less than 21 years left to run on the lease which has been assigned, it will need to be registered following completion. Where the superior title is unregistered, this will constitute a *first* registration and the same rules as to time limits apply as for first registration of freehold land (*see* Chapter 17, para. 17.2.3).

The documents which need to be delivered will be not only those relating to the lease itself, but all evidence relating to the superior title, in the form of abstracts or epitomes which have been marked as having been examined against the originals.

Notice to landlord and custody of documents   25.11.3
These matters are covered in Chapter 24, paras. 24,11.3–4 – which you should revise now.

Self-assessment questions

1 What title is a seller obliged to deduce to a buyer under the Standard Conditions of Sale?

2 Will a buyer find these conditions acceptable? If not, why not?

3 What searches will a buyer make pre-contract and pre-completion?

4 What is the time limit for registration following completion and what would be the consequences of failing to meet it?